# Student Support and Benefits Handbook: England, Wales and Northern Ireland

12th edition

David Malcolm, Lynne Condell and Angela Toal

Child Poverty Action Group

CPAG promotes action for the prevention and relief of poverty among children and families with children. To achieve this, CPAG aims to: raise awareness of the causes, extent, nature and impact of poverty, and strategies for its eradication and prevention; bring about positive policy changes for families with children in poverty; and enable those eligible for income maintenance to have access to their full entitlement. If you are not already supporting us, please consider making a donation, or ask for details of our membership schemes, training courses and publications.

Published by Child Poverty Action Group
30 Micawber Street
London N1 7TB
Tel: 020 7837 7979
staff@cpag.org.uk
www.cpag.org.uk

A CIP record for this book is available from the British Library
ISBN: 978 1 910715 04 8

Child Poverty Action Group is a charity registered in England and Wales (registration number 294841) and in Scotland (registration number SC039339), and is a company limited by guarantee, registered in England (registration number 1993854). VAT number: 690 808117

Cover design by Colorido Studios
Typeset by David Lewis XML Associates Ltd
Content management system by Konnectsoft
Printed and bound by CPI Group (UK) Ltd, Croydon CR0 4YY

# The authors

**David Malcolm** is Assistant Director at the National Union of Students (NUS), responsible for its work on student finance policy among other areas. He has worked on student finance at the NUS for over a decade. Previously, he was the sabbatical Vice President Welfare at the University of Strathclyde Students' Association.

**Lynne Condell** is Student Funds Manager at Liverpool John Moores University, and a former chair of the National Association of Student Money Advisers. She has worked in higher education funding for over 20 years, and in 2013 was awarded an MBE for services to higher education.

**Angela Toal** is a welfare rights worker with CPAG in Scotland, working on its Benefits for Students Project.

# Acknowledgements

The authors would particularly like to thank Lindsey Moffatt, Jayne Aldridge, Keith Houghton, Jeanette Jones and Carolyn George for their work on previous editions of this *Handbook*.

Grateful thanks are due to Connie Craig, Rob Ellis, Ian Williamson and Wayne Dewick for lending their time and expertise in checking and advising on this *Handbook*.

For editing the book and managing its production, thanks go to Alison Key. Thanks also to Kathleen Armstrong for proofreading the text and Anne Ketley for compiling the index.

The law covered in this book was correct on 1 September 2015 and includes regulations laid up to this date.

# Contents

# Foreword

This twelfth edition of CPAG's *Student Support and Benefits Handbook* is published at a time of uncertainty, austerity and change for both funding for education and social security provision.

The Browne Review of higher education funding and the subsequent response by the coalition government have radically changed the nature of higher education, shifting far more of the cost of courses onto the individual and placing emphasis on price competition as a means of improving quality. The full impact of these changes is not yet apparent, but higher fees and higher debt for higher education students in England are now a reality, and the impact on Welsh and Northern Irish higher education is slowly making itself felt. In England, the government now intends to abolish maintenance grants completely from 2016/17. Elsewhere, grant and loan rates have either been frozen or have failed to keep pace with inflation.

At the same time, the education maintenance allowance and adult learning grant have both been scrapped in England, and the cost of adult further education has been shifted to the individual. Meanwhile, many postgraduates struggle to find any funding whatsoever, although a new loan scheme may be introduced in England from 2016/17.

The Department for Work and Pensions has also embarked on an equally radical reform of social security, with the new universal credit beginning to replace many benefits and tax credits, although its introduction has been far from smooth. Meanwhile, personal independence payment is replacing disability living allowance – but with a 20 per cent cut to total funding. The post-election Budget in 2015 heralds further cuts to provision for many.

In this context, it has never been more important to understand how both education funding and social security work, and how they interrelate.

Politicians, rightly, see education and work as crucial routes out of poverty, and vital to the economic health of the nation. Yet students from the poorest backgrounds are still hugely under-represented in further and higher education, even more so in the elite institutions.

Although we know that, over the last two decades, there has been a significant improvement – the majority of school leavers now continue in education – this expansion does not extend in anywhere near the same proportion to families living in poverty.

Low-income students still face formidable barriers to their participation and to their achievement. They often have to work more during term time, are able to rely less on family support (both financial and otherwise), and must navigate the ever-changing and quite bewildering student support and social security benefits systems, often with little or no guidance. The ongoing reductions in benefit entitlement for lone parents are likely to make matters worse.

And when people on low incomes do enter education, they tend to follow a more complicated path, taking more breaks, deferring enrolment and switching, repeating or restarting their courses for non-academic reasons. We know these people are also more likely to drop out or forego opportunities to progress to more advanced courses. All this complicates even further their financial support and adds to the pressures they face in determining their entitlement.

'How will study affect my benefits?' is a key question for anyone who is living on benefits and thinking about going into education. No one can make a decision to start or continue studying without knowing they can support themselves and their family.

Fair access to education – indeed, education itself – is about much more than money, but clear, relevant information on financial support for students is vital. This is why the National Union of Students (NUS) is proud to collaborate with CPAG in producing this *Handbook*.

Good advice is critical. Student support across England, Wales, Northern Ireland and Scotland differs and, as a devolved issue, these differences are ever more apparent. Advisers, therefore, need information that relates specifically to the different nations across the UK. This book covers students in England, Wales and Northern Ireland, complementing CPAG's *Benefits for Students in Scotland Handbook*. We hope it will aid advisers, act as a tool to help break down barriers and, in the process, help people from disadvantaged backgrounds enter and complete further and higher education courses.

Of course, this *Handbook* is no silver bullet. If the government seriously wishes to eradicate child poverty, education must be a priority. It must commit to action on a number of levels: fairer access to student support; increased capacity in the student advice sector; further development in childcare services; continued, far-reaching change in some of our older and larger educational institutions; a raising of aspirations and achievement in schools in disadvantaged areas; and more resources channelled into our community support services. All remain substantial challenges.

When access to education is truly equal for people from both poor and rich backgrounds, we will know that poverty is on its way to being eradicated. Until then, NUS is fully committed to supporting our members, breaking down financial barriers and fighting injustice in the education funding system.

**Megan Dunn**, NUS President
**Shelly Asquith**, NUS Vice President Welfare

# How to use this *Handbook*

This *Handbook* is intended for those who advise students in England, Wales and Northern Ireland about their entitlement to student support, benefits, tax credits and other financial issues, such as tax and health benefits. It covers both further and higher education.

The *Handbook* covers rules affecting students studying in England, Wales and Northern Ireland who are eligible for support through English, Welsh and Northern Irish funding bodies such as the Department for Business, Innovation and Skills and the National Assembly for Wales. It does not cover the rules for students getting support from Scotland or elsewhere outside England, Wales or Northern Ireland.

**Note:** the benefits system in Northern Ireland is separate from that in the rest of the UK, though differences are usually minor. Any significant differences are highlighted. For the sake of simplicity, we refer to the Department for Work and Pensions as the responsible department in this *Handbook*, but this should be read as the Department for Social Development in Northern Ireland.

CPAG publishes a companion volume entitled *Benefits for Students in Scotland Handbook*. Details can be found in Appendix 1.

## Rates of government support

The *Handbook* is up to date at 1 September 2015 and is intended to be used for the academic year 2015/16, with information provided for 2016/17 where available.

Rates of student support, benefits and tax credits used are those for the 2015/16 academic year, and the 2016/17 year where available. Where applicable, benefit and tax credit rates will be uprated in April 2016 (these rates are usually available from January, though the government intends to freeze many rates for the next few years), whereas student support rates will be uprated, where applicable, in September 2016.

## Full-time students: definitions

Most full-time students are excluded from benefits – mainly those benefits for which entitlement relies on a means test. There is one definition of 'full-time student' used for income support, jobseeker's allowance and housing benefit. Other definitions are used for council tax, carer's allowance and employment and support allowance. And some students can still claim means-tested benefits, despite being classed as full time. So you should not assume that because a student is excluded from one benefit, s/he is excluded from them all. Who counts as a 'full-time student' is explained in detail in the relevant chapters.

## Means testing students

Government support systems do not necessarily treat student income in the same way. Different means tests apply to means-tested benefits, tax credits, health benefits and student support. It is always worth checking across these systems when calculating a student's total entitlement to government support. To help students and their advisers do this, this *Handbook* has separate chapters covering the treatment of income.

## Structure of the *Handbook*

**Part 1** looks at students' entitlement to student support. **Part 2** covers students' entitlement to benefits and tax credits. **Part 3** considers how income affects the amount of benefits or tax credits, with a particular focus on how student support is treated. **Part 4** covers other matters, such as tax and taking time out from studying.

Chapters are endnoted with references to the legal authorities. Where an abbreviation is used in the endnotes or in the text, this is explained in Appendix 3 and on pxv. If you are appealing against a benefit or tax credit decision, you may want to refer to the law. Appendix 1 suggests where you can obtain copies of Acts, regulations and caselaw.

## Your feedback counts

NUS and CPAG hope that this publication will serve as a useful resource for students and their advisers to help them deal with the complexity of financial support. We are aiming for a publication that is clear and that responds to the needs of its audience. The book has expanded with every edition, and we would appreciate any comments on how it may be improved for future years. Please contact CPAG's publications department or David Malcolm at NUS: david.malcolm@nus.org.uk.

# Abbreviations

| | | | |
|---|---|---|---|
| AHRC | Arts and Humanities Research Council | HNC | higher national certificate |
| BA | Batchelor of Arts | HND | higher national diploma |
| BBSRC | Biotechnology and Biological Sciences Research Council | IB | incapacity benefit |
| | | IS | income support |
| BEd | Bachelor of Education | JSA | jobseeker's allowance |
| BSA | Business Services Authority | MA | maternity allowance |
| BSc | Batchelor of Science | MRC | Medical Research Council |
| BTEC | Business and Technology Education Council | NERC | Natural Environment Research Council |
| CA | carer's allowance | NHS | National Health Service |
| CCW | Care Council for Wales | NI | national insurance |
| CTB | council tax benefit | NUS | National Union of Students |
| CTC | child tax credit | NVQ | national vocational qualification |
| DARD | Department of Agriculture and Rural Development | Ofsted | Office for Standards in Education |
| | | OSS | Office of Social Services |
| DELNI | Department for Employment and Learning Northern Ireland | PAYE | pay as you earn |
| | | PC | pension credit |
| DHSSPS | Department of Health, Social Services and Public Safety | PGCE | Postgraduate Certificate in Education |
| DLA | disability living allowance | PGDE | Postgraduate Diploma in Education |
| DSD | Department for Social Development | PIP | personal independence payment |
| DWP | Department for Work and Pensions | PPMS | Professional Preparation Master's Scheme |
| EEA | European Economic Area | RPI | retail price index |
| EFA | Education Funding Agency | SAP | statutory adoption pay |
| EHIC | European health insurance card | SDA | severe disablement allowance |
| EPSRC | Engineering and Physical Sciences Research Council | SFA | Skills Funding Agency |
| | | SMP | statutory maternity pay |
| ESA | employment and support allowance | SPP | statutory paternity pay |
| ESRC | Economic and Social Research Council | SSP | statutory sick pay |
| | | SSPP | statutory shared parental pay |
| EU | European Union | STFC | Science and Technology Facilities Council |
| FE | further education | | |
| HB | housing benefit | UC | universal credit |
| HEFCE | Higher Education Funding Council for England | UKCISA | UK Council for International Student Affairs |
| HMRC | Her Majesty's Revenue and Customs | WTC | working tax credit |

# Means-tested benefit rates 2015/16

## Income support and income-based jobseeker's allowance

### Personal allowances

|  |  | £pw |
|---|---|---|
| Single | Under 25 | 57.90 |
|  | 25 or over | 73.10 |
| Lone parent | Under 18 | 57.90 |
|  | 18 or over | 73.10 |
| Couple | Both under 18 (maximum) | 87.50 |
|  | One 18 or over (maximum) | 114.85 |
|  | Both 18 or over | 114.85 |

### Premiums

|  |  |  |
|---|---|---|
| Carer |  | 34.60 |
| Pensioner | Single (jobseeker's allowance only) | 78.10 |
|  | Couple | 116.00 |
| Disability | Single | 32.25 |
|  | Couple | 45.95 |
| Enhanced disability | Single | 15.75 |
|  | Couple | 22.60 |
| Severe disability | One qualifies | 61.85 |
|  | Two qualify | 123.70 |

### Children (pre-6 April 2004 claims with no child tax credit)

|  |  |  |
|---|---|---|
| Dependent children | Under 20 | 66.90 |
| Family premium |  | 17.45 |
| Disabled child premium |  | 60.06 |
| Enhanced disability premium |  | 24.43 |

### Pension credit

|  |  |  |
|---|---|---|
| Standard minimum guarantee | Single | 151.20 |
|  | Couple | 230.85 |
| Severe disability addition | One qualifies | 61.85 |
|  | Two qualify | 123.70 |
| Carer addition |  | 34.60 |
| Savings credit threshold | Single | 126.50 |
|  | Couple | 201.80 |

## Housing benefit

### Personal allowances

|  |  | £pw |
|---|---|---|
| Single | Under 25 | 57.90 |
|  | Under 25 (on main phase ESA) | 73.10 |
|  | 25 or over | 73.10 |
| Lone parent | Under 18 | 57.90 |
|  | Under 18 (on main phase ESA) | 73.10 |
|  | 18 or over | 73.10 |
| Couple | Both under 18 | 87.50 |
|  | Both under 18 (claimant on main phase ESA) | 114.85 |
|  | One or both 18 or over | 114.85 |
| Children | Under 20 | 66.90 |
| Over qualifying age for pension credit | Single under 65 | 151.20 |
|  | Single 65 or over | 166.05 |
|  | Couple both under 65 | 230.85 |
|  | Couple one or both 65 or over | 248.30 |

### Premiums

| | | |
|---|---|---|
| Family | Ordinary rate | 17.45 |
|  | Some lone parents | 22.20 |
| Carer |  | 34.60 |
| Disability | Single | 32.25 |
|  | Couple | 45.95 |
| Disabled child |  | 60.06 |
| Severe disability | One qualifies | 61.85 |
|  | Two qualify | 123.70 |
| Enhanced disability | Single | 15.75 |
|  | Couple | 22.60 |
|  | Child | 24.43 |

### Components

| | |
|---|---|
| Work-related activity | 29.05 |
| Support | 36.20 |

## Employment and support allowance

| Personal allowances | Assessment phase £pw | Main phase £pw |
|---|---|---|
| Single |  |  |
| Under 25 | 57.90 | 73.10 |
| 25 or over | 73.10 | 73.10 |

| Lone parent | | £pw | £pw |
|---|---|---|---|
| Under 18 | | 57.90 | 73.10 |
| 18 or over | | 73.10 | 73.10 |
| Couple | | | |
| Both under 18 (maximum) | | 87.50 | 114.85 |
| Both 18 or over | | 114.85 | 114.85 |

**Premiums**

| | £pw | £pw |
|---|---|---|
| Carer | 34.60 | 34.60 |
| Severe disability (one qualifies) | 61.85 | 61.85 |
| Severe disability (two qualify) | 123.70 | 123.70 |
| Enhanced disability | | |
| Single | 15.75 | 15.75 |
| Couple | 22.60 | 22.60 |
| Pensioner | | |
| Single, usual rate | 78.10 | 49.05 |
| Single, support group | | 41.90 |
| Couple, usual rate | 116.00 | 86.95 |
| Couple, support group | | 79.80 |

**Components**

| | |
|---|---|
| Work-related activity | 29.05 |
| Support | 36.20 |

**Universal credit**

**Standard allowance**

| | | £pm |
|---|---|---|
| Single | Under 25 | 251.77 |
| | 25 or over | 317.82 |
| Couple | Both under 25 | 395.20 |
| | One or both 25 or over | 498.89 |

**Elements**

| | | |
|---|---|---|
| First child | | 277.08 |
| Second and each subsequent child | | 231.67 |
| Disabled child | Lower rate | 126.11 |
| | Higher rate | 367.92 |
| Limited capability for work | | 126.11 |
| Limited capability for work-related activity | | 315.60 |
| Carer | | 150.39 |

**Childcare costs**

| | |
|---|---|
| One child | up to £532.29 |
| Two or more children | up to £912.50 |
| Percentage of childcare costs covered | 70% |

# Non-means-tested benefit rates 2015/16

|  | £pw |
|---|---|
| **Attendance allowance** | |
| Higher rate | 82.30 |
| Lower rate | 55.10 |
| **Bereavement benefits** | |
| Bereavement payment (lump sum) | 2,000.00 |
| Bereavement allowance (maximum) | 112.55 |
| **Carer's allowance** | 62.10 |
| **Child benefit** | |
| Only/eldest child | 20.70 |
| Other child(ren) | 13.70 |
| **Disability living allowance** | |
| **Care component** | |
| Highest | 82.30 |
| Middle | 55.10 |
| Lowest | 21.80 |
| **Mobility component** | |
| Higher | 57.45 |
| Lower | 21.80 |
| **Employment and support allowance (contributory)** | |
| **Assessment phase** | |
| Basic allowance (under 25) | 57.90 |
| Basic allowance (25 or over) | 73.10 |
| **Main phase** | |
| Basic allowance (16 or over) | 73.10 |
| Work-related activity component | 29.05 |
| Support component | 36.20 |

### Guardian's allowance 16.55

### Incapacity benefit (short-term)
Lower rate 79.45
Higher rate 94.05

### Incapacity benefit (long-term) 105.35
Age addition (under 35) 11.15
Age addition (35–44) 6.20

### Jobseeker's allowance (contribution-based)
Under 25 57.90
25 or over 73.10

### Maternity allowance
Standard rate 139.58
Variable rate 90% of earnings

### Personal independence payment
#### Daily living component
Enhanced rate 82.30
Standard rate 55.10

#### Mobility component
Enhanced rate 57.45
Standard rate 21.80

### Retirement pension 115.95

### Statutory adoption pay 139.58

### Statutory maternity pay
Standard rate 139.58
Variable rate 90% of earnings

### Statutory paternity pay 139.58

### Statutory shared parental pay 139.58

### Statutory sick pay 88.45

# Tax credit rates 2015/16

| Child tax credit | £ per day | £ per year |
|---|---|---|
| Family element | 1.49 | 545 |
| Child element | 7.60 | 2,780 |
| Disability element | 8.58 | 3,140 |
| Severe disability element | 3.49 | 1,275 |

| Working tax credit | | |
|---|---|---|
| Basic element | 5.36 | 1,960 |
| Couple element | 5.50 | 2,010 |
| Lone parent element | 5.50 | 2,010 |
| 30-hour element | 2.22 | 810 |
| Disability element | 8.12 | 2,970 |
| Severe disability element | 3.49 | 1,275 |
| Childcare element | Eligible childcare costs to a weekly maximum of: | |
| | One child | 70% of £175 |
| | Two or more children | 70% of £300 |

| Income thresholds | |
|---|---|
| Working tax credit only or with child tax credit | 6,420 |
| Child tax credit only | 16,105 |

# Student support rates 2015/16

| **Further education** | *Maximum amounts* |
|---|---|
| Care to Learn childcare bursary | |
| England (London) | £175 per child a week |
| England (outside London) | £160 per child a week |
| Northern Ireland | £165 per child a week |
| Education maintenance allowance | |
| Wales and Northern Ireland | £60 per fortnight |
| Maintenance bursary (Northern Ireland) | £2,092 per year |
| Welsh government learning grant | £1,500 per year |
| Vulnerable student bursay (England) | £1,200 per year (minimum) |

## Higher education

### Full-time undergraduates

| Adult dependants' grant | |
|---|---|
| England | £2,757 per year |
| Wales | £2,732 per year |
| Northern Ireland | £2,695 per year |
| **Childcare grant** | |
| One child: | |
| England | £155.24 per week |
| Wales | £161.50 per week |
| Northern Ireland | £148.75 per week |
| Two or more children: | |
| England | £266.24 per week |
| Wales | £274.55 per week |
| Northern Ireland | £255 per week |
| **Disabled students' allowance** | |
| England: | |
| Non-medical personal helper | £20,725 per academic year |
| Major items of specialist equipment | £5,212 for duration of course |
| Other expenditure | £1,741 per academic year |
| Additional expenditure on travel | Full reimbursement |

Wales:

| | |
|---|---|
| Non-medical personal helper | £21,181 per academic year |
| Major items of specialist equipment | £5,332 for duration of course |
| Other expenditure | £1,785 per academic year |

Northern Ireland:

| | |
|---|---|
| Non-medical personal helper | £20,938 per academic year |
| Major items of specialist equipment | £5,266 for duration of course |
| Other expenditure | £1,759 per academic year |
| Additional expenditure on travel | Full reimbursement |

**Higher education bursary (Northern Ireland)** £2,000 per year

**Maintenance grant**

England:

| | |
|---|---|
| 2012 cohort | £3,387 per year |
| Other cohorts | £3,110 per year |
| Northern Ireland | £3,475 per year |

**Parents' learning allowance**

| | |
|---|---|
| England | £1,573 per year |
| Wales | £1,557 per year |
| Northern Ireland | £1,538 per year |

**Special support grant**

England:

| | |
|---|---|
| 2012 cohort | £3,387 per year |
| Other cohorts | £3,110 per year |

Wales

| | |
|---|---|
| 2012 and 2010 cohorts | £5,161 per year |
| 2011 cohort | £5,780 per year |
| Pre-2010 cohorts | £3,000 per year |
| Northern Ireland | £3,475 per year |

**Student loan**

England, 2012 cohort:

| | Full year | Final year |
|---|---|---|
| Living away from home, studying in London | £8,009 | £7,294 |
| Living away from home, studying outside London | £5,740 | £5,338 |
| Living at home | £4,565 | £4,195 |

**Note:** 35 per cent of the student loan is means tested. The rate of loan may be reduced if you are eligible for a maintenance grant.

England, 2009, 2010 and 2011 cohorts:

| | Full year | Final year |
|---|---|---|
| Living away from home, studying in London | £7,230 | £6,582 |
| Living away from home, studying outside London | £5,167 | £4,782 |
| Living at home | £4,005 | £3,634 |

**Note:** 28 per cent of the student loan is means tested. The rate of loan may be reduced if you are eligible for a maintenance grant.

| England, pre-2009 cohort students: | Full year | Final year |
|---|---|---|
| Living away from home, studying in London | £6,933 | £6,312 |
| Living away from home, studying outside London | £4,952 | £4,582 |
| Living at home | £3,832 | £3,463 |

**Note:** 25 per cent of the student loan is means tested. The rate of loan may be reduced if you are eligible for a maintenance grant.

| Wales: | Full year | Final year |
|---|---|---|
| Living away from home, studying in London | £7,532 | £6,858 |
| Living away from home, studying outside London | £5,376 | £4,980 |
| Living at home | £4,162 | £3,767 |

**Note:** 25 per cent of the student loan is means tested. The rate of loan may be reduced if you are eligible for a Welsh government learning grant.

| Northern Ireland: | Full year | Final year |
|---|---|---|
| Living away from home, studying in London | £6,780 | £6,170 |
| Living away from home, studying outside London | £4,840 | £4,480 |
| Living at home | £3,750 | £3,390 |

**Note:** 25 per cent of the student loan is means tested. The rate of loan may be reduced if you are eligible for a higher education bursary or maintenance grant.

**Tuition fee grant (Wales)**

| | |
|---|---|
| Study in UK, 2012 cohort | £5,190 per year |
| Study in Wales, pre-2010 cohorts | £2,085 per year |
| **Tuition fee loan (all domiciles)** | £9,000 per year |

**Welsh government learning grant**

| | |
|---|---|
| 2012 and 2010 cohorts | £5,161 per year |
| 2011 cohort | £5,780 per year |
| Pre-2010 cohorts | £3,000 per year |

## Part-time undergraduates

**Course costs grant**

| | |
|---|---|
| England (pre-2012) | £280 per year |
| Northern Ireland | £265 per year |

**Tuition fee grant**

England (pre-2012):
Course intensity equivalent to:

| | |
|---|---|
| 50–59 per cent of a full-time course | £855 per year |
| 60–74 per cent of a full-time course | £1,025 per year |
| 75 per cent or more of a full-time course | £1,285 per year |

Wales (pre-2014):
Course intensity equivalent to:

| | |
|---|---|
| 50–59 per cent of a full-time course | £690 per year |
| 60–74 per cent of a full-time course | £820 per year |
| 75 per cent or more of a full-time course | £1,025 per year |

Northern Ireland:
Course intensity equivalent to: £820 per year
  50–59 per cent of a full-time course
  60–74 per cent of a full-time course £985 per year
  75 per cent or more of a full-time course £1,230 per year
**Tuition fee loan**
England (post-2012) and Wales for study £6,750 per year
elsewhere in UK (post-2014)
Wales for study in Wales (post-2014) £2,625 per year
**Welsh government learning grant** £1,155 per year

## Healthcare students
**Means-tested bursary**
England and Wales (30-week rates):
Studying in London
  2012 system £3,191 per year
  2007 system £3,571 per year
  Pre-2007 system £3,230 per year
Studying elsewhere
  2012 system £2,643 per year
  2007 system £2,958 per year
  Pre-2007 system £2,630 per year
Living in parental home
  2012 system £2,207 per year
  2007 system £2,470 per year
  Pre-2007 system £2,151 per year
Northern Ireland:
  Living away from parental home £2,355 per year
  Living in parental home £1,920 per year
**Non-means-tested grant** £1,000 per year
**(England and Wales, 2012 system)**
**Nursing and midwifery bursary** £5,165 per year
**(Northern Ireland)**
**Reduced-rate student loan**

| England: | Full year | Final year |
| --- | --- | --- |
| Studying in London | £3,263 | £2,498 |
| Studying outside London | £2,324 | £1,811 |
| Living in parental home | £1,744 | £1,324 |
| Wales: | | |
| Studying in London | £3,703 | £2,831 |
| Studying outside London | £2,634 | £2,053 |
| Living in parental home | £1,976 | £1,501 |

Northern Ireland:

| | | |
|---|---|---|
| Living away from parental home | £2,324 | £1,811 |
| Living in parental home | £1,744 | £1,324 |

**Note:** there is a range of supplementary grants for healthcare students not listed here. See Chapter 6 for further details.

## Social work students

NHS Business Services Authority social work
bursary (England)

| | |
|---|---|
| Studying in London, 2013 system | £5,262.50 per year |
| Studying in London, pre-2013 system | £4,975 per year |
| Studying elsewhere, 2013 system | £4,862.50 per year |
| Studying elsewhere, pre-2013 system | £4,575 per year |
| Care Council for Wales social work bursary (Wales) | £2,500 per year |
| Office of Social Services social work bursary (Northern Ireland) | £4,000 per year |

## Teacher training students

Teacher training bursary (England and Wales)
Amount depends on subject studied and undergraduate degree held
**Welsh medium improvement supplement (Wales)**

| | |
|---|---|
| Maths, chemistry and physics | £2,000 per year |
| Other subjects | £1,600 per year |

## Postgraduates

See p71 for a table of research council and research board stipend rates.

## Other sources

| | |
|---|---|
| Professional and career development loan | £300 to £10,000 for duration of course |

# Part 1

## Student support

# Chapter 1

# Further education student support

**This chapter covers:**
1. Student support in England (below)
2. Student support in Wales (p12)
3. Student support in Northern Ireland (p16)

*Basic facts*
- Financial support available for further education students is generally split between those aged 16 to 19 and those aged 19 and over.
- The support is different in England, Wales and Northern Ireland. In England, most support is discretionary; you are not guaranteed any assistance. In Wales and Northern Ireland, support usually depends on your income, but may not be guaranteed.

In this chapter, the term 'student' is used to refer to someone on a further education course or programme. You may be referred to as a 'learner' by your college or learning provider, or by other agencies.

## 1. Student support in England

There have been significant changes to funding policy for students in England over the last few years. Funding is now largely in the form of discretionary awards made by individual colleges and local providers, with few national schemes. Students aged 24 or over are also likely to have to pay more for their courses than under previous rules, although loans have been introduced to support them.

Support for students in England is funded by the Education Funding Agency (EFA) and the Skills Funding Agency (SFA).

## Support for 16–19-year-olds

### Tuition fees

Subject to certain residency conditions, which are broadly the same as for the 16–19 bursary fund (see below), if you are under 19 on the 31 August prior to your enrolment and you are starting either a full- or part-time further education course funded by the EFA, you do not have to pay tuition fees. Some private colleges or providers, however, may charge a fee.

### 16–19 bursary fund

The 16–19 bursary fund is the main form of support for the costs of learning for those aged 16 to 19. To be eligible, you must have been aged under 19 on the 31 August in the academic year you start your course.

The fund pays a guaranteed amount to a small number of students who meet specific criteria (see below). For most people, however, payment is at the discretion of the local learning provider – ie, your college, school or work-based learning provider. Amounts are not guaranteed, and funding in general is limited.

#### Who is eligible

You must be studying at a recognised school, sixth-form college, further education college or with a work-based learning provider. This can include traineeship programmes, but you cannot receive bursary funding if you are undertaking a waged apprenticeship. You must also meet certain residency requirements. You must be:

- a UK citizen or a person who is 'settled' in the UK within the meaning of the Immigration Act 1971 (ie, you have the right of abode or indefinite leave to enter or remain), and ordinarily resident in the UK for the three years prior to the start of the course; *or*
- a European Union (EU) citizen (or her/his spouse, civil partner or child) and ordinarily resident in the European Economic Area (EEA – see p22) or Switzerland for three years prior to the start of the course; *or*
- an EEA or Turkish migrant worker (or her/his spouse, civil partner or child) ordinarily resident in the UK at the start of the course and ordinarily resident in the EEA for the three years prior to the start of the course; *or*
- an officially recognised refugee (or her/his spouse, civil partner or child), or you must have been granted humanitarian protection; *or*
- the child of a diplomat.

**Note:** some temporary absences abroad may be disregarded when assessing your entitlement. Rules on residency are complicated, so if you are in doubt, speak to an adviser in the student services department in your college or contact either UKCISA or the National Union of Students (NUS). See Appendix 2 for the addresses.

There are special rules if a student from England studies in Wales or Scotland, and vice versa. If you are a student living in Wales, but travelling to

England for your course, you should first apply for an education maintenance allowance in Wales (see p13) if you are eligible. You are not entitled to apply for the guaranteed vulnerable students bursary (see below), although you can apply for a discretionary bursary. Any support received from Wales is taken into account when assessing need.

Students living in England and studying at a general further education college in Wales should apply for help through the Financial Contingency Fund (see p14). Students living in England and studying at a sixth-form college or special college in Wales should apply to their home local authority for help from the 16–19 bursary fund. Students living in England are not entitled to apply for a Welsh education maintenance allowance.

If you are a student living in Scotland, but travelling to England for your course, you should apply for an education maintenance allowance in Scotland. See CPAG's *Benefits for Students in Scotland Handbook* for more details. You are not entitled to support from the 16–19 bursary fund in England. Students living in England, but travelling to Scotland for their course, should apply to their home local authority for help from the 16–19 bursary fund as below, and are not entitled to apply for a Scottish education maintenance allowance.

**Guaranteed funding**

You can receive a guaranteed bursary of at least £1,200 a year if you are:

- in local authority care, including if you are an unaccompanied asylum-seeking child; *or*
- a care leaver; *or*
- in receipt of income support (IS), or universal credit (UC) in place of IS, in your own name; *or*
- a disabled young person getting employment and support allowance (ESA) and disability living allowance (DLA) or personal independence payment (PIP).

You must provide evidence that you qualify – eg, a letter from your local authority confirming you were in care, or from Jobcentre Plus confirming you get a relevant benefit.

The bursary can be paid in one lump sum or in instalments. The total amount must be at least £1,200, although providers can pay more if they consider it appropriate. Payment may be made in one lump sum, regular cash payments, or in the form of travel passes or other in-kind support, or a combination of these. If your course lasts less than a year, your bursary payment is reduced pro rata. Payment is withheld if you stop attending your course.

Guaranteed bursaries are not taken into account when calculating your entitlement to means-tested benefits (see Chapter 21).

## General funds

For most students, support from the 16–19 bursary fund is not guaranteed. However, providers can make payments to support students who would otherwise face barriers to participation. This might include funding to meet the cost of books, equipment and transport, or other costs as appropriate.

Providers have the discretion to decide who should receive support, how much to pay and whether any conditions should be attached – eg, relating to attendance or behaviour.

Providers can also choose to buy books or equipment on behalf of individuals or groups of students, if they consider them to be in need (the fund should not be used to buy equipment for all students regardless of their situation). In other words, you may not receive any support in cash and you may have to return any books or equipment provided in this way.

Providers should take care to ensure that payments are not made in such a way as to make them count as income for means-tested benefit purposes (see Chapter 21).

If you are unhappy about a provider's decision, you can complain through its standard complaints procedure.

## Education maintenance allowance

The education maintenance allowance is no longer available to students in England. Wales (see p13) and Northern Ireland (see p16) still have education maintenance allowance schemes, as does Scotland. For details of the Scottish scheme, see CPAG's *Benefits for Students in Scotland Handbook*.

## Armed forces bereavement scholarship scheme

The armed forces bereavement scholarship scheme provides additional support for children of servicemen/women killed on active duty since 1990. The scheme offers an annual grant of £1,500 per year (2012/13 rates – more recent figures are not available) to help pay for the costs of learning on further education courses lasting up to three years. It does not pay for repeat years.

To qualify, your parent must have died while in service with the UK armed forces and her/his death must be attributable to that service.

### Parent

A person counts as your parent if s/he was your biological or adoptive parent, or you were the subject of a special guardianship order, or if s/he was your step-parent and had financial responsibility for you. A foster parent does not count.

If your parent dies while you are in further education, support can be backdated to the start of the current term, or it starts from the next term if s/he dies during a vacation.

Support is not means tested. You must study at an institution in the UK, although you do not have to be resident in the UK. If you go on to university, you can receive further help from the scheme (see p97).

You can download an application form and get further information at www.gov.uk/government/publications/afbss-form-1.

## Care to Learn

Care to Learn is a scheme funded by the EFA to help young parents in England pay for their childcare costs while in full-time or part-time further education, Foundation Learning or other non-employed work-based learning schemes. If you are eligible, the scheme pays for the costs of registered childcare while you are at school, college or on placement, including fees that must be paid during holidays, plus the cost of transport to and from the childcare provider. You can claim up to a maximum of £175 a week per child if you live in London or up to £160 a week per child if you live elsewhere.

The amount you receive is not taken into account as income when working out your entitlement to social security benefits and tax credits.

However, if you are in receipt of childcare help through working tax credit, UC or a learning programme funded by the European Social Fund, you cannot get help from Care to Learn. You are also expected to take up your full entitlement to a government-funded early education place, but Care to Learn can pay for any additional costs. Your local authority can advise you on your entitlement.

You can apply if you were aged under 20 at the start of your course, living in England and caring for your own child(ren). You must want to start or continue a publicly funded course at school or sixth-form college, or to start a course at a further education college. If you are studying on a course in Scotland or Wales, you can receive help, but your usual place of residence must be in England.

The scheme only funds registered or approved childcare. If you are uncertain whether or not your childcare is registered or approved, speak to your college's student services department. If you have informal childcare arrangements, you can apply for support through the discretionary support funds (see p11).

You must meet residency conditions similar to those for higher education support (see p21). However, there are some differences – eg, asylum seekers under the age of 18 can receive help from Care to Learn if they are care leavers.

For further information, including how to apply, see www.gov.uk/care-to-learn or phone 0800 121 8989.

## Transport

Local authorities have responsibility for ensuring appropriate provision of home-to-school or home-to-college transport for those aged 16 to 18.[1] This might not be free of charge. Contact your college or local authority for further information, or see www.gov.uk/subsidised-college-transport-16-19 for details of local policies.

Many colleges and sixth-form colleges provide subsidised transport, and you should also ask them for details.

## Meals

From the 2015/16 academic year, all further education providers are required to provide free meals to disadvantaged young people. You are eligible if you meet the residency conditions for learner support (see p4), and are either aged 16–18 on the 31 August prior to the academic year, or are aged 19–25 and subject to a learning difficulty assessment or an education health and care plan. To receive free meals, you must be regarded as 'disadvantaged'. This means that either you or your parents receive certain benefits or your/their income is below £16,910 for the purposes of tax credits (see Chapters 19 and 20).

The free meal does not have to be a lunch if, because of the pattern of your course, breakfast would be more suitable. Ask your college or learning provider for more information on its policy. Guidance for colleges and providers is at www.gov.uk/guidance/16-to-18-education-free-meals.

## Residential bursaries

If a course you want to do is not available locally, you may be able to get help with accommodation for one further afield. Some specialist colleges that concentrate on agriculture, horticulture or art and design offer residential bursaries through the discretionary support funds. There are 50 of these colleges – a list is available at www.gov.uk/guidance/16-to-18-residential-bursary-fund. See p11 for more information about assistance from the discretionary support funds. The bursaries are available for full-time study and are also for travel costs if you have to live at home but travel significant distances to college.

If you wish to study a course not on the above list, but which is not available locally, you may be able to receive help under the residential support scheme. This offers up to £3,458 a year (£4,079 in London) for accommodation costs, provided the course is your first level two or level three qualification, requires 15 hours' attendance a week, is at least 10 weeks long and is not available within 15 miles or a two-hour return journey from your home. You must also be ordinarily resident in England. The amount you receive depends on your family income. More information is available from www.gov.uk/residential-support-scheme or phone 0800 121 8989.

## Disabled students

Colleges administer funds for students with learning difficulties or disabilities. If you have additional needs or costs related to a learning difficulty or disability, ask your college or learning provider for information about how to access extra help.

## Asylum seekers

Although most public funds are not available to you, if you are an unaccompanied asylum seeker aged under 18, you can apply to the 16–19 bursary fund (see p4) for assistance. This can only be in-kind support and not cash. If you are under 18 (or under 20 and a care leaver) and have childcare costs, you can also apply for help from the Care to Learn scheme (see p7).

For other sources of funding, contact the the Ruth Hayman Trust at www.ruthhaymantrust.org.uk.

## Support for students aged 19 and over

### Tuition fees

There is no universal free tuition for those in further education who are 19 and over.

Free tuition is available in certain circumstances, including if you are:

- studying a basic literacy or numeracy course;
- aged 19 or over and undertaking GCSE maths and/or English, provided you do not already hold these at grades A–C;
- aged 19–23 at the start of a course of vocational training that leads to your first level two qualification (the equivalent of five GCSEs at grades A*–C, but note that the GCSEs themselves are not funded under this provision);
- aged 19–23 at the start of a course for your first full level three qualification;
- aged 19–23 at the start of your course and you are a level four 'jumper' – ie, you have a level two qualification and are moving directly onto your first level four course without having studied for a level three qualification;
- aged 19–23 at the start of your course and undertaking an apprenticeship (intermediate, advanced or higher level);
- aged 24 or over at the start of your course and undertaking an apprenticeship;
- aged 19–24 and have a section 139a learning difficulty assessment for certain courses that meet the aims of the assessment;
- aged 19 or over at the start of your course and you get jobseeker's allowance, or ESA and you are in the work-related activity group, or UC and you must undertake skills training;
- aged 19 or over at the start of your course and get another social security benefit, at the discretion of your college or learning provider;
- aged 24 or over and you have left the British armed forces after 10 years' service or you have been medically discharged due to injury in active service, for the first full level two or level three qualification; *or*
- studying an English as a second or other language qualification, in certain circumstances.

If you qualify, the SFA pays your tuition fees for the course. The rules are complicated, so check whether you are eligible with your college or learning provider. There are also residency conditions.

If you are not in any of the above groups, you may have to pay tuition fees. Students aged 24 or over at the start of the course and undertaking qualifications at level two or above, other than apprenticeships, must pay fees in most cases, but there are now loans available to help with level three and four qualifications (see below). If you have difficulty meeting the costs of your fees, get advice from your student services department on your options.

## 24+ advanced learning loan

If you are aged 24 or over at the start of your further education course and are charged fees, you may be eligible for a student loan to cover the cost.

The loans are administered by the Student Loans Company on behalf of the SFA.

You can take out up to four loans, either concurrently in the case of A levels (ie, you can have four at once, if you are taking up to four A levels in one year), or consecutively (ie, four separate years of loan funding) for other qualifications. The minimum loan you can get is £300; the maximum cannot exceed the 'funding rate' stipulated by the SFA for the course, which can be several thousand pounds. You may also be restricted to the amount your college or learning provider is willing or able to make available, and your loan may therefore be lower than the fee you are charged.

The residency rules that apply to higher education student support (see p21) also apply. The rules can be complicated, so if you are in any doubt about your entitlement, get advice from your student services department.

Repayment terms and conditions are the same as those for loans in higher education taken out by students who started their courses on or after 1 September 2012 (see p32). Repayments will not start until April 2016 at the earliest and only once you have completed your course. Although it is possible to make voluntary repayments before or after this date, you should consider whether this is of financial benefit to you, given that outstanding loans are written off after 30 years and many people may not repay their loans in full. Ask your student services department for advice.

If you take out one or more 24+ advanced learning loans in order to pay for an 'access to higher education' course, these are written off if you proceed to higher education and complete the course. However, if you take out loans for other further education courses, these are not written off if you go on to complete a higher education course.

More information on 24+ advanced learning loans, including links to the application form and guidance documents, and resources for advisers and other intermediaries, are available at www.gov.uk/advanced-learning-loans.

## Disabled students

The system for disabled students aged over 19 is the same as for younger students (see p8). **Note:** additional funding for disabled students in receipt of a 24+ advanced learning loan should come from the Loan Bursary Fund instead (see p11).

## Discretionary support funds

You may be able to get additional help for your living or course costs through discretionary learner support funds. These are amounts of money given to colleges and other providers by the SFA for students in need. You must meet the same residency criteria as for higher education to receive any support (see p21). If you get a 24+ advanced learning loan, you must apply to a separate bursary scheme (see below), although in practice the rules of both schemes are similar. You can receive help from these funds if you are undertaking a traineeship, but not if you are receiving help for childcare and/or travel through Jobcentre Plus. There are three types of payments:

- hardship funds (see below);
- residential bursaries (see p8); *and*
- childcare support (see below).

### Hardship funds

These are general funds to enable students to access or stay on their courses, or to encourage attainment. They can pay for books and equipment, transport, course-related trips, emergencies or, in exceptional circumstances, tuition fees.

Your college or learning provider has discretion on how to prioritise spending and on the assessment criteria, so the support available to you depends on your college. If you want to challenge a decision, your college or learning provider must have an appeals procedure.

### Childcare support

Support can be offered to meet the costs of any registered childcare for students aged 20 or over. The support available is unlikely to be more than that available through the Care to Learn scheme (approximately £5,000 a child), but this may differ between colleges and providers. Funds are often oversubscribed and no particular sum is guaranteed. Payments can be made directly to the childcare provider or to you, depending on your college's/provider's policy. If you are aged under 20 and starting a new course, apply to the Care to Learn scheme (see p7) for help with registered childcare.

## Loan Bursary Fund

The Loan Bursary Fund provides support for disadvantaged and vulnerable students. All students who have had a loan approved by Student Finance England and have registered for their course are potentially eligible to apply, depending on their needs and circumstances.

The Fund provides discretionary support for students in hardship and for other expenses, such as childcare and travel. It can be used at the discretion of the provider to cover a student's needs in an emergency. Additional learning support is also available – eg, for teaching assistant support, specialist equipment, technology and necessary adjustments under the Equality Act 2010.

The bursaries are granted at the discretion of each college.

## Other grants

### City and Guilds bursary

A small number of bursaries are available to help with the costs of study for students on qualifying City and Guilds or former National Proficiency Tests Council courses. To qualify, you must be living in the UK and intending to study in the UK. Applications are considered twice a year, in April and September. For more information, see www.cityandguilds.com/bursaries.

### Work Programme training allowance

If you are on the Work Programme, you may be able to get a training allowance to help you gain qualifications to improve your employability. You are exempt from work-related activity requirements for benefits while you are in receipt of the training allowance.

### Apprenticeships

If you are undertaking an apprenticeship at any level, your employer must pay you at least the minimum wage for apprenticeships. If you are under 19, this is £3.30 per hour. If you are aged 19 or over, the minimum wage is £3.30 an hour for the first year of the apprenticeship, after which you must be paid at the standard rate for your age. This is at least £5.30 an hour if you are aged 20, or at least £6.70 an hour if you are aged 21 or over. See www.gov.uk/topic/further-education-skills/apprenticeships for further information. The minimum wage rates apply from 1 October 2015 and are reviewed annually.

### Professional and career development loan

Students on further education courses can apply for a professional and career development loan (see p97). However, consider carefully whether or not this is the most affordable option for you and seek financial advice.

---

## 2. **Student support in Wales**

### Support for 16–19-year-olds

#### Tuition fees

Subject to certain residency conditions, if you are under 19 on the 31 August prior to your enrolment and you are starting either a full- or part-time further education course funded by the Welsh government, you do not have to pay tuition fees. Some private colleges or providers, however, may charge a fee.

## Education maintenance allowance

The education maintenance allowance is a payment of £30 a week (paid fortnightly) to eligible students who meet certain course, residence and income conditions.

To receive an education maintenance allowance:

- you must be participating in a programme of full-time education (at least 12 guided learning hours for at least 10 weeks) at a recognised school, sixth-form college or further education college;
- you must meet certain residence conditions (see p47). You do not have to study in Wales to qualify, provided you live in Wales and your school or college is participating in the scheme;
- you must have been aged between 16 and 18 on 31 August 2015.

In addition, your gross (before tax) household income must be below £20,817 if you are the only child in the household, or £23,077 if there are additional young people studying full time and eligible for child benefit in the household. The income assessed is usually that of your parents or guardians. If you live with only one parent, your other parent's income is not assessed and any maintenance s/he pays is not counted as income. Benefits (including child benefit) and tax credits are disregarded when calculating your household income. The household income figure used is that for the previous tax year. For applications for 2015/16, this is the 2013/14 tax year. Any income you have (eg, from a part-time job) is not included.

Provided you meet the other standard conditions, if you are an 'independent student' (see below), you automatically receive the full allowance of £30.

### Independent students

You count as an 'independent student' if you:

– are responsible for a child; or
– live apart from your parents and are estranged from them, and you are not under the care of the local authority; or
– are under the care of the local authority – eg, with foster parents; or
– are classed as a young person in custody.

Payments are available for up to three full academic years and depend on your meeting the conditions set out in your agreement (see p14).

Applications made after the start of the course can only be backdated for 28 days, so it is important to apply within 28 days of the start of your course.

Education maintenance allowance payments are disregarded when calculating your family's entitlement to means-tested benefits. Therefore, you can receive an education maintenance allowance in addition to any benefits you or your family are claiming.

**Education maintenance allowance agreement**

To receive your weekly payments, you are required to sign an education maintenance allowance agreement provided by your college or learning provider (this may be referred to as a contract or something similar). It sets out what you are expected to achieve in terms of attendance and academic work and is signed by you, your parents (or another responsible adult) and the college/learning provider. If you fail to meet part of the contract in any week (eg, you do not attend classes or hand in homework), you are not paid your allowance for that week.

Although payments depend on 100 per cent attendance, some types of absence are permitted or 'authorised'. However, it is advisable to notify your college or learning provider of any absences if you want to be considered for your payment and any bonuses, particularly if you know in advance that you will be absent.

Authorised absences can include sickness, unavoidable medical appointments, religious holidays, emergency caring duties, driving tests, family funerals or representative duties such as a college governors' meeting. **Note:** jury service is not normally considered to be an authorised absence, as the guidance states you should seek to defer your service to a holiday period or until after the course.

Holidays are not generally considered acceptable reasons for absence. Colleges make the final decision on authorised absences, and you should discuss with your own provider any absence you may have to take.

## Passport to Study grant

Some local authorities in Wales offer extra funding for young people in further education whose parents are out of work, or receiving benefits because of having a low income or a disability. These are usually called Passport to Study grants and normally come in the form of assistance with travel costs. Contact your local authority to see if it offers such funding, and what terms and conditions apply.

## Financial Contingency Fund

If you are studying at a college, you may be able to get additional help for your living or course costs from the Financial Contingency Fund. This operates in a broadly similar manner to the discretionary support funds in England. See p11 for more details.

## Support for students aged 19 and over

### Tuition fees

There is no guaranteed help with fees if you are aged 19 or over. However, some colleges may run schemes providing full or partial remission if, for example, you are on a low income, are disabled or are in receipt of means-tested benefits. Ask your college what it provides.

## Welsh government learning grant

If you are aged 19 or over and on a low income, you may be eligible for a means-tested Welsh government learning grant for further education (formerly an Assembly learning grant) of up to £1,500.[2] A grant of at least £450 is available if you are on a full-time course (500 contact hours or more a year) and your household income is below £18,371. If your household income is below £12,236, £750 is available. The full £1,500 is available if your household income is less than £6,121. Part-time students (those who have between 275 and 499 contact hours a year) can receive a reduced grant of £300, £450 or £750 on the same income bands. The household income figure used is that for the previous tax year. For applications in 2015/16, this is the tax year 2013/14.

The grants are administered through Student Finance Wales, but students may attend any institution in the UK. More information is available at www.studentfinancewales.co.uk/fe.

## Pathways to Apprenticeship scheme

If you are aged between 16 and 25 and on a Pathways to Apprenticeship course of at least one year in length and 21 hours a week study, you can get an education maintenance allowance (see p13).

## Financial Contingency Fund

If you are studying at a college, you may be able to get additional help for your living or course costs from the Financial Contingency Fund. This operates in a broadly similar manner to the discretionary support funds in England. See p11 for more details.

## Other grants

### Work Programme training allowance

Welsh students may be able to receive the Work Programme training allowance (see p12).

### Apprenticeships

Apprentices in Wales must be paid the minimum wage at the appropriate rates (see p12). Apprentices in Wales do not pay tuition fees. More information is available from Careers Wales at www.careerswales.com.

## Professional and career development loan

Students on further education courses can apply for a professional and career development loan (see p97). However, consider carefully whether or not this is the most affordable option for you and seek financial advice.

# 3. Student support in Northern Ireland

## Support for 16–19-year-olds

### Tuition fees

If you are a full-time student, your tuition fees are paid in full. If you are a part-time student, concessionary tuition fees may apply.

### Education maintenance allowance

In Northern Ireland, the education maintenance allowance scheme is similar to that in Wales (see p13). However, there are some differences. Students in Northern Ireland are entitled to an education maintenance allowance if they turned 16, 17, 18 or 19 between 2 July 2014 and 1 July 2015. Your course must consist of at least 15 guided learning hours a week.

You are eligible for a payment of £30 a week if you are the only young person in your household or are an 'independent' student (see p36) and your gross (before tax) annual household income is £20,500 or less. If you have one or more siblings either aged under 16, or under 20 and in full-time education or training, your gross (before tax) annual household income must be £22,500 or less.

As in Wales, you are paid fortnightly.

A £100 bonus is available if you have met the goals in your education maintenance allowance agreement (see p14). This is usually provided in January and June.

More information on Northern Irish education maintenance allowances is at www.nidirect.gov.uk/education-maintenance-allowance-ema.

### Care to Learn

The Department for Employment and Learning's Care to Learn scheme is designed to help young parents in Northern Ireland pay for childcare costs while in full- or part-time further education. If you are eligible, the scheme pays for the costs of registered childcare while you are at school, college or on placement, including fees that must be paid during holidays, plus the cost of transport to and from the childcare provider, up to a maximum of £165 per child a week. It does not affect, nor is it affected by, benefits and tax credits.

You can apply if you are aged 16 or over but under 20 at the start of your course, live in Northern Ireland and fulfil certain residency requirements, and you care for your own child(ren). You must wish to start or continue a publicly funded course at school or a sixth-form college, or to start a further education or higher education course at a further education college. If you are already receiving childcare funding from other government sources (eg, through working tax credit), you are not eligible for this scheme and should apply to the college's support fund if you need further help.

The scheme only funds childcare from a provider registered with the Health and Social Care Trust. If you have informal childcare arrangements, you can still apply for support through your college's support fund.

## Support for students aged 19 and over

### Tuition fees

Tuition fee remission (ie, your fees are paid for you) is available if you are studying a full-time eligible vocational course up to level three – eg, NVQ level three.

> **Full time course**
> A 'full-time course' is defined as a course lasting for a minimum of 30 weeks and consisting of at least 15 hours and at least seven sessions a week, or 21 hours a week with no sessional requirement. GCSE, A level or AS level subjects are not eligible, except when studied in combination with a relevant vocational qualification at a similar level.

If your course does not qualify for tuition fee remission, you may be able to receive help from your college support fund.

### Further education awards

If you are on a full-time further education course, you can apply to the regional Education Authority office for a non-repayable maintenance grant, called a further education award (previously known as a discretionary award). These can also provide additional help with tuition fees, if required. There are also extra allowances, similar to those available in higher education (see p65), for students with dependants, disabled students and care leavers. All these grants (except for disabled students' allowances) are means tested.

There are residency requirements, and you cannot be in receipt of another award, such as an education maintenance allowance (see p16) or a Department of Agriculture and Rural Development grant (see p18), at the same time. Although the awards are no longer referred to as 'discretionary', they remain so – funds are insufficient to provide all applicants with grants and you should apply as soon as possible.

**Note:** the closing date for applications for each year is the end of June prior to the start of the course for full-time students, and the end of September for part-time students.

For further information, see www.eani.org.uk, or contact Student Finance NI, 1 Hospital Road, Omagh, Co Tyrone BT79 0AW, tel: 028 8225 4546 or email: feawards@welbni.org.

### Bursary for maintenance

You may qualify for a means-tested bursary for maintenance of up to £2,092. The maximum amount is available if your household income is less than £21,331, and a partial amount if your household income is between £21,331 and £38,805. No maintenance grant is payable if your household income exceeds £38,805.

### Support for childcare

If you have children and incur childcare costs, you can claim a childcare grant. How much you receive depends on your household income and the number of children you have. See www.eani.org.uk for more details.

If you are aged under 20 at the start of the course, you should apply to the Care to Learn scheme in Northern Ireland to cover your childcare costs (see p16).

### Disabled students

Disabled students who require additional support should apply to their college or learning provider for assistance. Contact the disability adviser at the college in the first instance.

### Part-time courses

Part-time courses attract funding at lower levels. If fees are charged, you may qualify for fee support of up to £465 a year. A means-tested course costs grant of up to £265 is available. You cannot receive any help if your income exceeds £25,000 a year. See www.eani.org.uk for more details.

## Support funds

There are two discretionary funds administered by colleges that offer additional help if you are a part-time or full-time further education student aged 19 or over. Support funds are aimed at those experiencing financial difficulties and may include help with living costs and/or fees. Eligibility criteria apply. The additional support funds are aimed at students with learning difficulties who are not in receipt of other help for disabled students, such as a disabled students' allowance, and can be used to pay for additional human or technical support, such as IT hardware.

## Other grants

### Department of Agriculture and Rural Development grant

If you are attending a further education course at the Enniskillen, Greenmount or Loughry campuses of the College of Agriculture, Food and Rural Enterprise, you may be eligible for financial support from the Department of Agriculture and Rural Development.

To be eligible, you must be ordinarily resident in Northern Ireland and meet certain other residency requirements. You can be any age.

A means-tested living costs grant of up to £1,659 is available if you live in your parents' home, or up to £2,362 if you do not. Further allowances may be available if you have children or adult dependants, or if you are a care leaver or have a disability.

Further information can be found at www.cafre.ac.uk/study-at-cafre/financial-support.

## Professional and career development loan

Students on further education courses can apply for a professional and career development loan (see p97). However, consider carefully whether or not this is the most affordable option for you and seek financial advice.

# Notes

**1. Student support in England**
1  s509 EA 1996

**2. Student support in Wales**
2  E(ALGS)(W) Regs

# Chapter 2

## Undergraduate student support: England

**This chapter covers:**
1. Full-time undergraduates (p21)
2. Part-time undergraduates (p41)
3. Discretionary and institutional funds (p43)

### Basic facts

- Undergraduate students can apply for a mixture of grants and loans, depending on their personal circumstances.
- The type of financial support available depends on several factors, including when the course starts, its length, the discipline and whether the course is full time or part time.
- Separate provision is available for social work, healthcare and initial teacher training students.
- Institutions should have funds for students in hardship and to support retention and progression.

**Note:** English, Welsh, Northern Irish and Scottish students are funded under separate systems. See Chapter 3 for details of the system in Wales, Chapter 4 for details of the system in Northern Ireland and CPAG's *Benefits for Students in Scotland Handbook* for details of the system in Scotland.

Students domiciled in England who wish to study in Wales, Northern Ireland or Scotland receive the same package of support as though they were studying in England.

**Note:** the rates of most forms of maintenance support described in this chapter have increased by 3.34 per cent for 2015/16. However, fees have remained frozen.

### Future changes

The government has recently announced plans to abolish both the maintenance grant and special support grant for all new entrants to higher education from the 2016/17 academic year. The changes are still subject to parliamentary approval, but are likely to involve increasing maintenance loan rates to compensate for their abolition. Although this will give some students more money overall, such support will have to be repaid according to the standard rules.

The Department for Business, Innovation and Skills is also consulting on freezing the student loan repayment threshold for all students who started in the 2012/13 academic year or later.

# 1. Full-time undergraduates

Full-time undergraduates in England on eligible courses (see p24), and who are personally eligible (see below), can apply for financial assistance from the Department for Business, Innovation and Skills. Funding is administered by Student Finance England on its behalf. There have been a number of changes to student funding and support over the last 10 years, and so the tuition fees you can be charged and the support you can receive for fees and maintenance depends on when you started your course.

Separate provision is available for part-time undergraduates (see p41) and those studying degree or higher diploma courses in healthcare (see p76).

## Who is eligible for support

To receive help under any system, you must be 'personally eligible' by meeting residence conditions (see below) and be studying an eligible course (see p24).

### Residence conditions

To be eligible for support, you must meet residence conditions.[1] This usually means that you must:

- be settled in the UK within the meaning of the Immigration Act 1971 (this includes those with British citizenship, right of abode or indefinite leave to enter/remain in the UK); *and*
- be resident in England on the first day of the first academic year; *and*
- have lived in the 'UK and islands'[2] for three years immediately before the start of the course, although temporary absences for reasons such as vacations or temporary employment abroad can be disregarded. Service abroad in the regular UK armed forces is always disregarded; *and*
- not have spent any of the three years in the 'UK and islands' mainly for the purpose of receiving full-time education. If you were in full-time education during the three years, you can still receive support if you can prove this was not the main reason for your being in the UK.

**Note:** there are exceptions to these rules, including for people with settled status who have exercised their right of free movement in the European Economic Area

(EEA). However, residency rules are complex and you may wish to speak to an adviser in your institution or students' union.

---

### Home students

A '**home student**' is someone who meets the required residence conditions and is treated as a domestic student for fee and student support purposes (although it is possible for someone to be treated as a home student for fee purposes and not receive student support). Home students are usuallly charged a lower fee than overseas students, and overseas students have very limited access to student support for fees or maintenance.

---

## European Union nationals

Broadly, if you are a European Union (EU) national, you can count as a home student and be eligible for support with both tuition fees and living costs if you have been resident in the UK for the three years immediately before the start of the course and you are resident in England or Wales on the first day of the first academic year. If any of this time was spent mainly for the purpose of receiving full-time education, you must have been ordinarily resident in the UK, elsewhere in the EEA or Switzerland immediately before the three-year period began.

---

### The European Economic Area

The '**European Economic Area**' comprises the member states of the EU plus Norway, Liechtenstein and Iceland.

The current member states of the EU are: Austria, Belgium, Bulgaria, Croatia, Cyprus, Czech Republic, Denmark, Estonia, Finland, France, Germany, Greece, Hungary, Ireland, Italy, Latvia, Lithuania, Luxembourg, Malta, Netherlands, Poland, Portugal, Romania, Slovenia, Slovakia, Spain, Sweden and the UK.

---

Alternatively, if you have permanent residence after having become settled in the UK, you may qualify as a home student. This can also be granted if you are a 'relevant family member' of a person with permanent residence and you have been resident in the UK for three years or more.[3] However, if any of this time was spent mainly for the purpose of full-time education, you must have been resident in the UK or elsewhere in the EEA or Switzerland immediately before the three-year period.

If you are a national of an EU member state (or a 'relevant family member' of an EU national) and coming to the UK to undertake higher education, you may be eligible for help with fees only. You must have lived in the EEA and/or Switzerland for three years before the start of your course, and no part of the three-year period should have been mainly for the purposes of full-time education.

*Relevant family member*

A '**relevant family member**' includes children, a spouse or civil partner or, for EEA workers only, dependent direct 'ascendants', such as parents or grandparents. If you are an eligible direct descendant of an EEA worker who is no longer working in the UK, you may still be eligible for student support if you came to the UK to accompany your parent.

If a new country joins the EU, it is considered to have always been in the EEA when determining the three-year period. For example, although Bulgaria and Romania joined the EU on 1 January 2007 and Croatia on 1 July 2013, they are regarded as having always been part of the EEA for the purposes of assessing support.

## Migrant workers

If you are a non-UK, EEA or Swiss migrant worker and are, or have been, working in the UK (employed, self-employed or as a frontier worker), or you are a 'relevant family member' (see above) of such a migrant worker, you may be eligible for support with both tuition fees and living costs as a home student. You must also have three years' residence in the EEA and/or Switzerland.

If you are a UK national or the relevant family member of a UK national and have been living in another EEA country or Switzerland and you return to the UK to study, you may be eligible for support as a home student if you were ordinarily resident and settled in the UK immediately prior to leaving, and you are now settled and ordinarily resident in the UK on the first day of the first year of your course. You or your family member must have been resident in another EEA country as a student, worker, self-sufficient or self-employed person. You must apply for support in the part of the UK in which you were living before you left.[4]

If you are the child of a Turkish migrant worker, you can also pay home fees and receive support if your parents have been ordinarily resident in the UK and lawfully employed, and if you are ordinarily resident in the UK on the first day of the first academic year of the course and have been ordinarily resident in the EEA, Switzerland and/or Turkey for the three years before the start of the course.[5]

If you are the child of a Swiss worker still living in the UK as a worker, student, self-employed or self-sufficient person, you may qualify for student support if you have been resident in the UK or elsewhere in the EEA/Switzerland for the three years before the first day of the first academic year of your course, and you are ordinarily resident in the UK by that date. If, during the three years, your main purpose for being in the UK or EEA/Switzerland was for full-time education, you must have been ordinarily resident before this date.

**Refugees**

If you are recognised as a refugee by the UK government and have lived in the 'UK and islands' since being granted this status, or you are a 'relevant family member' of such a person (see p23), you should be treated as a home student and be eligible for support with both tuition fees and living costs (see pp27–34).[6]

If you applied for asylum and have been granted humanitarian protection or discretionary (or exceptional) leave, you may be treated as a home student for support purposes if you received this leave before the start of the first day of the first academic year of your course, and you meet the three-year residency criteria (see p22).

## What is an eligible course

To be eligible for support, broadly the course must be full time (as defined by the education provider) and be:[7]

- a first degree (including foundation degrees);
- a diploma of higher education;
- a BTEC Higher National Certificate (HNC) or Higher National Diploma (HND);
- a course of initial teacher training;
- a course for the further training of teachers, or youth or community workers;
- a course to prepare for certain professional examinations of a standard higher than A level, or HNC/HND where a first degree is not required for entry;
- a course not higher than a first degree, but higher than those described in the above bullet point.

**Note:** some courses, particularly in art and design, can require the student to undertake a foundation year or course, which is different to a foundation degree. This is normally a course of one academic year in length which precedes the main higher education degree course.

Support for these courses is often much more limited, as they usually do not come within the definition of 'higher education'. You may be eligible for support as a further education student (see Chapter 1). Speak to an adviser in your students' union or institution for further guidance.

Some courses in science, engineering or technology can have an integrated foundation year which forms part of the higher education course, and these consequently attract higher education funding. If in doubt about your entitlement, speak to an adviser.

## Which system of student support applies

This chapter refers to students as 'old system' and 'current system' students, depending on when you started your course.

## Students who entered higher education between 1 September 1998 and 1 September 2006

If you began your course between 1 September 1998 and 1 September 2006 and do not fit into the gap year provision explained below, you receive financial help as an **'old system'** student.[8]

'Old system' students, including those regarded as 'gap year students' in the 2006/07 academic year (see p26), can apply for a package of support, which includes:

- grants and loans for tuition fees (see p27);
- a higher education grant (see p29);
- a student loan for living costs (see p30);
- supplementary grants in particular circumstances (see p33).

## Students who entered higher education on or after 1 September 2006

You qualify for support as a **'current system'** student if:[9]

- you entered higher education for the first time in 2006 or later and do not come under the gap year provisions outlined below;
- you started a Postgraduate Certificate in Education (PGCE) or Postgraduate Diploma in Education (PGDE) course on or after 1 September 2006;
- you have withdrawn from a previous course of study and did not arrange a transfer before leaving your previous course.

Changes have been made on several occasions since 2006/07, but there is transitional protection for those who entered higher education on different rules. In addition, different rates and income thresholds apply, depending on your year of entry. In this chapter:

- students who started their course in the 2006/07 or 2007/08 academic year are referred to as **'2006 cohort'** students;
- students who started their course in the 2008/09 academic year are referred to as **'2008 cohort'** students;
- students who started their course in the 2009/10, 2010/11 or 2011/12 academic year are referred to as **'2009 cohort'** students;
- students who started, or who will start, their course in the 2012/13, 2013/14, 2014/15 or 2015/16 academic year are referred to as **'2012 cohort'** students.

**Note:** the government has recently announced changes to student support for the 2016 academic year. If the legislation is passed in autumn 2015, there will be a '2016 cohort' added to the above.

'Current system' students can apply for a package of support, which includes:

- student loans for tuition fees (see p27);
- either a maintenance grant (see p29) or special support grant (see p30);
- a student loan for living costs (see p30);
- supplementary grants in particular circumstances (see p33).

## Gap year students

Some gap year students who began their course in the 2006/07 academic year are treated as 'old system' students if they deferred entry to higher education from the 2005/06 academic year and had confirmed their place at their institution by 1 August 2005.[10] You must still be on that course, or a course with similar content, to qualify. If you think you should qualify, speak to an adviser.

## Previous study

If you have previously attended a higher education course, the amount of support you can receive on any subsequent course may be affected by the rules on previous study.[11]

If you are a 'current system' student (see p25) and hold an honours degree, support for any new qualification is restricted to supplementary grants for travel costs, grants for dependants and grants for disability-related costs.[12]

Some exceptions apply: students who hold an honours degree and are undertaking a PGCE or PGDE course receive full funding, while those undertaking a further undergraduate course in certain professional subjects, such as medicine, veterinary science, architecture and social work, can receive a maintenance loan for that course,[13] although not a loan for tuition fees or a maintenance or special support grant. For further details of medicine and dentistry courses, see p28.

Students eligible for a means-tested NHS bursary continue to be eligible for a reduced-rate loan, whether or not they already hold an equivalent or higher level qualification. If you wish to study a qualification of an equivalent or lower level to one you already hold, financial support may be further restricted, as the Higher Education Funding Council for England does not provide funding to the higher education institution in the form of a teaching grant, and tuition fees may therefore exceed the £3,465 or £9,000 cap. Again, some professional courses are exempt. Check your entitlement with an adviser.

If you do not already hold an honours degree, in general the maximum number of years of tuition fee loan and maintenance or special support grant funding you can receive is equivalent to the ordinary length of your course plus one year, less any years of study previously undertaken.[14] If you have studied part of a year, you are treated as if you have undertaken a full year of study. Maintenance loans are, however, unaffected.

If you are transferring courses, or undertaking an 'end-on' course, these previous study rules affect you. You may be able to secure additional years of 'full' funding if you were unable to complete a previous year or course for 'compelling personal reasons', such as illness or caring responsibilities.[15] You must provide evidence of this to Student Finance England.

Rules for 'old system' (see p25) students are slightly different, but have broadly the same effect.

Further information on previous study is available from www.gov.uk/student-finance or from your student adviser.

# Grants and loans for tuition fees

## 'Old system' students

If you are an 'old system' student (see p25), you may be liable to pay a contribution towards your tuition fees, up to a maximum of £1,380 per academic year (potentially rising each year with inflation).

'Old system' students with a low household income can receive help with all, or some, of their contribution to their tuition fees.[16] You may be entitled to a grant from Student Finance England towards the costs of your fees, depending on your and (where appropriate) your parents' or partner's income (see p37).

Once this income assessment for the tuition fee grant has been carried out, you may be eligible for a loan for the remaining tuition fees.[17] For example, if Student Finance England has agreed to pay £600 towards your fees due on the basis of your household income, you can apply for a tuition fee loan for the remaining £780.

Tuition fee loans must be repaid on the same basis as loans for living costs (see p32).

## 'New system' students

In 2012, major changes were made to student funding. Colleges and universities can now charge new entrants (2012 cohort) fees of up to £9,000 per academic year, unless you are undertaking a sandwich (placement) year, in which case fees are restricted to 20 per cent of the maximum (you can be charged a maximum of £1,800), or unless you are on an Erasmus placement, in which case fees are restricted to 15 per cent of the maximum (£1,350 per year). Continuing students who started between 1 September 2006 and 31 August 2012 (2006, 2008 and 2009 cohorts) can be charged fees of up to £3,465 a year. Different rules apply to 'old system' students who started before 1 September 2006 (see above).

If you are a home (see p22) or EU student, you can apply for a tuition fee loan to cover all, or part, of the cost of the fees.[18] Your income is not assessed for this.

The repayment terms of a tuition fee loan are the same as for an income-contingent maintenance loan (see p32).

In addition, you may be eligible for a maintenance grant of up to £3,110 (2006, 2008 and 2009 cohorts) or £3,387 (2012 cohort) (see p29) and, in some circumstances, a bursary from your institution (see p44).

The rules that determine how much you are charged are complex. In 2015/16, colleges and universities can charge fees of up to £9,000 a year in certain circumstances.[19] These circumstances are not necessarily the same as those for receiving student support for fees to that level, so it is important to check the amount of tuition fees you will be charged by your institution.

For example, if you began a course before 1 September 2006 and transfer to a similar course at the same institution, you are charged no more than £1,380 for your tuition fees in 2015/16. If, however, you transfer to a similar course at a different institution or a different course at the same institution, you can be charged up to £9,000 in 2015/16. However, because you were receiving student support before 1 September 2006 and have not withdrawn from education, you receive the student support package that you have always received – eg, an income-assessed tuition fee grant of a maximum of £1,380 and up to £1,000 higher education grant, in addition to the maintenance loan and other supplementary grants for which you may be eligible.

In 2015/16, an institution can charge '2012 cohort' students up to £6,000 a year for their courses and, if the university or college has an approved access agreement with the Office for Fair Access, up to £9,000. The same transfer arrangements apply, as above. So, if you entered higher education before 2012/13, but are considering transferring in 2015/16 or later, you are strongly advised to obtain advice before doing so.

If you choose to study outside England, the same arrangements concerning fees and funding apply. In 2015/16, 2012 cohort students may be charged up to £9,000 a year in Scotland, Wales and Northern Ireland.

**Note:** there is no requirement to take out a tuition fee loan. If you wish, you can pay all, or part of, the fee in cash in advance. Your institution generally expects some indication of how you intend to pay your fees when you register.

## Medicine and dentistry students

There are special fee arrangements for medicine and dentistry students, and these differ depending on whether you are undertaking a standard five-year undergraduate medicine or dentistry course, or the four-year graduate entry course.[20] **Note:** in both cases, some students may study an extra year in a specialist area of medicine.

If you are on a standard five-year undergraduate course, you pay fees at the rate charged by the institution until the fifth year of study, after which you move to the NHS bursary scheme (see Chapter 6). The NHS then pays your fees in the fifth and any subsequent years. Those starting in 2012/13 or later will see the maximum fee rise to £9,000 in years one to four, in line with other students, but will continue to have their fees paid in the fifth and subsequent years by the NHS. **Note:** this system is under review and students entering higher education after the 2015/16 academic year may face different rules.

If you are on the four-year graduate entry course and started your course in 2011/12 or earlier, you must pay the fee charged by the institution upfront in your first year, up to a maximum of £3,465. There is no loan available to help with your fees for this year. However, after the first year, you are then funded through the NHS bursary scheme.

If you started a four-year graduate entry course in 2012/13 or later, the maximum fee is £9,000 a year. In your first year, you must pay the first £3,465 of your fees. A student loan is available to cover any amount charged above this level. In your second and subsequent years, the NHS pays the first £3,465 (rising with inflation), and a student loan for fees is available for any amount charged above this.

**Note:** different arrangements may be introduced for those entering in 2016/17 or later.

Students who hold an honours degree and who wish to study the standard undergraduate course do not have access to fee support until they reach the NHS bursary-funded stage of the course in year five.

## Higher education grant

Students who started a new course between September 2004 and August 2006 (or who are treated as 'old system' students if they started their course in the 2006/07 academic year) are eligible for a higher education grant of up to £1,010.[21] Students on full-time, sandwich and part-time initial teacher training courses are eligible to apply. If you started your course before September 2004, you are not eligible.

## Maintenance grant

A maintenance grant is available to 'current system' students from low-income backgrounds who started their studies on or after 1 September 2006.[22] This grant is for maintenance costs, and the maximum amount in 2015/16 is £3,110 for the 2006, 2008 and 2009 cohorts and £3,387 for the 2012 cohort.[23] The amount of the grant for 2012 cohort students is higher to reflect the different rules on bursaries.[24]

In all cases, part of the grant substitutes part of the loan for living costs. How this is done depends on which cohort you are in. In 2015/16, if you started your course before the 2009/10 academic year, the loan is substituted pound for pound, up to a maximum of £1,400. For example, if you receive a £900 maintenance grant, the maximum amount of loan you can borrow is reduced by £900. Any maintenance grant in excess of £1,400 does not further reduce the loan.

In 2015/16 for 2009 cohort students, 50 pence of the loan is substituted for every pound of maintenance grant paid, so that the maximum substitution is £1,555 if the full maintenance grant is paid.[25]

In 2015/16, 2012 cohort students have a higher grant, with a maximum payment of £3,387. They have 50 pence of the loan substituted for every pound of maintenance grant paid, so that the maximum substitution is £1,693 if the full maintenance grant is paid.[26]

If you are eligible for means-tested benefits, the maintenance grant is taken into account as income when working out your entitlement, so if you are eligible you should ensure you receive the special support grant instead. An adviser in your university can help you with this.

**Note:** the government plans to abolish both the maintenance grant and special support grant for new students from the 2016/17 academic year and replace them with higher value maintenance loans. This change is still subject to parliamentary approval.

## Special support grant

The special support grant is available to 'current system' students from low-income backgrounds who started their studies on or after 1 September 2006 and who are eligible for means-tested benefits, such as income support or housing benefit.[27] The maximum amount in 2015/16 is £3,110 for the 2006, 2008 and 2009 cohorts and £3,387 for the 2012 cohort.[28] This grant is for course-related costs and is not taken into account as income when working out entitlement to means-tested benefits.

The special support grant is payable in addition to the full maintenance loan, with no loan substitution applied.

**Note:** the government plans to abolish both the maintenance grant and special support grant for new students from the 2016/17 academic year and replace them with higher value maintenance loans. This change is still subject to parliamentary approval.

## Student maintenance loans

Student maintenance loans are available to eligible 'old system' and 'current system' students to help with living costs, such as food and rent. There are two different types of loan.

**Mortgage-style loans** were available to those students who were eligible to receive mandatory awards (the system in place before 1998). These are no longer available to students currently in higher education, but see p32 for information on repayment.

**Income-contingent loans** form part of the help available to students under the current student support system. Part of the loan (35 per cent for 2012 cohort students, 28 per cent for 2009 cohort students, and 25 per cent for other students) is subject to an income assessment. The remaining 65 per cent, 72 per cent or 75 per cent is not income assessed. You may be entitled to an additional amount if your course exceeds 30 weeks and three days in the year (see p31).

The amounts available depend on the year of entry (or cohort) and have been increased by 3.34 per cent in 2015/16.

**Note:** the government plans to increase the amount of the maintenance loan available in 2016/17 to compensate for the proposed abolition of the maintenance grant and special support grant. Students who would have previously received a maintenance grant will see a 10.3 per cent increase and students who would have received a special support grant a 2.41 per cent increase. This change is still subject to parliamentary approval.

*Maximum amount of income-contingent loan 2015/16*

| 2012 cohort | Full year | Final year |
|---|---|---|
| London | £8,009 | £7,294 |
| Elsewhere | £5,740 | £5,338 |
| Parental home | £4,565 | £4,195 |
| Overseas rate | £6,820 | £5,927 |
| **2009 cohort**[29] | | |
| London | £7,230 | £6,582 |
| Elsewhere | £5,167 | £4,782 |
| Parental home | £4,005 | £3,634 |
| Overseas rate | £6,151 | £5,348 |
| **Other students**[30] | | |
| London | £6,933 | £6,312 |
| Elsewhere | £4,952 | £4,582 |
| Parental home | £3,832 | £3,463 |
| Overseas rate | £5,899 | £5,129 |

## Long courses loan

You may be entitled to additional amounts of loan for any extra weeks of attendance over the standard 30 weeks and three days. Your institution can clarify whether your course has additional weeks.

If you started before 1 September 2008, this additional amount is simply added to the standard amount of loan paid. For 2008, 2009 and 2012 cohort students, it is known specifically as the 'long courses loan' and is treated differently in the income assessment. Any additional amount payable is paid along with other forms of support at the start of each term, and is repaid along with other student loan debt.

The table below outlines the amount paid for each week your course exceeds the standard length. If your course year lasts 45 weeks or more, you are paid for a full 52 weeks of attendance. These rates have increased by 3.34 per cent for 2015/16.

*Amount of long courses loan 2015/16*

| | Weekly amount |
|---|---|
| London | £110 |
| Elsewhere | £86 |
| Parental home | £56 |
| Overseas rate | £119 |

## Repaying your loan

Both mortgage-style and income-contingent loans are repayable at the end of your studies. The repayment method differs for each type of loan.

### Mortgage-style loans

Mortgage-style loans are normally repaid over 60 fixed monthly instalments from the April following your graduation or the point you otherwise leave your course, or over 84 fixed monthly instalments if you had loans for five or more years.[31] However, you can request that repayments be deferred if you earn less than 85 per cent of the national average wage. In 2015/16, repayments can be deferred if your gross earnings are not more than £28,828 per year or £2,356 per month.

Liability to repay mortgage-style loans can be cancelled if:[32]

- you die;
- you are permanently incapacitated from work because of a disability;
- you reach the age of 50 (or 60 if you were 40 or over when you last took out a loan);
- 25 years have passed since the April following your graduation or the point at which you otherwise left your course,

whichever comes first.

Interest on mortgage-style loans is set at the rate of inflation, measured by the retail price index (RPI) in March, applied for a year from the following September.

### Income-contingent loans

The amount of money you pay back each month on an income-contingent loan depends on your earnings and when you started your course.

If you have an income-contingent loan and started your course in 2011/12 or earlier, you begin to make repayments from the April after you graduate or otherwise leave your course, once you earn above £17,335 a year. Repayments start at a rate of 9 per cent of all income above that threshold.[33] For example, if you earn £18,335 a year, you pay back 9 per cent of £1,000 – ie, £90 a year or £7.50 a month.

This threshold is set to increase with inflation each year until at least 2016.

If you started your course before 2012/13, interest is set at the rate of inflation, measured by the RPI in March, applied for a year from the following September, with a cap of 1 per cent above the base rates of certain nominated banks.

If you started your course in 2012/13 or later, you begin to repay your loan no earlier than April 2016, although you can choose to make voluntary repayments before this date.

From April 2016, repayments will start at a rate of 9 per cent of any income above £21,000 a year. **Note:** the government intended that this threshold would rise each year thereafter, in line with average earnings, but it is now consulting on freezing this for at least five years (to April 2021). At the time of writing, the outcome of this consultation was not known.

Interest on income-contingent loans for 2012 cohort students is variable. During the period of study, up to the April following graduation or otherwise leaving the course, the interest rate is set at the rate of inflation, measured by the RPI in March, plus 3 per cent. Thereafter, it is at: RPI if you earn less than the repayment threshold of £21,000; RPI plus 3 per cent if you earn more than £41,000 a year before tax; and an amount on a sliding scale between RPI and RPI plus 3 per cent if you earn between £21,000 and £41,000 a year. The cap on the interest rates is set at 'the rate prevailing on the market', but it is not clear how this will be measured in practice.

Liability to repay an income-contingent loan can be cancelled if you die or are permanently incapacitated from work because of a disability. If you are an 'old system' student, liability is also cancelled when you reach the age of 65.

'Current system' students who started before 2012/13 have their liability cancelled 25 years after the April following their graduation or when they otherwise left the course,[34] while 2012 cohort students have liability cancelled 30 years after the April following their graduation or when they otherwise left the course.

## Supplementary grants

A number of additional grants are available to both 'old system' and 'current system' students in certain circumstances.

### Adult dependants' grant

If you have an adult dependant(s) 'wholly or mainly financially dependent' on you, you may be eligible for an adult dependants' grant.[35] Eligible adult dependants include your spouse or civil partner, or (if you are aged 25 or over) a cohabiting partner. The maximum grant is £2,757 in 2015/16, and it is intended that the grant will be frozen at this rate for 2016/17, but the amount you receive depends on your situation and the income of your dependant(s). The amount you are eligible to receive is halved if your spouse/partner receives full-time student support from the Department for Business, Innovation and Skills.

### Parents' learning allowance

If you are a parent with dependent children, you may be eligible for a parents' learning allowance to help cover your course-related costs.[36] How much you get depends on your income and that of your partner, spouse and any other dependants. It is not counted as income when assessing your benefit and tax credit entitlement.

The maximum entitlement in 2015/16 is £1,573, and it is intended that the allowance will be frozen at this rate for 2016/17. If a couple are both full-time students, both can claim the full allowance, subject to their household income.

## Childcare grant

If you have responsibility for a child under the age of 15 (or 17 if s/he has special educational needs) and you use registered or approved childcare, you can apply for a childcare grant.[37] You cannot receive the childcare grant if you receive the childcare element in working tax credit (WTC – see Chapter 20) or universal credit (UC – see Chapter 18). You are also ineligible if your partner receives the childcare allowance in an NHS bursary (see p79).

### Registered or approved childcare

A 'registered childcare provider'is a person who is registered under the Children Act and who provides daycare.[38] The person must care for one or more children aged under eight for more than two hours a day for payment. The care must be provided on domestic premises used wholly or mainly as a private dwelling. A relative who provides childcare for your child qualifies, provided s/he is registered with the Office for Standards in Education (Ofsted) and s/he is also looking after other children who are unrelated to her/him. Nurseries, out-of-hours school clubs and holiday playschemes also count.

'Approved childcare'covers provision for children aged eight or over. The childcare must be approved by an accredited organisation under the Working Tax Credit (Entitlement and Maximum Rate) Regulations 2002 (as amended). This definition includes carers who are approved under the voluntary childcare approval scheme. This covers childcare in the parent's home for children of any age, and childcare for children aged eight or over provided by a childminder in her/his own home or other domestic premises.

The grant can cover up to 85 per cent of your actual costs for childcare. In 2015/16 the maximum amount you can receive is £155.24 a week for one child or £266.24 a week for two or more children. It is intended that the childcare grant will be frozen at this rate for the 2016/17 academic year. The maximum amount of grant available annually in 2015/16 is £8,072 for one child and £13,844 for two or more children.

The amount you receive depends on your income and the income of any dependants.

## Grant for travel costs

If you are a medical or dental student undertaking clinical placements, or if you have to study abroad as a compulsory part of your course, you may be able to claim help with your travel costs if they are more than £303 in the year. The help is means tested (see p35).

## Disabled students' allowance

If you incur additional course-related costs as a consequence of a disability, you can apply for disabled students' allowance.[39] This is a needs-based allowance and you must provide medical evidence of your disability, such as a letter from your doctor, educational psychologist or other specialist, when you apply to Student Finance England for assistance under this scheme. If Student Finance England accepts this proof, it (and/or the adviser in your university or college) helps you to arrange a needs assessment with a recognised assessor. S/he recommends what additional support or equipment you should be supplied with. The maximum rates for the different elements of the allowance in 2015/16 are listed below. It is intended that these will also apply for the 2016/17 academic year.

---

*Maximum amount of disabled students' allowance 2015/16*[40]

| | |
|---|---|
| Non-medical personal helper(s) | £20,725 per academic year |
| Major items of specialist equipment | £5,212 for the duration of the course |
| Other expenditure | Up to £1,741 per academic year |
| Extra travel expenditure resulting from disability | Full reimbursement |

---

At the time of writing, the disabled students' allowance for students domiciled in England was going through some major changes. Although the basic structure of the allowance remains the same, the government intends to 'rebalance' the support it provides, potentially placing greater responsibility on universities and colleges to provide non-medical personal helpers, and restrict the types of computer and other IT equipment it funds. In 2015/16, the allowance no longer covers the first £200 of the cost of a computer and students applying for the disabled students' allowance for the first time must fund this themselves. Some institutions have hardship funds or bursaries to help students with this additional cost. Other changes are still being consulted on and are likely to be introduced in 2016/17. You should speak to an adviser in your university or students' union for more information.

## Assessing income for student support

Most elements of student support for both 'current system' and 'old system' students are subject to an income assessment.[41] You may be assessed as either a dependent (see p36) or an independent student (see p36).

Your own income is always assessed, plus that of your:
- parent(s), if you do not have independent status (see p36); *or*
- spouse, if you are married; *or*
- civil partner, if you are in a civil partnership; *or*
- cohabiting partner of the opposite sex, if you are aged 25 or over and started your course in September 2000 or later; *or*
- cohabiting partner of the same sex, if you are aged 25 or over and started your course in September 2005 or later.

## Dependent students

If you are considered a dependent student, Student Finance England looks at your parents' gross taxable income over the previous full tax year (for the academic year 2015/16, this is 6 April 2013 to 5 April 2014), then subtracts pension scheme and superannuation payments, which attract tax relief. A further £1,130 is deducted for each additional dependent child or if your parent is a student her/himself.[42]

The remaining amount is added to your estimated gross taxable income for the 2015/16 academic year (if any, and subject to various disregards, including all earnings from part-time or casual work) to form your household income figure.[43]

The household income figure is then used to determine how much the household is expected to contribute to your costs and, therefore, how much support you can receive from the government.

**Note:** if the level of your parents' income falls by at least 15 per cent during the academic year, you can request a reassessment (a current year income assessment) from Student Finance England.[44]

If your parents are separated, divorced or widowed and you are not deemed independent, the income of the parent with whom you live is taken into account. If you do not live with either parent, Student Finance England decides which parent's income is the most appropriate to use.

If you started your course after September 2004, the income of a parent's new spouse or partner is also assessed, even if that person is not your parent.

## Independent students

You are assessed as an independent student if:[45]

- you are either aged 25 before the beginning of the academic year in which your course begins or you become 25 during the academic year (in which case, you have independent status from the beginning of the following academic year); *or*
- you are married or in a civil partnership before the course begins, or you marry or form a civil partnership during the course (in which case, you become independent from the beginning of the following academic year); *or*
- you have been financially self-reliant for any three years before the academic year in which your course begins (this qualifying period can include periods of unemployment and participation in training schemes for the unemployed, such as modern apprenticeships); *or*
- you have responsibility for one or more children; *or*
- you are 'irreconcilably estranged' from your parents (see p37); *or*
- you have been in the care of a local authority for a certain period; *or*
- your parents cannot be found; *or*
- it is not reasonably practicable for your parents to send parental contributions to the UK, or they would be placed in jeopardy if they did so; *or*
- you have no living parents; *or*

- you are a member of a religious order living in a house of that order, and you started your course before 1 September 2009.

If you are considered an independent student, your parents' income is not taken into account. Your gross taxable income for the academic year, less various disregards (including earnings from part-time work), is taken into account. If you have a spouse or partner, her/his income may be taken into account (see below).

### Estrangement

If your relationship with your parents has completely broken down, and you do not meet any of the other criteria for independent status, you can apply for 'estrangement' status so that their income is not taken into account.

If you can provide evidence that you have had no contact with your parents for at least a year, you should be treated as estranged. If you have become estranged but have had contact within the last 12 months, you can still use other evidence to prove your estrangement – eg, letters from social services or medical or other professionals.[46] You cannot usually be assessed as estranged part way through the year. Instead, you must wait until you reapply the next academic year and provide evidence of your circumstances at that time.

Your students' union or institution advice centre can assist you to apply for estrangement status.

## Spouses and partners

If your spouse or civil/cohabiting partner is considered part of the assessable household, her/his income is assessed in a similar way to that of a student's parents (see p36).[47]

Any income from your spouse or civil/cohabiting partner is added to your income to form the household income to be taken into account. However, if you have separated from your spouse or civil partner, her/his income is not assessed.

As with dependent students, the household income figure is used to determine how much the household is expected to contribute to your costs and, therefore, how much support you can receive from the government.

## How income affects student support

### 'Current system' students: pre-2008 cohorts

If you started your course in the 2006/07 or 2007/08 academic years, and are not subject to any of the gap year provisions (see p26), your assessed income first reduces any maintenance grant or special support grant you are due to receive. In 2015/16, the following applies.[48]

- If your household income is £18,360 or less, you receive the maximum maintenance or special support grant.
- If your household income is between £18,361 and £39,571, you receive a reduced amount of the grant (the minimum amount is £50).

- For every £5.68 of household income between £18,361 and £28,075, £1 is deducted from the grant.
- For every £8.51 of household income above £28,075, £1 is deducted from the grant until the maximum household income of £39,571 is reached.
- No grant is payable if your household income is more than £39,571.

Income above £39,796 reduces other student support at a rate of £1 for every £8.97 of income above £39,796.[49] Any supplementary grants for dependants are reduced first, then the 25 per cent of the student loan that is means tested and, finally, any grant for travel costs.[50]

This assessment also applies if you started a course in the 2008/09 academic year or later but have previously studied at higher education level.

## 'Current system' students: 2008 cohort

If you started your course in the 2008/09 academic year and have not previously studied at higher education level, your assessed income first reduces any maintenance grant or special support grant you are due to receive. In 2015/16, the following applies.[51]

- If your household income is £25,000 or less, you receive the maximum maintenance or special support grant.
- If your household income is between £25,001 and £61,047, you receive a reduced amount of the applicable grant (the minimum amount is £50).
  - For every £5.68 of household income between £25,001 and £34,713, £1 is deducted from the grant.
  - For every £19.50 of household income above £34,713, £1 is deducted from the grant until the maximum household income of £61,047 is reached.
- No grant is payable if your household income is more than £61,047.

Income above £61,062 reduces the income-assessed 25 per cent of the applicable basic rate of your student loan at a rate of £1 for every £8.88 of additional income.[52]

Other income-assessed student support is reduced in a different way. Support is reduced at a rate of £1 for every £8.97 of income above £39,796.[53] Any supplementary grants for dependants are reduced first, then any long courses loan payable and, finally, any grant for travel costs.[54]

## 'Current system' students: 2009 cohort

If you started your course in the 2009/10 academic year or later (but before 1 September 2012) and have not previously studied at higher education level, your assessed income first reduces any maintenance grant or special support grant you are due to receive. In 2015/16, the following applies.[55]

- If your household income is £25,000 or less, you receive the maximum maintenance or special support grant.

- If your household income is between £25,001 and £50,706, you receive a reduced amount of the applicable grant (the minimum amount is £50).
  - For every £4.85 of household income between £25,001 and £34,264, £1 is deducted from the grant.
  - For every £14.29 of household income above £34,264, £1 is deducted from the grant until the maximum household income of £50,706 is reached.
- No grant is payable if your household income is more than £50,706.

Income above £50,778 reduces the income-assessed 28 per cent of the applicable basic rate of student loan (see p31) at a rate of £1 for every £4.79 of additional income.[56]

Other income-assessed student support is reduced in a different way. Support is reduced at a rate of £1 for every £8.97 of income above £39,796.[57] Any supplementary grants for dependants are reduced first, then any long courses loan payable and, finally, any grant for travel costs.[58]

## 'Current system' students: 2012 cohort

If you start your course in the 2012/13 academic year or later and have not previously studied at higher education level, your assessed income first reduces any maintenance grant or special support grant you are due to receive. In 2015/16, the following applies.[59]

- If your household income is £25,000 or less, you receive the maximum maintenance or special support grant.
- If your household income is between £25,001 and £42,620, you receive a reduced amount of the applicable grant (the minimum amount is £50). For every £5.28 of household income above £25,000, £1 is deducted from the grant until the maximum household income of £42,620 is reached.
- No grant is payable if your household income is more than £42,620.

Income above £42,875 reduces the income-assessed 35 per cent of the applicable basic rate of student loan (see p31) at a rate of £1 for every £9.59 of additional income.[60]

Other income-assessed support is reduced in a different way. Support is reduced at a rate of £1 for every £8.97 of income above £39,796.[61] Any supplementary grants for dependants are reduced first, then any long courses loan payable and, finally, any grant for travel costs.[62]

## 'Old system' students

If you are funded under the system available to students who started courses between 1998 and 2005, the following applies.

### Higher education grant

The income assessment for the higher education grant is separate from that for other support.[63]

- If your household income is £16,750 or less, you receive the maximum grant.
- If your household income is between £16,751 and £22,735, you receive a reduced amount of the grant (the minimum amount is £50). For every £6.23 of household income above £16,751, £1 is deducted from the grant until the maximum household income of £22,735 is reached.
- No grant is payable if your household income is £22,736 or more.

### Dependent students

If you are a dependent student (see p36), your parents' or your spouse's/partner's income is taken into account and your household income is calculated as for 'current system' students.

If your household income is less than £23,660, no contribution applies. Once your household income reaches £23,660, your parents or spouse/partner must pay an annual £45 contribution towards your support. After this, £1 is deducted from your support for every £9.27 of household income above this amount.[64]

The contribution is applied first to the grant for tuition fees, then to any grants for dependants, then to the income-assessed portion of the student loan and, finally, to any grant for tuition fees, until all income-assessed support is eliminated.[65]

### Independent students

If you are a single, independent student (see p36), as with 'current system' students, only your own estimated gross taxable income (less various disregards) for the current academic year is taken into account. If your income is less than £11,020 no contribution is payable, but your student support is reduced by £1 for every £9.27 of income above this level in the same order as for dependent students.[66]

## Overpayments

If you have been overpaid student support either by your local authority (when it had responsibility for student finance applications) or by Student Finance England, the overpayment can be recovered.[67] This is the case even if the overpayment was the result of a mistake made by Student Finance England or the local authority. Both have the discretion not to recover the overpayment, but they normally attempt to do so.

Usually, any overpayment of student support is recovered by reducing the support you are due to receive in future instalments. If you are not due to receive any further instalments, Student Finance England can use any other methods available to it. In practice, this means either asking you to repay the money in full directly, agreeing a repayment plan with you or adding the overpayment to your student loan debt.

If you have been overpaid fee support, in the past it was usually reclaimed from the academic institution and the institution then discussed any amount owed

**2**

with you directly. However, this changed in the 2012/13 year, and fee overpayments are normally recovered via Student Finance England.[68]

If you have received equipment through the disabled students' allowance and it is subsequently decided that you have been 'overpaid', it may be acceptable to return the equipment rather than repay its cash value.[69]

Contact your students' union or advice service for help checking whether an overpayment has been made, and for help negotiating with Student Finance England or your institution if this is the case.

# 2. Part-time undergraduates

Support for part-time students is different from that available to full-time students, and is focused on course-related costs rather than living costs. The support available depends on when you started your course. The same course and personal eligibility requirements apply as for full-time students (see pp21–24).[70]

In addition, if you started your course on or after 1 September 2012, the course must be at least 25 per cent of a full-time course – ie, it takes no more than four times the equivalent length of the full-time course to complete. If you started your course before this date, it must be least 50 per cent of a full-time course – ie, it takes no longer than twice the time of the equivalent full-time course to complete.[71]

## Loans for tuition fees: 2012 entrants or later

Student loans for fees are available for part-time study for new students (including students from the European Union (EU) – see p22) starting from September 2012/13. Your course must be at an intensity of at least 25 per cent of the equivalent full-time course, and you can receive support for a maximum of 16 years.[72]

You can receive a loan of up to £6,750 to cover the cost of the fees charged.[73] From 1 September 2012, part-time fees for new students are regulated, so your fees should not exceed this amount. Fee loans to part-time students must be repaid in the same way as loans to full-time 2012 cohort students, with the same arrangements for interest (see p32).

Your income and the income of your parents or partner does not affect your entitlement to a tuition fee loan.

## Grants for tuition fees: pre-September 2012 entrants

If you started your course in 2011/12 or earlier and are a part-time undergraduate student (including students from the EU – see p22), you may be eligible for an income-assessed tuition fee grant.[74] The maximum amount of grant for which you are eligible depends on the intensity of study for each academic year of the course.

**Maximum grant for part-time fees 2015/16**

| Course intensity | Maximum grant available |
| --- | --- |
| Less than 60% | £855 |
| 60–74% | £1,025 |
| 75% or more | £1,285 |

Part-time students whose tuition fees are higher than the amount covered by the grant for fees should apply to their institution for help from its hardship fund. Although hardship funds were part of the Access to Learning Fund, which is no longer funded by the Higher Education Funding Council for England, many institutions offer transitional protection for continuing part-time students. Ask your advice centre or students' union for further information.

## Grants for course costs: pre-September 2012 entrants

A grant of up to £280 is available for students from low-income backgrounds to help with the costs of books, equipment and travel.[75] The amount of grant available is not affected by the intensity of study. This is not available for EU students.

## Disabled students' allowance

If you are a part-time student and studying at an intensity of at least 50 per cent (pre-2012 entrants) or 25 per cent (2012 or later entrants) of an equivalent full-time course and have a disability, you can apply for a disabled students' allowance. However, the amount Student Finance England can award for non-medical help and other general expenditure is reduced according to the workload of a part-time course.

**Maximum amount of disabled students' allowance 2015/16[76]**

| | |
| --- | --- |
| Non-medical personal helper(s) | £15,543 per academic year |
| Major items of specialist equipment | £5,212 for the duration of the course |
| Other expenditure | Up to £1,305 per academic year |
| Extra travel expenditure resulting from disability | Full reimbursement |

At the time of writing, the disabled students' allowance for students domiciled in England was going through some major changes. Although the basic structure of the allowance remains the same, the government intends to 'rebalance' the support it provides, potentially placing greater responsibility on universities and colleges to provide non-medical personal helpers, and restrict the types of computer and other IT equipment it funds. In 2015/16, the allowance no longer covers the first £200 of the cost of a computer and students applying for the disabled students' allowance for the first time must fund this themselves. Some institutions have hardship funds or bursaries to help students with this additional cost. Other changes are still being consulted on and are likely to be introduced in 2016/17. You should speak to an adviser in your university or students' union for more information.

### How income affects student support: pre-September 2012 entrants

**Note:** if you are funded under the new rules in place since September 2012, no income assessment applies.

In 2015/16, the following applies.

- If your income is below £16,845, you are eligible for the maximum grant for fees and course costs.
- If your income is between £16,846 and £25,419, you receive some help with fees and course costs.
- If your income is between £25,420 and £28,065, you receive some help with course costs, but not with fees. The exact amount you receive depends on your income.
- If your income is £28,065, you receive a course grant of £50. If your income is above this amount, you receive no support.

Only your and your partner's income is taken into account as household income. Your parents' income is ignored, regardless of your age.[77]

If you are married or in a civil partnership, or aged 25 or over and living with a partner (including a same-sex partner) or have dependent children, the following amounts are deducted from your income:[78]

- £2,000 for your partner;
- £2,000 for your eldest child;
- £1,000 for every other child.

---

## 3. **Discretionary and institutional funds**

Before 2014 all higher education institutions were allocated money from the Higher Education Funding Council for England (HEFCE) to provide discretionary hardship funds for 'home' (see p22) undergraduate and postgraduate students in financial difficulty. The funds (the Access to Learning Fund) were also used to help part-time undergraduate students who started before 1 September 2012 with fee support. The funds provided both repayable loans and non-repayable grants. However, from September 2014 these funds have no longer been provided by HEFCE. Instead, institutions are expected to provide their own funds to alleviate student hardship and to support retention and progression. As these funds are no longer provided or reported on centrally, it is likely that they no longer have common assessment criteria. You should therefore contact your institution for information on how to apply and how you will be assessed.

## Additional fee support scheme

This scheme was previously part of the Access to Learning Fund, which was abolished in 2014. However, all institutions are expected to continue to identify funds to support retention and progression, and so funds should still be available to help part-time 'home' and European Union students who started their course before 1 September 2012 to meet the costs of their tuition fees, where these fees are higher than the amount covered by the government grant for fees. Local fund administrators have discretion on how much assistance to pay and to whom. For more information, speak to an adviser in your university or college or contact the fund administrator.

## Institutional bursaries

If you are a 'current system' student who started in September 2011 or earlier, you are receiving the full maintenance or special support grant of £3,110 in 2015/16 and your university or college charges fees of more than £3,110, you are eligible for a minimum non-repayable bursary.

The Office for Fair Access, which governs bursary rules, has stated that the minimum mandatory bursary must be equivalent to 10 per cent of the tuition fees charged by the university or college. Therefore, in 2015/16, if the fee charged is £3,465, the mandatory minimum bursary is £347.[79] However, many institutions offer more than this. Contact your university or college for more information.

There is no minimum bursary for students who started in 2012/13 or later.

# Notes

1. **Full-time undergraduates**
   1. Sch 1 Part 2 E(SS) Regs
   2. 'Islands' in this context are the Channel Islands and the Isle of Man
   3. For a definition of 'relevant family member', see Sch 1 para 1 E(SS) Regs
   4. Sch 1 para 8 E(SS) Regs
   5. Sch 1 para 12 E(SS) Regs
   6. Sch 1 para 4 E(SS) Regs
   7. Reg 5 and Sch 2 E(SS) Regs
   8. Reg 2 E(SS) Regs
   9. Reg 2 E(SS) Regs
   10. Reg 2 E(SS) Regs
   11. Regs 21-23 E(SS) Regs
   12. Regs 20, 56, 60 and 67 E(SS) Regs
   13. Reg 67 E(SS) Regs
   14. Regs 20 and 21 E(SS) Regs
   15. Regs 19(10) and 30(2) E(SS) Regs
   16. Reg 25 E(SS) Regs
   17. Reg 34 E(SS) Regs
   18. Reg 19 E(SS) Regs
   19. s25 HEA 2004
   20. Letter from David Willetts and Andrew Lansley to the British Medical Association, 28 June 2011
   21. Reg 64 E(SS) Regs
   22. Reg 56 E(SS) Regs
   23. Regs 57, 58 and 60 E(SS) Regs
   24. Reg 59 E(SS) Regs
   25. Reg 72(8)-(10) E(SS) Regs
   26. Reg 76 E(SS) Regs
   27. Reg 61 E(SS) Regs
   28. Regs 62, 63 and 65 E(SS) Regs
   29. Reg 74 E(SS) Regs
   30. Reg 72 E(SS) Regs
   31. Sch 2 para 5 E(SL) Regs. **Note:** if you have taken out more than five student loans, you repay your loan in 84 monthly instalments.
   32. Sch 2 para 12 E(SL) Regs
   33. Reg 44 E(SL)(R) Regs
   34. Reg 19 E(SL)(R) Regs
   35. Reg 44 E(SS) Regs
   36. Reg 46 E(SS) Regs
   37. Reg 45 E(SS) Regs
   38. s79(f) CA 1989
   39. Reg 40 E(SS) Regs
   40. Reg 41 E(SS) Regs
   41. Sch 4 E(SS) Regs
   42. Sch 4 para 3 E(SS) Regs
   43. Sch 4 paras 3 and 4 E(SS) Regs
   44. Sch 4 para 5(3)-(4) E(SS) Regs
   45. Sch 4 para 2 E(SS) Regs
   46. Sch 4 para 2(1)(e) E(SS) Regs
   47. Sch 4 para 6 E(SS) Regs
   48. Reg 59 E(SS) Regs
   49. Sch 4 para 9 E(SS) Regs
   50. Regs 98 and 101 E(SS) Regs
   51. Reg 57 E(SS) Regs
   52. Reg 70 E(SS) Regs
   53. Sch 4 para 9 E(SS) Regs
   54. Regs 97 and 100 E(SS) Regs
   55. Reg 58 E(SS) Regs
   56. Reg 72 E(SS) Regs
   57. Sch 4 para 9 E(SS) Regs
   58. Regs 97 and 100 E(SS) Regs
   59. Reg 59 E(SS) Regs
   60. Reg 76 E(SS) Regs
   61. Sch 4 para 9 E(SS) Regs
   62. Regs 99 and 100 E(SS) Regs
   63. Reg 65 E(SS) Regs
   64. Sch 4 para 8(1) E(SS) Regs
   65. Reg 99 E(SS) Regs
   66. Sch 4 para 8(2) E(SS) Regs
   67. Regs 117-19 E(SS) Regs
   68. Reg 157 E(SS) Regs
   69. Regs 117, 156 and 168 E(SS) Regs

2. **Part-time undergraduates**
   70. Reg 137 E(SS) Regs
   71. Reg 139 E(SS) Regs
   72. Reg 144 E(SS) Regs
   73. Reg 145 E(SS) Regs
   74. Reg 141 E(SS) Regs
   75. Reg 142 E(SS) Regs
   76. Reg 147 E(SS) Regs
   77. Reg 142 E(SS) Regs
   78. Reg 143 E(SS) Regs

3. **Discretionary and institutional funds**
   79. Letter from the Office for Fair Access to higher education institutions, 23 July 2009

# Chapter 3

································································

# Undergraduate student support: Wales

**This chapter covers:**
1. Full-time undergraduates (below)
2. Part-time undergraduates (p54)
3. Discretionary hardship funds (p57)

································································

*Basic facts*

– Undergraduate students can apply for a mixture of grants and loans for fees and living costs, depending on their personal circumstances.
– Different support is available for full-time and part-time students.
– Separate or additional provision is available for healthcare, social work and initial teacher training students.
– Support from hardship funds may be available for those in financial difficulty.

································································

**Note:** English, Welsh, Northern Irish and Scottish students are funded under separate systems. See Chapter 2 for details of the system in England, Chapter 4 for details of the system in Northern Ireland and CPAG's *Benefits for Students in Scotland Handbook* for details of the system in Scotland.

Students domiciled in Wales who wish to study in England, Northern Ireland or Scotland receive the same package of support as though they were studying in Wales. The exception to this are Welsh-domiciled students who started courses between 2006 and 2009 and who are eligible for the tuition fee grant, which is only payable if they study in Wales.

---

## 1. Full-time undergraduates

Full-time undergraduates in Wales on eligible courses (see p47) and who are personally eligible (see p47) can apply for financial assistance from the Welsh government. Separate provision is available for part-time undergraduates (see p54). There have been a number of changes to student funding and support during the last 10 years, and so the support you can receive depends on when you started your course.

## Who is eligible for support

To receive financial support, you must be 'personally eligible' by meeting residence conditions (see below) and be studying an eligible course (see below).

### Residence conditions

To be personally eligible for support from the Welsh government, you must meet residency conditions.[1] These are generally the same as for England (see p21), except that, where appropriate, you must be normally resident in Wales on the first day of the first academic year. In addition, in Wales, students with certain forms of leave to remain can receive support, unlike in England. Ask an adviser for information.

### What is an eligible course

To be eligible for support, broadly the course must be full time (as defined by the education provider) and be:[2]
* a first degree;
* a higher education diploma;
* a BTEC Higher National Certificate (HNC) or Higher National Diploma (HND);
* a course of initial teacher training;
* a course for the further training of teachers, or youth or community workers;
* a course to prepare for certain professional examinations of a standard higher than A level, or HNC/HND where a first degree is not required for entry;
* a course not higher than a first degree, but higher than those described in the above bullet point.

**Note:** some courses, particularly in art and design, can require you to undertake a 'foundation' year or course, which is different to a foundation degree. This is normally a course of one academic year in length which precedes the main higher education degree course.

Support for these courses is often much more limited as they usually do not come within the definition of 'higher education'. You may be eligible for support as a further education student (see Chapter 1). Speak to an adviser in your students' union or institution for further guidance.

## Which system of student funding applies

This chapter refers to 'old system' and 'current system' students, depending on when you started your course.

## Students who entered higher education between 1 September 1998 and 1 September 2006

If you began your course between 1 September 1998 and 1 September 2006 and are not covered by the gap year provision explained on p26, you receive financial help as an 'old system' student.[3]

Broadly, the support to which you are entitled is identical to that available for 'old system' students in England (see pp27–34).[4]

## Students who entered higher education on or after 1 September 2006

You qualify for support as a 'current system' student if: [5]

- you entered (or are entering) higher education for the first time in September 2006 or later and are not covered by the gap year provisions outlined on p26; *or*
- you started a Postgraduate Certificate in Education (PGCE) course on or after 1 September 2006; *or*
- you have withdrawn from a previous course of study and did not arrange a transfer before leaving your previous course.

Changes have been made on several occasions since 2006/07, but the Welsh government has maintained transitional protection for those who started studying on different rules. Although the underlying structure of student support is broadly the same, there are differences depending on your year of entry. In this chapter:

- students who started their course between 2006/07 and 2009/10 are referred to as '**2006 cohort**' or '**new system**' students;
- students who started their course in the 2010/11 academic year are referred to as '**2010 cohort**' students;
- students who started their course in the 2011/12 academic year are referred to as '**2011 cohort**' students;
- students who started their course in the 2012/13 academic year or later are referred to as '**2012 cohort**' students.

**Note:** if you defer entry from one year, you may be treated as being part of an earlier cohort, even if you start studying a year later. For example, if you deferred entry from 2009/10 to 2010/11, you are treated as a 2006 cohort student, even though you started in 2010/11. Similarly, if you applied in 2011, but deferred entry until 2012, you are treated as a 2012 cohort student.

## Previous study

If you have previously attended a higher education course, the amount of support you can receive may be affected by the rules on previous study.[6]

If you are a 'current system' student (see above) and hold an honours degree from a UK institution, support for any new qualification is restricted to supplementary grants for travel costs, students with dependants and disabled students.[7]

Some exceptions apply: students who hold an honours degree and who are undertaking a PGCE course receive full funding, while those undertaking a further undergraduate course in certain professional subjects, such as social work, medicine, dentistry, architecture, town planning or veterinary science, can receive a maintenance loan for that course,[8] although not a loan for tuition fees or a maintenance or special support grant.

If you do not already hold an honours degree, in general the maximum number of years of tuition fee loan and maintenance or special support grant funding you can receive is equivalent to the ordinary length of your course plus one year, less any years of study previously undertaken.[9] If you have studied part of a year, you are treated as if you have undertaken a full year of study. Maintenance loan funding is, however, unaffected.

If you are transferring courses, or undertaking an 'end-on' course, these previous study rules affect you. You may be able to secure additional years of 'full' funding if you were unable to complete a previous year or course for 'compelling personal reasons', such as illness or caring responsibilities.[10] You must provide evidence of this to Student Finance Wales. You may also request another year on top of this if you can supply evidence. Rules for 'old system' students are slightly different, but have broadly the same effect.

Further information on previous study is available from your student adviser or www.studentfinancewales.co.uk.

## Grants and loans for tuition fees

### 2012 cohort

If you started your course on or after 1 September 2012 and are an eligible 'current system' Welsh-domiciled student studying anywhere in the UK, or a non-UK European Union (EU) student studying in Wales only, you may be charged fees of up to £9,000 a year. In 2015/16, if you are charged more than £3,810, you can claim a fee grant from the Welsh government of up to £5,190 so that your liability does not exceed £3,810.[11] You can then take out a loan to pay for all or part of this amount.[12]

### 2006, 2010 and 2011 cohorts

If you are an eligible 'current system' Welsh-domiciled student or a non-UK EU student studying in Wales and you started your course before 1 September 2012, you pay fees of up to £3,465 in the 2015/16 academic year.

If you are a 2006 cohort student, you can receive a tuition fee grant of up to £2,085, so that the most you pay is £1,380 for the year.[13] You are eligible to take out a tuition fee loan to cover the remainder.[14]

If you are a 2010 or 2011 cohort student, or otherwise eligible for fee support but not for a fee grant, you can receive a fee loan of up to the amount of the fee charged.[15]

If you choose to study in England, you pay up to £3,465, and in Northern Ireland £3,805. Fees for Welsh-domiciled students in Scotland are fixed at £1,820 a year for all courses except medicine, which is fixed at £2,895 a year in 2014/15. In all cases, eligible Welsh-domiciled students can take out tuition fee loans to cover the cost.

## All students

The maximum loan available matches the fee you are charged, less any fee grant. The fee loan is not means tested on your income or the income of anyone in your household. However, the loan is added to your total student loan debt (including any loans taken out for living costs). You must start your repayments once you have graduated or otherwise left the course, and are earning at least £21,000 a year (2012 cohort) or £17,335 a year (pre-2012 cohorts) and are working in the UK.

If you wish to pay all or part of your fees in cash in advance, you can do so. Your institution will generally expect some indication of how you intend to pay your fees when you register.

Help with tuition fees for part-time courses is also available (see p55).

## Welsh government learning grant

### 2010 and 2012 cohorts

In 2015/16, the Welsh government learning grant (previously the Assembly learning grant) for 2010 and 2012 cohort students is a non-repayable, means-tested allowance of up to £5,161.[16] The maximum amount is payable to students with a household income of less than £18,371 a year, and a partial amount is paid on a sliding scale to students with a household income of up to £50,020.

Part of the grant substitutes the student loan for living costs. If you receive a Welsh government learning grant, the amount of loan for living costs you can receive is reduced by 50 pence for every £1 you receive, up to a maximum of £2,580. See p52 for more details on loans for living costs.

*Example*
Rhys receives an Welsh government learning grant of £1,540. The maximum amount of loan for living costs he can receive is reduced by £770.

If you are entitled to apply for means-tested benefits, the Welsh government learning grant is taken into account as income when working out your (or your partner's) entitlement, so you should apply for a special support grant instead (see below). See Chapters 21, 22, 23 and 24 for more details of how your income is treated.

## 2011 cohort

2011 cohort students are entitled to a higher Welsh government learning grant of up to £5,780 in 2015/16.[17] Otherwise, conditions are the same as for 2010 and 2012 cohort students (see p50).

## 2006 cohort

Other 'current system' students can receive a slightly different Welsh government learning grant of a non-repayable, means-tested allowance of up to £3,000.[18] The maximum amount is payable to students with a household income of less than £18,371 a year, and a partial amount is paid on a sliding scale to students with a household income of up to £39,329.

As for 2010 cohort students (see p50), part of the grant substitutes the student loan for living costs. In this case, if you receive a Welsh government learning grant, the amount of loan for living costs you can receive is reduced by £1 for every pound of learning grant, up to a maximum of £1,329 (see p52 for more details).

*Example*
Hadeel receives a Welsh government learning grant of £770. The maximum amount of loan for living costs she can receive is reduced by £770.

If you are entitled to apply for means-tested benefits, the Welsh government learning grant is taken into account as income when working out your (or your partner's) entitlement, so you should apply for a special support grant instead (see below). See Chapters 21, 22, 23 and 24 for more details of how your income is treated.

## Special support grant

A special support grant is available to provide extra support for students regarded as particularly vulnerable. You must be a full-time student eligible to claim means-tested social security benefits.[19]

Most full-time students cannot receive such benefits. Some students, however, can claim – eg, if you are a lone parent, or you and your partner are both full-time students and have one or more children, or you receive disability living allowance or personal independence payment, or you are deaf. When universal credit (UC) is rolled out in Wales, those claiming UC may also be eligible. See the relevant benefits chapter for details of which students can claim means-tested benefits.

If you are entitled to means-tested benefits, you should claim the special support grant rather than the Welsh government learning grant. Like the Welsh government learning grant for 'current system' students, the special support grant is a non-repayable, means-tested allowance of up to £5,780 for 2011 cohort students,[20] £5,161 for 2010 and 2012 cohort students,[21] and £3,000 for other 'current system' students.[22] The special support grant is based on the same income scales as the maintenance grant for each cohort (see pp53–54).

Unlike the Welsh government learning grant, however, the special support grant does not substitute any part of the student loan, and it is not taken into account when calculating your entitlement to means-tested benefits.

## Student loan for living costs

Student loans for living costs are available to eligible Welsh-domiciled students. The amount for all cohorts of students are the same (see below). However, if you receive a Welsh government learning grant, the loan is reduced by an amount, depending on your cohort (see p50).

*Maximum amount of income-contingent loan 2015/16*[23]

|  | Full year | Final year |
|---|---|---|
| London | £7,532 | £6,858 |
| Elsewhere | £5,376 | £4,980 |
| Parental home | £4,162 | £3,767 |
| Overseas rate | £6,410 | £5,575 |

Repayment terms are the same as for English students. As in England, there are different rules depending on whether you started your course before or after 1 September 2012 (see p32).

## Partial cancellations

Eligible Welsh-domiciled students who have taken out a maintenance loan since 2010/11 may be eligible to have up to £1,500 of the loan cancelled when they reach the point when they begin making repayments. This cancellation can only be applied once, and is not multiplied by the number of academic years in which you took out a loan. If the balance of your loan is less than £1,500, the cancellation is equal to the loan balance less the first repayment you make. **Note:** cancellation is not automatic and you should speak to Student Finance Wales to ensure it is applied.

If you have any outstanding penalties or charges on your loan, are in breach of your loan agreement or 'are shown by your conduct to be unfit to receive a cancellation', it will be refused. You might be considered 'unfit' if, for example, you provided false information when applying for the loan.

## Supplementary grants

A number of additional grants and allowances are available to both 'old system' and 'current system' students who have extra needs.

### Students with dependants

Students with dependent children may be able to receive a **parents' learning allowance**[24] of up to £1,557 and/or a **childcare grant**[25] of 85 per cent of actual costs of their childcare, up to a maximum of £161.50 a week for one child or 85 per cent of actual costs up to a maximum of £274.55 a week for two or more children.

If you have an adult dependant(s) 'wholly or mainly financially dependent' on you, you may be eligible for a means-tested **adult dependants' grant** up to a maximum of £2,732.[26] Students with children should also apply for child benefit (see Chapter 8), child tax credit (see Chapter 19) or UC once this has been introduced in your area (see Chapter 18).

### Disabled students' allowance

If you are disabled and have extra costs associated with your course because of your disability, you may be entitled to extra help to pay for them. This is awarded on the same basis as in England (see p34). **Note:** there are higher rates in Wales: the maximum general allowance is £1,785; the maximum grant for equipment is £5,332; and the maximum non-medical helper allowance is £21,181 per year.[27]

### Grant for travel costs

Medical and dental students on placement and students who must travel abroad may be entitled to help with the cost of travel. This is awarded on the same basis as in England (see p34).[28]

## How income affects student support

Much of the support you receive is based on your household income. The definition of household income in Wales is the same as that in England (see p35).

Once your household income is assessed, it first reduces any maintenance grant or special support grant you are due to receive. The assessment is different, depending on which cohort of students you are in.

### 2010 and 2012 cohorts

In 2015/16, the following applies.[29]
- If your household income is £18,370 or less, you receive the maximum maintenance or special support grant.
- If your household income is between £18,371 and £50,020, you receive a reduced amount of the applicable grant (the minimum amount is £50).
  - For every £3.653 of household income between £18,371 and £26,500, £1 is deducted from the grant.

- For every £4.18 of household income between £26,501 and £34,000, £1 is deducted from the grant.
- For every £14.67 of household income above £34,000, £1 is deducted from the grant until the maximum household income of £50,020 is reached.
- No grant is payable if household income is £50,021 or more.

Income above £50,753 reduces other support at a rate of £1 for every £5 of additional income.[30] Any supplementary grants for dependants are reduced first, then the 25 per cent of the student loan that is means tested, and finally any grant for travel costs.[31]

### 2011 cohort

In 2015/16, your household income affects your student support as above, except that grants are reduced by £1 for every £9.36 of household income above £34,000.[32] Income above £50,448 reduces other support at a rate of £1 for every £5 of additional income.[33]

### Other 'current system' students

In 2015/16, the following applies.[34]

- If your household income is £18,370 or less, you receive the maximum maintenance or special support grant.
- If your household income is between £18,371 and £39,329, you receive a reduced amount of the applicable grant (the minimum amount is £50).
  - For every £5.674 of household income between £18,371 and £27,852, £1 is deducted from the grant.
  - For every £8.97 of household income above £27,852, £1 is deducted from the grant until the maximum household income of £39,329 is reached.
- No grant is payable if household income is £39,330 or more.[35]

Income above £39,778 reduces other support at a rate of £1 for every £8.97 of income above £39,778 until 75 per cent of the full maintenance loan remains.[36] Any supplementary grants for dependants are reduced first, then the 25 per cent of the student loan that is means tested, and finally any grant for travel costs.[37]

---

## 2. Part-time undergraduates

Support for part-time students is different from that available to full-time students. New and existing part-time undergraduate students can qualify for support for fees and living costs. The course and personal eligibility requirements are the same as for full-time students (see p47).

The support offered depends on when you started your course. If you started your course before 1 September 2014, to be eligible for support, you must be studying a course that is at least 50 per cent of a full-time course – ie, it takes no longer than twice the time of the equivalent full-time course to complete. If you started your course on or after 1 September 2014, to be eligible for fee loans or the part-time disabled students' allowance, your course must be at least 25 per cent of a full-time course – ie, it takes no more than four times the equivalent length of the full-time course to complete. Other support for living costs still requires a course intensity of 50 per cent.

## Loan for tuition fees

In 2015/16, Welsh-domiciled part-time students who started their course on 1 September 2014 or later can access fee loans. These are similar to the arrangements for part-time students in England since 2012/13 (see p41), but with some differences. In particular, maximum loans for study in Wales are lower, and there is no regulation of part-time fees in Wales. This means that the fee charged may be higher than the loan you can receive.

Eligible Welsh-domiciled and non-UK European Union (EU) students starting courses on or after 1 September 2014 can access a non-means-tested fee loan for part-time study in Wales of up to £2,625 per year.[38] If your course is at an institution in England, Scotland or Northern Ireland, the loan can be up to £6,750 per year.[39] If your course fee is lower than these amounts, you can take out a loan up to the value of your fees. Repayment arrangements are the same as for full-time students starting their course after 1 September 2012 (see p32).

If you started your course before 1 September 2014, you remain on the old system of part-time funding, as outlined below.

## Grant for tuition fees

If you are a part-time undergraduate student (including a student from the EU – see p22), and you started your course before 1 September 2014, you may be eligible for a means-tested grant for your fees.[40] The maximum amount of grant to which you are eligible depends on the intensity of study for each academic year of the course (see below).

## Grant for course costs

A grant for course costs of up to £1,155 is available to students from low-income backgrounds to help with the costs of books, equipment and travel.[41] The amount of grant available depends on family income. You must be studying a course that is at least 50 per cent intensity of a full-time course. The exact amount you recieve depends on your household income (see below). This grant is not available to EU students. It does not affect your entitlement to means-tested benefits.

*Maximum grant for part-time fee and course costs 2015/16*

| Course intensity | Maximum fee grant ('old system' students only) | Maximum course grant |
|---|---|---|
| 50–59% of the equivalent full-time course | £690 | £1,155 |
| 60–74% of the equivalent full-time course | £820 | £1,155 |
| 75% or more of the equivalent full-time course | £1,025 | £1,155 |

## Disabled students' allowance

If you are studying at an intensity of at least 25 per cent of an equivalent full-time course and have a disability, you can apply for a disabled students' allowance.[42] The amount Student Finance Wales can award for non-medical help and other general expenditure is, however, reduced according to the workload of a part-time course.

## Grants for dependants

If you are studying at an intensity of at least 50 per cent of an equivalent full-time course and have dependent children or an adult dependant, you may also apply for the **childcare grant**, **parents' learning allowance** or **adult dependants' grant**.[43] See p53 for further information. The amount you can receive depends on your income and that of your household.

The amount Student Finance Wales can award is reduced pro rata according to the workload of the part-time course.

## Fee waiver

This is available to part-time students undertaking at least 10 credits and fewer than 30, who are in receipt of a means-tested benefit, and whose sole income is benefits or who are registered jobseekers. Students who already have a first degree are not eligible. This scheme is administered by universities and colleges.

## How income affects student support

If you started your course on or after 1 September 2014, your course is at least 50 per cent intensity of an equivalent full-time course, and you are single and have no dependants, the following applies.[44]

- If your income is below £26,095, you receive the full course costs grant.

- If your income is between £26,096 and £28,180, you receive a partial grant.
- If your income exceeds £28,180, you do not receive any grant.

If you started your course before 1 September 2014, and you are single and have no dependants, the following applies.[45]

- If your income is £16,864 or less, you are eligible for the maximum grant for fees and course costs.
- If your income is between £16,865 and £25,435, you receive some help with fees and course costs.
- If your income is between £25,436 and £28,180, you receive some help with course costs, but not with fees. The exact amount you receive depends on your income.
- If your income exceeds £28,180, you cannot receive support with fees or course costs.

Only your and your partner's income is taken into account as household income. Your parents' income is ignored.

In either case, if you are married or in a civil partnership, or aged 25 or over and living with a partner (including a same-sex partner) or have dependent children, the following amounts are deducted from your income:[46]

- £2,000 for your partner;
- £2,000 for your eldest child;
- £1,000 for every other child.

If you are entitled to a grant for a dependant (see p56), a different income assessment applies.

Student Finance Wales has published further information on its website www.studentfinancewales.co.uk.

# 3. **Discretionary hardship funds**

Higher education institutions provide discretionary hardship funds for 'home' (see p22) undergraduate and postgraduate students in financial difficulty. The funds issue both repayable loans and non-repayable grants.

Non-repayable grants are available on a needs-assessed basis if you are experiencing financial difficulty serious enough to mean you may have to leave your course. Previously, central funding was given to Welsh higher education institutions and the funding was known as the Financial Contingency Fund. In 2015/16, higher education institutions are expected to make their own provision, although they may still keep this name.

In most cases, hardship funds can help with living and study costs, such as childcare, rent, course costs and utility bills, or with large one-off and exceptional costs, such as major housing repairs and emergency situations such as fire or bereavement. The institution has discretion and makes the final decision.

Priority is usually given to students with children, mature students, students from low-income families, disabled students, final-year students and those who have left care. Usually, you must have applied for your full entitlement of a student loan, if you are eligible for one.

Individual institutions have different application processes and different pressures on the funds available and no sum is guaranteed. However, there is normally an appeals process if you want to challenge the fund administrator's decision.

# Notes

1. **Full-time undergraduates**
   1  Sch 1 E(SS)(W) Regs
   2  Reg 5 and Sch 2 E(SS)(W) Regs
   3  Reg 2 E(SS)(W) Regs
   4  E(SS)(W) Regs
   5  Reg 2 E(SS)(W) Regs
   6  Regs 6 and 7 E(SS)(W) Regs
   7  Reg 7 E(SS)(W) Regs
   8  Reg 7(4) E(SS)(W) Regs
   9  Reg 6 E(SS)(W) Regs
   10  Reg 6 E(SS)(W) Regs
   11  Reg 17 E(SS)(W) Regs
   12  Reg 21 E(SS)(W) Regs
   13  Reg 16 E(SS)(W) Regs
   14  Reg 20 E(SS)(W) Regs
   15  Reg 19 E(SS)(W) Regs
   16  Reg 38 E(SS)(W) Regs
   17  Reg 39 E(SS)(W) Regs
   18  Reg 37 E(SS)(W) Regs
   19  Reg 40 E(SS)(W) Regs
   20  Reg 43 E(SS)(W) Regs
   21  Reg 42 E(SS)(W) Regs
   22  Reg 41 E(SS)(W) Regs
   23  Regs 46-49 E(SS)(W) Regs
   24  Reg 29 E(SS)(W) Regs
   25  Reg 28 E(SS)(W) Regs
   26  Reg 27 E(SS)(W) Regs
   27  Reg 25 E(SS)(W) Regs
   28  Regs 33-35 E(SS)(W) Regs
   29  Reg 38 E(SS)(W) Regs
   30  Sch 5 E(SS)(W) Regs
   31  Reg 61 E(SS)(W) Regs

   32  Reg 39 E(SS)(W) Regs
   33  Sch 5 E(SS)(W) Regs
   34  Reg 37 E(SS)(W) Regs
   35  Reg 37 E(SS)(W) Regs
   36  Sch 5 E(SS)(W) Regs
   37  Reg 61 E(SS)(W) Regs

2. **Part-time undergraduates**
   38  Reg 91(3) E(SS)(W)Regs
   39  Reg 91(4) E(SS)(W)Regs
   40  Reg 90 E(SS)(W) Regs
   41  Regs 90 and 92 E(SS)(W) Regs
   42  Reg 93 E(SS)(W) Regs
   43  Regs 94-98 E(SS)(W) Regs
   45  Reg 90(5) E(SS)(W) Regs
   46  Reg 9(8) E(SS)(W) Regs

# Chapter 4

· · · · · · · · · · · · · · · · · · · · · · · · · · · · · · · · · · · · · · · · · · ·

# Undergraduate student support: Northern Ireland

**This chapter covers:**
1. Full-time undergraduates (below)
2. Part-time undergraduates (p67)
3. Discretionary support funds (p68)

· · · · · · · · · · · · · · · · · · · · · · · · · · · · · · · · · · · · · · · · · ·

*Basic facts*
– Undergraduate students can apply for a mixture of grants and loans for fees and living costs, depending on their personal circumstances.
– The type of financial support available depends on several factors, including when the course starts, its length, the discipline and whether the course is full time or part time.
– Separate or additional provision is available for healthcare, social work and initial teacher training students.
– Discretionary funds are available for those in financial difficulty, but funding is not guaranteed.

· · · · · · · · · · · · · · · · · · · · · · · · · · · · · · · · · · · · · · · · · ·

**Note:** English, Welsh, Scottish and Northern Irish students are funded under separate systems. See Chapter 2 for the details of the system in England, Chapter 3 for details of the system in Wales and CPAG's *Benefits for Students in Scotland Handbook* for details of the system in Scotland.

Students domiciled in Northern Ireland who wish to study in England, Wales or Scotland receive the same package of support as though they were studying in Northern Ireland.

## 1. Full-time undergraduates

Student awards for Northern Irish-domiciled students studying in Northern Ireland, mainland Britain or the Republic of Ireland are administered by the Department for Employment and Learning (DELNI). Applications for support are processed by the Education Authority, under the 'brand' of Student Finance NI.

You should apply via the Student Finance NI website, or to the Education Authority regional office that covers the area in which you normally live, rather than where you intend to study. A list of offices is at www.studentfinanceni.co.uk.

## Who is eligible for support

In order to receive financial support, you must be 'personally eligible' by meeting residence conditions (see below) and be studying an eligible course (see below).

### Residence conditions

To be eligible for support from Student Finance NI, you must meet the residence conditions.[1] These are the same as for England (see p21), except that, where appropriate, you must be normally resident in Northern Ireland on the first day of the first academic year. Also, in Northern Ireland, students from overseas with certain forms of leave to remain can receive support, unlike in England. Ask an adviser for information.

### Course eligibility

To be eligible for support, broadly the course must be full time (as defined by the education provider) and be:[2]

- a first degree;
- a higher education diploma;
- a BTEC HNC or HND;
- a course of initial teacher training;
- a course for the further training of teachers, or youth or community workers;
- a course to prepare for certain professional examinations of a standard higher than A level, or HNC/HND where a first degree is not required for entry;
- a course not higher than a first degree, but higher than those described in the above bullet point.

**Note:** some courses, particularly in art and design, can require the student to undertake a foundation year or course, which is different to a foundation degree. This is normally a course of one academic year in length which precedes the main higher education degree course.

Support for these courses is often much more limited as they usually do not fall within the definition of 'higher education'. You may be eligible for support as a further education student (see Chapter 1). Contact an adviser in your students' union or institution for further guidance.

## Which system of student support applies

This chapter refers to 'old system' and 'current system' students, depending on when you started your course.

### Students who entered higher education in the UK between 1 September 1998 and 1 September 2006, or before 1 September 2013 in the Republic of Ireland

If you began your course on or after 1 September 1998, or were counted as a gap year student in the 2006/07 academic year (see p26), you receive financial help as an **'old system'** student.[3]

This also applies if you are a student who is attending an institution in the Republic of Ireland and you started your course before 1 September 2013.

### Students who entered higher education in the UK on or after 1 September 2006, or on or after 1 September 2013 in the Republic of Ireland

If you began your course on or after 1 September 2006 and you are not treated as if you started before this date (eg, if you secured a deferred entry place from the 2005/06 academic year), you receive financial help as a **'current system'** student under the current rules for student support.[4]

If you are studying in the Republic of Ireland, you are funded under this system if you started your course on 1 September 2013 or later. If you started before this date, you are funded as an 'old system' student.

## Previous study

If you have previously attended a higher education course, the amount of support you can receive may be affected by the rules on previous study.[5]

If you are a 'current system' student (see above) and hold an honours degree, support for any new qualification is restricted to supplementary grants for travel costs, students with dependants and disabled students.[6]

Some exceptions apply: students who hold an honours degree and who are undertaking a Postgraduate Certificate in Education (PGCE) course receive full funding, while those undertaking a further undergraduate course in certain professional subjects, such as medicine or veterinary science, can receive a maintenance loan for that course,[7] although not a loan for tuition fees or a maintenance or special support grant.

If you do not already hold an honours degree, in general the maximum number of years of tuition fee loan and maintenance or special support grant funding you can receive is equivalent to the ordinary length of your course plus one year, less any years of study previously undertaken.[8] If you have studied part of a year, you are treated as if you have undertaken a full year of study. Maintenance loan funding is, however, unaffected. Students on social work courses are also exempt from these rules.

If you are transferring courses, or undertaking an 'end-on' course, these previous study rules affect you. You may be able to secure additional years of 'full' funding if you were unable to complete a previous year or course for 'compelling personal reasons' such as illness or caring responsibilities.[9] You must provide evidence of this to Student Finance NI.

Rules for 'old system' students (see p61) are slightly different, but have broadly the same effect.

Further information on previous study is available from your students' union or institution.

## Grants and loans for tuition fees

### 'Old system' students

The maximum fee you pay in the 2015/16 academic year is £1,510.[10] The government may meet some, or all, of the fee depending on your family's income. If you are assessed to make a contribution, you may be eligible for a student loan up to the amount of the fee charged.[11]

If you are a Northern Irish student attending a course at a publicly funded college in the Republic of Ireland, your tuition fees are paid by the Irish government. In addition, the college may charge a registration fee (known as a contribution charge) of €3,000 (in 2015/16) to cover examination and student services fees, which can be refunded from Student Finance NI.[12] This help is not means tested. It is important, therefore, that you apply to Student Finance NI to ensure the charge will be paid for you, even if you do not intend to apply for other financial help towards your living costs.

### 'Current system' students

Eligible 'current system' Northern Irish-domiciled students studying in Northern Ireland pay variable fees of up to £3,805 in the 2015/16 academic year. You are eligible for a tuition fee loan to cover these.[13]

If you started your course on 1 September 2012 or later and study in England, Scotland or Wales, you are charged up to £9,000 in the 2015/16 academic year. You are eligible for a loan to cover these fees.[14]

If you started your course before 1 September 2012 and study in England and Wales, you pay variable fees of up to £3,465 per year in 2015/16. Fees for Northern Irish-domiciled students who started a course in Scotland before this date are fixed at £1,820 a year for all courses except medicine, in which case the fee is fixed at £2,895 a year. In all cases, eligible Northern Irish-domiciled students can take out a tuition fee loan to cover this cost.

If you start your course in the Republic of Ireland on or after 1 September 2013, you are charged a student contribution of €3,000 in 2015/16. This is not paid by Student Finance NI as it is for 'old system' students. Instead, you can apply for a student contribution loan to cover the cost. The terms and conditions of student contribution loans are identical to those for tuition fee loans for students studying in the UK (see p65).[15] If you started your course on or after 1 September 2013, you can also apply for a maintenance grant or loan (see p63).

The maximum fee loan or institution charge loan available matches the fee or contribution you are charged. Neither loan is means tested on your or your household income. However, the loan is added to your total student loan debt (including any loans taken out for living costs – see p65) and you must start repayments once you have graduated or otherwise left the course and are earning at least £17,335 a year.

If you wish to pay all or part of the fee upfront yourself, you can do so. Your institution will expect some indication of how you intend to pay your fees when you register.

Help with tuition fees for part-time courses is also available (see p67).

## Higher education bursary

If you are an 'old system' student and have a low income, you may be eligible for a non-repayable, means-tested bursary of up to £2,000 to help with your living costs.[16]

The full amount is available if your household income is £11,805 or less; a partial amount is available on a sliding scale if your household income is between £11,806 and £23,605. If you have a household income of more than £23,605, you are not eligible to receive the bursary.

Any bursary you receive affects the amount of student loan you can have (see p65).

Your bursary is paid in three instalments over the course of the academic year.

## Maintenance grant

The maintenance grant for 'current system' students is a non-repayable, means-tested allowance of up to £3,475. The maximum amount is payable to students with a household income of £19,203 or less a year, and a partial amount is paid on a sliding scale up to a household income of £41,065.[17]

If you are entitled to apply for means-tested benefits, the maintenance grant is treated as income when working out your (or your partner's) entitlement, so you should apply for the special support grant instead (see p64).

Part of the maintenance grant substitutes the student loan for living costs (see p65). This means that if you receive any maintenance grant, the amount of loan for living costs you can receive is reduced, up to a maximum of £1,887.[18] The formula for this can be complex, so get advice if you are uncertain whether it has been applied correctly.

If you get a full maintenance grant of £3,475, the maximum amount of student loan for living costs is reduced by £1,887. If you get a maintenance grant of more than £1,318 but less than £3,475, your loan is reduced by an amount equal to £1,887 less £1 for every £17.25 that your household income exceeds £19,203. See p35 for how your household income is calculated and p66 for how it affects your student support. If your grant is £1,318 or less, the loan is reduced by the amount of maintenance grant paid.

Teacher training students are treated slightly differently. Check with Student Finance NI, or your students' union or university advice service.

*Examples*

Laura is a single, independent student studying in Belfast. She starts her course in October 2014. She has an assessable household income of £2,000. She receives the maximum grant of £3,475 and can take out a student loan of up to £2,953 (the maximum rate of £4,840 *less* £1,887).

Anne is 18 and lives with her parents in Armagh. She starts her course in Belfast in October 2014. Her assessable household income is £21,500, which means she receives a maintenance grant of £2,921.

Her household income is £2,297 above the lower limit of £19,203. This £2,297 is divided by 17.25 to give £133. This is subtracted from the maximum loan deduction of £1,887 to give £1,754.

Anne's maximum loan entitlement is therefore £3,750 – £1,754 = £1,996

Iain is 19 and starts his course in Coleraine in October 2014. He receives a maintenance grant of £800. The maximum amount of loan he can receive is reduced by £800.

## Special support grant

The special support grant is available to 'current system' full-time students entitled to claim means-tested benefits who are regarded as particularly vulnerable.[19]

Most full-time students are not entitled to means-tested benefits. However, you may be entitled if, for example, you are a lone parent, or you and your partner are both full-time students and have one or more children, or you receive disability living allowance or personal independence payment, or you are deaf. See Chapters 10, 12, 13, 14 and 18 for details of which students can claim means-tested benefits.

If you get a means-tested benefit, you should claim the special support grant instead of the maintenance grant. Like the maintenance grant, the special support grant is a non-repayable, means-tested allowance of up to £3,475. The maximum amount is payable to students with a household income of £19,203 or less a year. A partial amount is paid on a sliding scale up to a household income of £41,065.

Unlike the maintenance grant, however, the special support grant does not substitute any part of the student loan and it is not taken into account as income when calculating your entitlement to means-tested benefits.

## Student loans

Both 'old system' and 'current system' students can apply for a partially means-tested student loan to help cover their living costs and other expenses. These are income-contingent loans (see p30).

*Maximum amount of income-contingent loan 2015/16[20]*

|  | Full year | Final year |
|---|---|---|
| London | £6,780 | £6,170 |
| Elsewhere | £4,840 | £4,480 |
| Parental home | £3,750 | £3,390 |
| Overseas rate | £5,770 | £5,015 |

You may be entitled to additional amounts of loan for any extra weeks of attendance over the standard 30 weeks and three days.

A quarter of the loan is means tested on your household income. In addition, if you are an 'old system' student and are entitled to the full rate of bursary (see p63), the amount you can borrow is reduced by £1,500. If you are entitled to a partial bursary, the amount of loan you can take out is reduced by the amount of the bursary you receive.[21]

If you are a 'current system' student and get a maintenance grant, up to £1,887 of the loan may be substituted for the maintenance grant paid. See p63 for details of the loan substitution. If you receive a special support grant, no part of your loan is substituted.

The loan is repayable at the end of your studies. The amount of money you pay back each month depends on your earnings. Once you earn above £17,335 a year, repayments begin at the rate of 9 per cent of all income above this threshold. For example, if you earn £18,335 a year, you pay back 9 per cent of £1,000 – ie, £90 a year or £7.50 a month.

## Supplementary grants

The **childcare grant, parents' learning allowance, adult dependants' grant** and **disabled students' allowance** are all available to Northern Irish undergraduates on the same basis as for students in England (see p33).[22]

Except for the disabled students' allowance, all these grants are means tested. **Note:** the rates for some of these grants are slightly different in Northern Ireland than in England.

*Maximum amounts of supplementary grants 2015/16*

| | |
|---|---|
| Parents' learning allowance | £1,538 a year |
| Childcare grant (one child) | £148.75 a week |
| Childcare grant (two or more children) | £255 a week |
| Adult dependants' grant | £2,695 a year |
| Disabled students' allowance (non-medical personal help) | £20,938 a year |
| Disabled students' allowance (equipment) | £5,266 for the duration of the course |
| Disabled students' allowance (general allowance) | £1,759 a year |

Medical and dental students on placement and students who must travel abroad may be entitled to help with the cost of travel. This is awarded on the same basis as in England (see p82).

You may also be entitled to a bursary from your institution (see p63).

## How income affects student support

Much of the support you receive is based on your household income. The definition of household income in Northern Ireland is the same as that in England (see p35).

Once your household income is assessed, it first reduces any maintenance grant or special support grant you are due to receive.

In 2015/16, the following applies.[23]

- If your household income is £19,203 or less, you receive the maximum maintenance or special support grant.
- If your household income is between £19,204 and £41,065, you receive a reduced amount of the applicable grant (the minimum amount is £50).
  - For every £4.55 of household income between £19,204 and £29,019, £1 is deducted from the grant.
  - For every £9.50 of household income above £29,019, £1 is deducted from the grant until the maximum household income of £41,065 is reached.
- No grant is payable if your household income is £41,066 or more.

Income above £41,540 reduces other support at a rate of £1 for every £9.50 of income above that figure.[24] Any supplementary grants for dependants are reduced first, then the 25 per cent of the student loan that is means tested and, finally, any grant for travel costs.[25]

## 2. Part-time undergraduates

Support for part-time students is different from that available for full-time students, although the course and personal eligibility requirements are the same (see p60).[26] To be eligible for support, you must be studying a course in the UK that is at least 50 per cent of a full-time course – ie, it takes no longer than twice the time of the equivalent full-time course to complete.[27]

**Note:** the Northern Ireland Executive is currently reviewing part-time student funding and changes may be made for future years.

### Grant for tuition fees

Part-time undergraduate students (including students from the European Union (EU) – see p22) may be eligible for an income-assessed grant for tuition fees.[28] The maximum amount of grant for which you are eligible depends on the intensity of study for each academic year of the course.

*Maximum grant for part-time fees 2015/16*

| Course intensity | Maximum grant available |
| --- | --- |
| Less than 60% | £820 |
| 60–74% | £985 |
| 75% or more | £1,230 |

### Grant for course costs

A grant of up to £265 is available to students from low-income backgrounds to help with the costs of books, equipment and travel.[29] The amount of grant available is not affected by the intensity of study. This grant is not available to EU students.

### Disabled students' allowance

If you are studying at an intensity of at least 50 per cent of an equivalent full-time course and have a disability, you can apply for a disabled students' allowance. The amount that can be awarded for non-medical help and other general expenditure is, however, reduced according to the workload of a part-time course.

*Maximum amount of disabled students' allowance 2015/16[30]*

| | |
| --- | --- |
| Non-medical personal helper(s) | £15,703 per academic year |
| Major items of specialist equipment | £5,266 for the duration of the course |
| Other expenditure | Up to £1,319 per academic year |
| Extra travel expenditure resulting from disability | Full reimbursement |

## How income affects student support

In 2015/16, the following applies.

- If your income is below £16,843, you are eligible for the maximum grant for fees and course costs.
- If your income is between £16,843 and £24,420, you receive some help with fees and course costs.
- If your income is between £25,421 and £28,067, you receive some help with course costs, but not with fees. The exact amount you receive depends on your income.
- If your income is £28,067, you receive a course grant of £50. If your income is above this amount, you receive no support.

Only your and your partner's income is taken into account as household income. Your parents' income is ignored, regardless of your age.[31]

If you are married or in a civil partnership, or are aged 25 or over and living with a partner (including a same-sex partner), or have dependent children, the following amounts are deducted from your income:[32]

- £2,000 for your partner;
- £2,000 for your eldest child;
- £1,000 for every other child.

---

## 3. **Discretionary support funds**

Higher education institutions are allocated money to provide hardship funds for 'home' (see p22) undergraduate and postgraduate students in financial difficulty. In Northern Ireland these are known as 'support funds'. Repayable loans and non-repayable grants can be issued, although support is not guaranteed. Additional hardship funds may be available – check with your institution or students' union.

Non-repayable grants are available on a needs-assessed basis if you are experiencing financial difficulty serious enough to mean you may have to leave your course. The funds can help with living and study costs such as childcare, rent, books and utility bills, or with large one-off and exceptional costs, such as major housing repairs and emergency situations, such as fire or bereavement.

Priority is usually given to students with children, mature students, students from low-income families, disabled students, final-year students and those who have left care. However, all students who meet the personal and course requirements for undergraduate student support can apply, including healthcare students. You must, however, have applied for your full entitlement of a student loan, if you are eligible for one.

The funds cannot be used to meet the costs of tuition fees or to make up for non-receipt of a parental contribution to a grant or loan.

Grants are not normally more than £3,500, although institutions have some discretion in exceptional circumstances. Individual institutions have different application processes and different pressures on the funds, and no sum is guaranteed. However, there is an appeals process if you want to challenge a decision.

# Notes

## 1. Full-time undergraduates
1   Sch 1 E(SS)(NI) Regs
2   Reg 5 and Sch 2 E(SS)(NI) Regs
3   Reg 2 E(SS)(NI) Regs
4   Reg 2 E(SS)(NI) Regs
5   Regs 14 and 15 E(SS)(NI) Regs
6   Regs 20, 57, 59 and 63 E(SS)(NI) Regs
7   Reg 63(2) E(SS)(NI) Regs
8   Reg 23 E(SS)(NI) Regs
9   Reg 20(10) E(SS)(NI) Regs
10  Reg 32 E(SS)(NI) Regs
11  Regs 35 and 36 E(SS)(NI) Regs
12  Reg 32(7) E(SS)(NI) Regs
13  Regs 20-25 E(SS)(NI) Regs
14  Reg 25(1) E(SS)NI Regs
15  Reg 25A E(SS)NI Regs
16  Reg 61 E(SS)(NI) Regs
17  Reg 58 E(SS)(NI) Regs
18  Reg 66 E(SS)(NI) Regs
19  Regs 59 and 60 E(SS)(NI) Regs
20  Reg 68 E(SS)(NI) Regs
21  Reg 68(3)-(4) E(SS)(NI) Regs
22  Regs 41-56 E(SS)(NI) Regs
23  Regs 58(5) and 60(5) E(SS)(NI) Regs
24  Sch 5 para 9 E(SS)(NI) Regs
25  Regs 88 and 90 E(SS)(NI) Regs

## 2. Part-time undergraduates
26  Regs 122-24 E(SS)(NI) Regs
27  Reg 124(1)(c) E(SS)(NI) Regs
28  Reg 126 E(SS)(NI) Regs
29  Reg 126(1)(b) E(SS)(NI) Regs
30  Reg 130 E(SS)(NI) Regs
31  Reg 127 E(SS)(NI) Regs
32  Reg 128 E(SS)(NI) Regs

# Chapter 5

# Postgraduate student support

This chapter covers:
1. Studentships (below)
2. Postgraduate Support Scheme (p72)
3. Disabled students' allowance (p72)
4. Postgraduate support in Northern Ireland (p73)

*Basic facts*
- UK students are entitled to financial support for a postgraduate course of initial teacher training – eg, a Postgraduate Certificate in Education.
- English and Welsh students may also be able to receive a bursary for postgraduate study in social work, but this is not available to Northern Irish students studying in England or Wales.
- State support for other postgraduate courses is limited. Individual scholarships or 'studentships' are available from seven research councils, and a new postgraduate support scheme is available for taught postgraduate courses, but the demand far outstrips supply and funding is not guaranteed.
- Disabled postgraduates may be able to receive help to meet their additional costs of learning through the disabled students' allowance.

**Note:** funding for postgraduate students in Northern Ireland is different from that in England and Wales (see p73).

See Chapter 6 for details on financial support for teacher training and social work courses.

## 1. Studentships

Research councils fund research and masters studentships (scholarships), covering fees and maintenance. The following are the basic rates for maintenance stipends in 2015/16. A grant for tuition fees is usually paid in addition to these (£4,052 in 2015/16). Other schemes may be available, and eligibility and residence conditions apply. Additional allowances may be available if you have dependants, and some research councils fund part-time study.

Contact the relevant research council for information on the funding it provides and to which universities (see Appendix 2). Applications for studentships are made directly to the university, not to the relevant research council. You

| Body | Research studentship | Masters studentship | |
|------|------|------|------|
| AHRC | £16,057 | £16,057 | London |
| | £14,057 | £14,057 | Outside London |
| AHRC PPMS | – | £16,057 | London |
| | – | £14,057 | Outside London |
| ESRC | £16,057 | – | London |
| | £14,057 | – | Outside London |
| NERC | £16057 | – | London |
| | £14,057 | – | Outside London |
| MRC | £16057 | £15,863 (2014/15 rate) | London |
| | £14,057 | £13,863 (2014/15 rate) | Outside London |
| EPSRC | £16,057 | – | Engineering doctorates only: London |
| | £14,057 | – | Engineering doctorates only: Outside London |
| STFC | £16,057 | – | London |
| | £14,057 | – | Outside London |
| BBSRC | £16,057 | – | London |
| | £14,057 | – | Outside London |

AHRC = Arts and Humanities Research Council
BBSRC = Biotechnology and Biological Sciences Research Council
EPSRC = Engineering and Physical Sciences Research Council
ESRC = Economic and Social Research Council

MRC = Medical Research Council
NERC = Natural Environment Research Council
PPMS = Professional Preparation Master's Scheme
STFC = Science and Technology Facilities Council

should apply as early as possible, as the application deadline for almost all awards is usually several months in advance of the start of the course. **Note:** funding for masters courses is becoming increasingly scarce.

The British Academy also offers studentships on a similar basis to research councils. See www.britac.ac.uk/funding for details.

## 2. **Postgraduate Support Scheme**

The Postgraduate Support Scheme supports students on taught postgraduate courses in England in the 2015/16 academic year only. The scheme aims to address some of the barriers to studying at postgraduate level faced by students from under-represented groups. It is anticipated that it will be a precursor to a new taught postgraduate loan scheme for English-domiciled students, expected to be introduced in 2016/17. However, the final details of this loan scheme are not yet known and are subject to parliamentary approval.

Postgraduate Support Scheme awards are worth £10,000 per student. They are paid as a combination of a fee waiver and/or a cash bursary, and do not have to be repaid. This is a match-funded initiative and therefore £5,000 per student is from the Higher Education Funding Council for England (HEFCE) and £5,000 from the higher education institution. The HEFCE criteria states that awards should be restricted to students who are:

* progressing from an undergraduate course for which they were charged the higher tuition fee, introduced in 2012/13;
* undertaking a taught masters courses in any subject;
* studying full time or part time for a maximum of two years;
* domiciled in the UK or European Union;
* from a group that is evidentially under-represented among the institution's taught masters population.

In addition to the above criteria, institutions should use their own evidence base to identify their own priorities.

The number of awards is fixed and they are likely to be oversubscribed. Check on the institution's website for the application process and criteria or contact an adviser in your students' union or university for more information.

## 3. **Disabled students' allowance**

Both full-time and part-time postgraduate students studying 'recognised' taught and research courses are eligible for a disabled students' allowance.

A 'recognised course' is one which normally requires a first degree, is at least one academic year long, is provided by a publicly funded institution and is not a course of initial teacher training. Your course must be eligible for an award from a research council or be equivalent to a course that is eligible for an award. However, if the course you are undertaking allows you to apply for its own equivalent allowance, you must apply for this.

Part-time courses must last for longer than one year, but no more than twice as long as an equivalent full-time course. There is no age limit, but residency conditions apply.

One allowance of up to £10,362 a year in 2015/16 is available for specialist equipment, non-medical personal helpers and/or additional travel costs, subject to a needs assessment.[1] Contact Student Finance England, Student Finance Wales or Student Finance NI for more details.

**Note:** at the time of writing, the disabled students' allowance for English-domiciled students was going through some major changes. Although the basic structure of the allowance remains the same, the government intends to 'rebalance' the support it provides, potentially placing greater responsibility on universities and colleges to provide non-medical personal helpers, and restrict the types of computer and other IT equipment it funds. In 2015/16, the allowance no longer covers the first £200 of the cost of a computer and students applying for the disabled students' allowance for the first time must fund this themselves. Some institutions have hardship funds or bursaries to help students with this additional cost. Other changes are still being consulted on and are likely to be introduced in 2016/17. You should speak to an adviser in your university or students' union for more information. The changes do not currently apply in Wales or Northern Ireland.

Students funded through one of the main studentship programmes (see p70) are not yet affected by these changes and are eligible for more generous disabled students' allowance funding through the research council. Contact the disability support office at your institution about an application.

---

# 4. Postgraduate support in Northern Ireland

There are no concessionary fees for postgraduate courses in Northern Ireland. Contact the university or college where you want to study to check any possible sources of funding for your course. **Note:** postgraduate funding is no longer available for UK students wishing to study in the Republic of Ireland.

Funding is generally in the form of studentship awards. To be considered for funding, you must comply with the three-year residency requirement for undergraduates (see p60).

The Department for Employment and Learning (DELNI) makes funding available to Queen's University Belfast and the University of Ulster for research and certain approved courses of full-time study leading to higher degrees. The universities are responsible for administering these awards and the application process is very competitive. Further information can be found on the DELNI website at www.nidirect.gov.uk/index/information-and-services/education-and-learning/higher-education/choices-after-you-graduate/postgraduate-awards.htm.

Closing dates for the different awards vary, but are strictly observed. Check the closing date with the postgraduate office at the university you will be attending.

## Studentships

These grants are awarded for postgraduate research degrees (eg, MPhils and PhDs) and for approved courses of advanced study – eg, masters degrees. You can obtain approved course lists from the universities. Most students benefiting from these awards have degrees awarded at 2:1 or above, although you may be accepted for a taught masters degree in science and technology if you have a lower second class honours degree.

Studentship awards are for fixed amounts and are not means tested. Approved fees and maintenance costs are included. The basic rate of the maintenance grant payable in 2015/16 is £14,057 for research studentships, and £7,028 for taught studentships. Additional allowances may also be paid for dependants and students with special needs.

If you are a science and technology student working on a research project, you may also apply through the DELNI for a co-operative award in science and technology that involves sponsorship from industry. Details are available from the DELNI. Further information at www.delni.gov.uk/fe-cast-awards. The basic maintenance grant is supplemented by a payment of at least 60 per cent from the collaborating body to the institution.

The Department of Agriculture and Rural Development (DARD) runs a separate scheme, providing postgraduate studentships in its priority research areas. See www.delni.gov.uk/postgrad-awards-leaflet-2014-2015.pdf for more details.

## Studying in Northern Ireland

If you are seeking research funding and want to study in Northern Ireland, you must apply directly to the university for a place on a course and an award. Being offered a place does not automatically mean that you will obtain funding. Closing dates for applications are at the discretion of the institution (and are generally around April/May), but late applications may be accepted subject to availability of places. Grants are awarded by the DELNI for all fields except agriculture and medicine.

## Studying elsewhere in the UK

If you plan to study elsewhere in the UK, you may be able to receive funding through various research councils (see p71). You must approach the university where you want to study, not the research council, but it is always worth checking with the research council to which universities it has allocated funding. Closing dates vary, but are normally well before the start of term.

## Disabled students' allowance

A postgraduate disabled students' allowance is available to eligible postgraduate students in Northern Ireland on the same basis as for postgraduate students in England and Wales (see p72). You should apply to Student Finance NI via your regional Education Authority office.

## Bursaries

### Postgraduate Certificate in Education

See the information on initial teacher training in Northern Ireland on p91.

# Notes

**3. Disabled students' allowance**
1  Reg 158 E(SS) Regs

# Chapter 6

••••••••••••••••••••••••••••••••••••••••••••••••••••

# Vocational courses and other sources of student support

**This chapter covers:**

••••••••••••••••••••••••••••••••••••••••••••••••••••

*Basic facts*
- Specific funding is provided for certain vocational courses, sometimes in addition to the standard student support available.
- The NHS in England and Wales, and the Northern Ireland Executive, provides support for healthcare students, including medicine, dentistry and social work students.
- Incentives are provided for teacher training in England and Wales.
- Dance and drama students in private colleges may qualify for support.
- Certain other sources of funding, including charitable support, are available.

••••••••••••••••••••••••••••••••••••••••••••••••••••

## 1. Healthcare students in England and Wales

Healthcare students who meet certain personal and residency criteria, and who are undertaking an eligible course (see p77) in England and Wales are funded by the NHS bursary scheme. The personal and residency criteria are similar to those for undergraduate study (see p21), although support for NHS courses is usually available even if you already hold a degree. **Note:** the English and Welsh schemes are separate, but follow the same rules. There are a few differences in the rates.

*Eligible courses*
– Allied health professions: chiropody, dietetics, occupational therapy, orthoptics, physiotherapy, prosthetics and orthotics, radiography, operating department practice, speech and language therapy
– Professions complementary to dentistry: dental hygiene, dental therapy
– Nursing and midwifery
– Medicine and dentistry (the latter stages of pre-registration training only)

The funding arrangements that apply to you depend on when you started your course.
- If you started your course on or after 1 September 2012, see below.
- If you started your course between 1 September 2007 and 31 August 2012, see p80.
- If you started your course before 1 September 2007, see p80.

**Note:** in their initial years of training, medicine and dentistry students are funded by Student Finance England or Student Finance Wales. When they move onto the NHS bursary scheme, they are funded under the rules that were in place when they started their course. Thus, a medical student who started in the 2011/12 academic year who moves onto the NHS bursary scheme in 2015/16 is funded under the 2007 rules.

## The 2012 bursary scheme

The 2012 bursary scheme applies to all eligible healthcare students, including medicine and dentistry students who started their course on or after 1 September 2012. The separate schemes previously available to degree-level and diploma-level study have now been merged.

**Note:** employed students (sometimes known as seconded students) do not usually qualify for bursaries, but may qualify for student support payable by the Department for Business, Innovation and Skills or the Welsh government (see Chapters 2 and 3).

### Tuition fees

Most healthcare students funded by the NHS do not pay tuition fees. Medicine and dentistry students on standard five-year undergraduate courses have their fees paid in the years they are funded by the NHS. Arrangements will be reviewed and may change for new students after the 2015/16 academic year.

Medicine and dentistry students on four-year graduate entry courses funded under the 2012 scheme are charged a fee element (see p28).

## Non-means-tested grant

All eligible students receive a non-means-tested bursary of £1,000. This is paid in monthly instalments over the year. The rate does not increase even if your course lasts longer than 30 weeks in the year.

## Means-tested bursary

Depending on your household income, you may be eligible for an additional means-tested bursary. If you receive support, it is paid monthly.

*Maximum amount of means-tested bursary 2015/16*

|  | Courses lasting 30 weeks in the year | Courses lasting 45 weeks or more in the year |
| --- | --- | --- |
| London | £3,191 | £5,567 |
| Elsewhere | £2,643 | £4,491 |
| Parental home | £2,207 | £3,439 |

## Extra weeks' allowance

The bursary is paid for a notional academic year of 30 weeks and three days. If your course requires additional attendance, a further allowance is paid.

*Extra weeks' allowance 2015/16 (per week)*

| London | £108 |
| --- | --- |
| Elsewhere | £84 |
| Parental home | £56 |

If your required attendance in an academic year is 45 weeks or more, an allowance for all 52 weeks is paid.

## Reduced-rate student loan

If you get a bursary, you may also be eligible for a reduced-rate undergraduate student loan. This is not subject to a means test. You should apply through Student Finance England or Student Finance Wales. **Note:** the rates in England and Wales are different.

*Reduced-rate student loan 2015/16*

| England | Full year | Final year |
| --- | --- | --- |
| London | £3,263 | £2,498 |
| Elsewhere | £2,324 | £1,811 |
| Parental home | £1,744 | £1,324 |

| Wales | | |
|---|---|---|
| London | £3,703 | £2,831 |
| Elsewhere | £2,634 | £2,053 |
| Parental home | £1,976 | £1,501 |

The loan must be repaid after graduation, with the same repayment conditions as for other higher education students who started new courses in the 2012/13 academic year or later (see p32).

## Dependants' allowance

If you have adults or children wholly or mainly financially dependent on you, you may be eligible for an extra dependants' allowance. Eligibility is means tested and depends on the income of your dependant(s).

**Note:** the NHS is currently reviewing the allowances for dependants and childcare. At the time of writing, the outcome of this was not known, but it was expected to be available in autumn 2015.

*Amount of dependants' allowance 2015/16*

Spouse or civil partner (or other adult dependant, or first child if there is no spouse or any adult dependants)    £2,448

Each additional dependant    £549

## Parents' learning allowance

If you have a dependent child, you can claim an additional £1,204 to support the costs associated with her/him. This is available to all student parents, including those with partners, but is means tested.

## Childcare allowance

If you have responsibility for a child under the age of 15 (or 17 if s/he has special educational needs) and you use registered or approved childcare, you can apply for a means-tested childcare allowance. You cannot receive this if you receive the childcare element in working tax credit (see p220) or childcare support through universal credit (see p206).

The grant can cover up to 85 per cent of your actual costs of childcare, with a maximum payment of £128.78 a week for one child or £191.45 a week for two or more children. In Wales, the maximum payment for two or more children is £209.95 a week.

## Practice placement costs

The cost of travel between your home and a practice placement site that is not part of the college, and additional residential costs where appropriate, may be reimbursed to you. Only the amount that exceeds the cost of travel between your term-time residence and the normal place of study is reimbursed.

## Disabled students' allowance

If you have a disability, you can claim a disabled students' allowance from the NHS on the same basis as higher education students in England, except that the equipment allowance is very slightly higher, at £5,212 for the course (see p34 – the same rates apply to NHS students in Wales).

## Students who started their course before 2012

**Note:** the bursary scheme changed in the 2007/08 academic year. This section therefore refers to 'old system' (ie, pre-2007 system students) and '2007 system' students – ie, those who started their course between 1 September 2007 and 31 August 2012.

The support available depends on the level of the course you are studying. If you are a diploma-level student, you can receive a non-means-tested bursary (see below). If you are a degree-level student, you are eligible for a means-tested award (see p82). Each type of bursary also has additional allowances for specific groups. To be eligible for either, you must also meet the personal residency conditions for higher education students in England (see p21). In both cases, the NHS pays your tuition fees.

Both types of bursary are funded in England by NHS Student Bursaries. In Wales, nursing and midwifery students are eligible for the non-means-tested bursary and this is processed by the university. The means-tested bursary and the childcare allowance for all students are processed by NHS Wales Student Awards Services.

In addition to receiving either of the two bursaries, all NHS students in Wales who meet the criteria can apply for financial support from their institution's local hardship fund (see p57). NHS students in England should check with their own university or college about its hardship scheme and whether they can apply (see p43).

## Diploma-level students

### Non-means-tested bursary

'Old system' and '2007 system' diploma-level students can receive a non-means-tested bursary. The amount of bursary you receive does not depend on your income. In England, the bursary is available to students on a nursing, midwifery or operating department practice higher education diploma course. In Wales, the bursary is available to nursing and midwifery students. In Wales, operating department practice diploma students have their tuition fees paid by the NHS and receive a training salary instead of a bursary.

If you are eligible for this bursary, the NHS also pays your fees. The bursary is paid in 12 equal monthly instalments across the academic year.

*Maximum amount of non-means-tested bursary 2015/16*

|  | *'Old system' students* | *'2007 system' students* |
|---|---|---|
| London | £7,810 | £8,242 |
| Elsewhere | £6,645 | £7,056 |
| Parental home | £6,645 | £7,056 |

There are also additional allowances available if you are a diploma student.

## Extra weeks' allowance

The bursary assumes that you are required to attend your course for 45 weeks a year, so no additional weeks' allowance is paid.

## Older students' allowance

If you are an 'old system' student and were aged 26 or over before the beginning of your first academic year,[1] you receive an additional £768. If you turn 26 during your course, you do not become eligible in later years. This allowance cannot be claimed in addition to the single parent addition (see p82). It is not available for '2007 system' students.

## Dependants' allowance

If you have an adult or child wholly or mainly financially dependent on you, you may be eligible for an extra dependants' allowance. Eligibility for this allowance is means tested and depends on the income of your dependant(s).

*Amount of dependants' allowance 2015/16*

**'Old system' students**

| | |
|---|---|
| Spouse or civil partner (or other adult dependant, or first child if there is no spouse or any adult dependants) | £2,283 |
| Child aged under 11 | £483 |
| Child aged 11–15 | £958 |
| Child aged 16–17 | £1,270 |
| Child aged 18+ | £1,798 |

**'2007 system' students**

| | |
|---|---|
| Spouse or civil partner (or other adult dependant, or first child if there is no spouse or any adult dependants) | £2,283 |
| Each additional dependant | £549 |

### Single parent addition

If you are an 'old system' student and a lone parent, you are entitled to an additional £1,126. This is not paid in addition to the older students' allowance. '2007 system' students should apply for the parents' learning allowance instead.

### Parents' learning allowance

If you are a '2007 system' student and have a dependent child(ren), you can claim an additional £1,126. This is available to all '2007 system' student parents, including those with partners, but is means tested.

### Childcare allowance

This is paid on the same basis as for '2012 system' students (see p79).

### Practice placement costs

The cost of travel between your home and a practice placement site that is not part of the college, plus additional residential costs, where appropriate, may be reimbursed to you. Only the amount that exceeds the cost of travel between your term-time residence and place of study is reimbursed.

### Disabled students' allowance

If you have a disability, you can claim a disabled students' allowance from the NHS on the same basis as students in other forms of higher education (the rates in England also apply to NHS students in Wales). For more information, see p34.

### Maintenance loan

Diploma-level students cannot apply for a maintenance loan, unless they are 'seconded' by an employer to attend the course and, therefore, not eligible for an NHS bursary.

## Degree-level students

### Means-tested bursary

A means-tested bursary is available if you are an 'old system' or '2007 system' student studying for a degree-level qualification in any of the healthcare disciplines outlined on p77. If you meet the personal eligibility criteria, your tuition fees are also paid. The amount you receive for living costs depends on your (and your partner's) income or, if you are a 'dependent student' (see p36), your parents' income.

If you are eligible for a means-tested bursary, you may also be eligible for a reduced-rate undergraduate student loan, as for '2012 system' students (see p78). This loan is not subject to a means test. Apply to Student Finance England or Student Finance Wales. The repayment conditions are the same as for other undergraduate students who started their course before 1 September 2012 (see p32).

Employed students do not usually qualify for bursaries, but may qualify for student support from the Department for Business, Innovation and Skills or Welsh government.

*Maximum amount of means-tested bursary 2015/16*

|  | *'Old system' students* | *'2007 system' students* |
|---|---|---|
| London | £3,230 | £3,571 |
| Elsewhere | £2,630 | £2,958 |
| Parental home | £2,151 | £2,470 |

As with other students, there is a range of additional allowances available.

### Extra weeks' allowance

The extra weeks' allowance for '2007 system' students is the same as for '2012 system' students (see p78). The rates for 'old system' students are £2 per week lower than for '2007' or '2012 system' students in each case.

### Older students' allowance

If you are an 'old system' student, and were aged 26 or over before the beginning of your first academic year,[2] you receive an additional allowance. If you turn 26 during your course, you do not become eligible in later years. This allowance cannot be claimed in addition to the single parent addition. It is also payable to diploma students attending accelerated programmes for graduates, regardless of age.

*Older students' allowance 2015/16*

| *Age before first academic year* | *Amount* |
|---|---|
| 26 | £457 |
| 27 | £793 |
| 28 | £1,176 |
| 29+ | £1,554 |

### Dependants' allowance

If you have adults or children wholly or mainly financially dependent on you, you may be eligible for extra dependants' allowances. However, the income of your dependants is taken into account and so eligibility for this allowance is means tested.

*Amount of dependants' allowance 2015/16*

**'Old system' students**

| | |
|---|---|
| Spouse (or other adult dependant, or first child if there is no spouse or any adult dependants) | £2,693 |
| Child aged under 11 | £564 |
| Child aged 11–15 | £1,126 |
| Child aged 16–17 | £1,498 |
| Child aged 18+ | £2,155 |

**'2007 system' students**

| | |
|---|---|
| Spouse or civil partner (or other adult dependant, or first child if there is no spouse or any adult dependants) | £2,693 |
| Each additional dependant | £549 |

### Single parent allowance

If you are an 'old system' student and a lone parent, you are entitled to an additional £1,329. This is not paid in addition to the older students' allowance. '2007 system' students should apply for the parents' learning allowance.

### Parents' learning allowance

If you are a 2007 system student and have a dependent child(ren), you can claim an additional £1,329. This is available to all student parents, including those with partners, but is means tested.

### Childcare allowance

This is paid on the same basis as for '2012 system' students (see p79).

### Practice placement costs

The cost of travel between your home and a practice placement site that is not part of the college, and additional residential costs where appropriate, may be reimbursed to you. Only the amount that exceeds the cost of travel between your term-time residence and place of study is reimbursed.

### Disabled students' allowance

If you have a disability, you can claim a disabled students' allowance from the NHS on the same basis as students in other forms of higher education (see p34 – the same rates apply to NHS students in Wales).

### NHS hardship grant

In addition to institutional hardship funds (see p43), the NHS operates a limited hardship fund for medicine and dentistry students eligible for the means-tested bursary. Contact NHS Student Bursaries or NHS Wales Student Awards Services to apply (see Appendix 2).

## European Union nationals

If you are a national of a European Union (EU) member state, you may be eligible for NHS bursary support.

If you or your parent(s) are non-UK EU nationals who satisfy the three-year residence criteria in the 'UK and islands' (see p21), you are treated as if you are a UK student and are eligible for support for both maintenance and fees. You are not required to have settled status. If your residence in the UK was mainly for the purpose of full-time higher education, you may still be eligible for an NHS bursary (maintenance grant and tuition fees) if you can show that you were ordinarily resident in a European Economic Area country or Switzerland immediately prior to your period of ordinary residence in the UK.

EU students who are not ordinarily resident in the UK under the terms described, may be awarded an 'EU fees only' award, under which they have the cost of their tuition fees met, but are not eligible for a student loan, hardship funds or the maintenance element of the NHS bursary.

You may also qualify for support as a migrant worker. The rules are complex, so seek advice from the advice centre in your university or students' union if you think this may apply to you.

## Part-time students

Part-time students on NHS-funded degree courses are eligible for support, which is paid pro rata, depending on the length of the part-time course.

The full rate is paid if you have additional costs resulting from a disability and for reimbursing the costs of attending a clinical placement.

## Students who are pregnant or who have recently given birth

If you are an NHS-funded student, have enrolled on your course and require maternity leave, you can be paid your bursary for a period of up to 45 weeks (known as a 'maternity allowance'). Seconded students and EU nationals on fees-only awards cannot receive this.

For more information, see www.nhsbsa.nhs.uk/students or contact NHS Wales Student Awards Services at www.nwsspstudentfinance.wales.nhs.uk (search for NHS bursaries).

---

# 2. Healthcare students in Northern Ireland

If you are planning to study an allied health professions degree course in Northern Ireland, you can apply for funding from the Department of Health, Social Services and Public Safety (DHSSPS). Under these arrangements, you do not pay tuition fees and can apply for an income-assessed bursary to cover your living costs and a reduced rate, non-income-assessed student loan. Medical and dental students in their final year of study are also funded through this system. Students from European Union countries who are studying in Northern Ireland are also exempt from paying tuition fees, but cannot get a bursary or loan to cover their living costs.

The amount of bursary you receive depends on your household income. Additional allowances may be available if you have dependants or a disability. **Note:** the bursaries are under review and changes may be made for future years.

*Bursary rates 2015/16*

| Full year | Bursary | Loan |
|---|---|---|
| Living away from parental home | £2,355 | £2,370 |
| Living at parental home | £1,920 | £1,780 |
| **Final year** | | |
| Living away from parental home | £2,355 | £1,850 |
| Living at parental home | £1,920 | £1,350 |

Regional education authority offices administer the bursary arrangements on behalf of the DHSSPS under the name Student Finance NI. If you are a Northern Irish student, you should, therefore, apply to your local Student Finance NI regional office. If you live in England, Scotland or Wales, apply to Student Finance NI at the address for the north eastern regional Education Authority office. For more information, see www.nidirect.gov.uk/nhs-and-social-work-students.

## Nursing and midwifery students

Full-time pre-registration nursing and direct-entry midwifery students taking up a commissioned DHSSPS place on a course leading to entry on the Nursing and Midwifery Council register can receive a bursary while undertaking the course. Students receiving a bursary do not pay tuition fees, but are not eligible for support from Student Finance NI. They can apply for discretionary help from their institution's support funds. Contact your students' union or advice centre for more details. You apply for a bursary via the Bursary Administration Unit, part of the Business Services Organisation at the DHSSPS (see Appendix 2).

The bursary system changed for new students after 1 September 2007, but students who started their course before this date remain funded under the old rules.

Both schemes comprise a non-means-tested basic rate, additional means-tested allowances, and travel expenses for costs incurred while on clinical placements. Disabled students' allowances are also payable, where appropriate, at the same rate as for other higher education students (see p67). The rates are set annually.

**Bursary rates 2015/16**

| | |
|---|---|
| Basic award (not means tested) | £5,165 |
| Additional dependants' additions (means tested) | |
|     Partner or other adult dependant (or first child if no other dependant) | £2,389 |
|     Each subsequent child | £567 |
| Parents' learning allowance (you must receive a dependants' addition to qualify for this) | £1,125 |
| Contribution to childcare | Up to £1,250 |

# 3. **Initial teacher training in England**

There are three main routes for initial teacher training in England that lead to qualified teacher status, each with different funding arrangements:

- Bachelor of Education (BEd): an undergraduate degree, usually for four years' full-time study or equivalent, with qualified teacher status gained after a year's successful teaching, although there are now some two-year and three-year undergraduate courses that lead to qualified teacher status;
- Postgraduate Certificate in Education (PGCE) or Postgraduate Diploma in Education (PGDE): a postgraduate degree, delivered either by a higher education institution or through a 'school-centred initial teacher training' provider, including the School Direct (non-salaried) programme, usually for one year (or the part-time equivalent), with qualified teacher status gained after a year's successful teaching;
- employment-based initial teacher training: this can be undertaken through the School Direct (salaried) programme.

## Bachelor of Education and Bachelor of Arts/Science with qualified teacher status

The main financial assistance available if you are studying for a BEd, BA or BSc qualification is the basic undergraduate student support package outlined in Chapter 2. This includes all supplementary grants and access to any hardship funds.

There are no further incentives for BEd, BA or BSc with qualified teacher status study in 2015/16.

## Postgraduate Certificate/Diploma in Education

If you are on a full- or part-time PGCE/PGDE course at a higher education institution or through a 'school-centred initial teacher training' provider, including the School Direct (non-salaried) programme, and meet the personal and residential eligibility criteria for undergraduate student support (see p21), you are entitled to the same support package as undergraduate students (see Chapter 2). You may also be able to apply for assistance from your university or college's hardship fund. There are also incentive packages for which you may be eligible.

### Tuition fees

Like all new undergraduates in England, PGCE/PGDE students are liable for variable fees of up to £9,000 in 2015/16. Eligible students can take out a non-means tested loan to cover the cost of these.[3]

### Teacher training bursary

The teacher training bursary aims to encourage 'high-quality' entrants to the teaching profession in England, as determined by the degree classification they receive at undergraduate level, or if they hold a postgraduate qualification. Those with the highest undergraduate classifications or who hold doctorate-level qualifications receive the highest bursary. The exact rates for different subject and classification combinations vary from year to year, depending on the Department for Education's priorities. For the current rates see https://getintoteaching.education.gov.uk/bursaries-and-funding.

If you are on a one-year course, you are paid in monthly instalments between October and June. If your course is part time, you are paid in instalments in accordance with the length of your training.

If you are a full-time trainee, the salary is not taxable and you do not have to pay national insurance contributions. If you are a part-time trainee, the salary may be taxable, depending on your total income for the year. It is included in any calculation for means-tested benefits.

Students from the European Union are also eligible for these incentives, plus a loan for tuition fees (although not for the standard maintenance support from Student Finance England).

Some subjects attract bursaries from 'subject association groups'. Where relevant, you should apply for these first. If you receive such a bursary, you are not eligible for the standard bursary. The details are as follows.

- Physics graduates with at least a first-class degree or PhD may qualify for an Institute of Physics scholarship of £25,000 to teach secondary physics.
- Chemistry graduates with at least a 2:1 may qualify for a Royal Society of Chemistry scholarship of £25,000 to teach secondary chemistry.

- Computer science graduates with at least a 2:1 may qualify for a BCS, the Chartered Institute for IT scholarship of £25,000 to teach secondary computing.
- Maths graduates with at least a 2:1 may qualify for an Institute of Mathematics and its Applications scholarship of £25,000 to teach secondary mathematics.

The exact nature of the scholarships may vary from year to year. Check with the relevant subject association group.

Full details of all scholarship programmes are available on the Department for Education website at: https://getintoteaching.education.gov.uk/bursaries-and-funding.

## Employment-based initial teacher training

### School Direct

The School Direct teacher training programme allows you to train as a teacher in academies or local authority-maintained schools while earning a salary. You must have at least three years' post-graduation work experience, although this does not need to be in an educational setting. Trainees on the scheme do not qualify for student support or bursaries, but are paid a salary. The salary rate depends on the type of school, and potentially the subject you are teaching.

More details are available at https://getintoteaching.education.gov.uk.

### Repayment of teachers' loans

This was a pilot scheme for newly qualified teachers who took teaching posts in the academic years 2002/03, 2003/04 and 2004/05. If you are eligible and you work in a shortage subject, your student loan is repaid for you. The scheme only applies if you spend at least half of your teaching time teaching the shortage subjects. To be eligible you must:

- be employed in England or Wales in a teaching post at a maintained school, a non-maintained special school, a city technology college, a city college for the technology of arts or a city academy;
- have begun employment between 1 July 2002 and 30 June 2005;
- be employed to teach one or more of the shortage subjects for at least half of your teaching time within a normal school week.

More information is available at www.studentloanrepayment.co.uk. The scheme is not available to teachers who started employment after 30 June 2005.

## 4. Initial teacher training in Wales

In Wales, there are three main routes for initial teacher training that leads to qualified teacher status:

- Bachelor of Education (BEd): an undergraduate degree, usually for four years' full-time study or equivalent, with qualified teacher status gained after a year's successful teaching;
- Postgraduate Certificate in Education (PGCE): a postgraduate degree, usually for one year (or the part-time equivalent), with qualified teacher status gained after a year's successful teaching;
- school-centred initial teacher training, through a graduate teacher programme.

## Bachelor of Education

The main financial assistance available if you are studying a BEd qualification is the basic undergraduate student support package for Welsh students, outlined in Chapter 3. This includes all supplementary grants and access to the hardship funds. There are no further incentives for undergraduate study.

## Postgraduate Certificate of Education

If you are on a full- or part-time PGCE course and meet the personal and residential eligibility criteria for undergraduate student support (see p47), you are entitled to the same support package as new undergraduate students in the relevant cohort (see p47), including support for fees. You can apply for assistance from the local hardship funds. There are also incentive packages for which you may be eligible.

### Teacher training grant

If you undertake a PGCE initial teacher training course in Wales, you may be eligible for a teacher training grant if you are studying a priority subject. How much you receive depends on your undergraduate degree classification, with bursaries of up to £20,000 available in 2015/16. The bursary rates for different subject and degree combinations vary each year, depending on the Welsh government's priorities. **Note:** students with lower classifications, particularly third-class degrees, may not be entitled to a bursary at all. For the latest rates, see http://teachertrainingcymru.org.

Students from the European Union (EU) are also eligible for these incentives.

The incentives are paid by the Welsh government to the provider, which then pays the relevant amount to eligible students on a monthly basis once they have enrolled and started their training.

### Welsh medium improvement supplement

To help those students who need additional assistance to raise their competence and confidence, a £1,600 grant is available to undergraduate or postgraduate students undertaking secondary initial teacher training in Wales using the Welsh language.[4] This increases to £2,000 for maths, chemistry and physics courses. Once qualified, you are expected to take up a secondary school teaching post using the Welsh language. Your institution assesses your eligibility and advises you on the application process.

## Graduate teacher programme

If you are a graduate aged 24 or over, the graduate teacher programme allows you to train as a teacher in maintained schools while still earning a living.

You receive a salary from the school in which you are based. The level of salary to be paid by the school is agreed by the governing body and may be at a rate based on the scales for either qualified or unqualified teachers, but must be no lower than the minimum salary grade for unqualified teachers of at least £16,136. If you are on this scheme, you are not eligible for the training bursary, outlined above. In addition, the school receives a grant for the cost of your training. This can be used to cover the cost of an initial training needs assessment, tuition fees, supply cover, mentoring training, learning resources and materials. This funding cannot be used as a wage supplement.

## Repayment of teachers' loans

The repayment of teachers' loans scheme has closed to new applicants. However, existing teachers on this scheme still benefit (see p89).

---

# 5. Initial teacher training in Northern Ireland

Students accepted on a course of initial teacher training in Northern Ireland in the 2015/16 academic year, including Postgraduate Certificate in Education (PGCE) courses, receive the same funding as 'new system' undergraduate students (see pp62–65). This means that PGCE students are liable for tuition fees, but can take out a loan to cover these.

You can make an application for funding through Student Finance NI.

The additional financial incentives available for undergraduate and PGCE study in England and Wales are not available in Northern Ireland, but Northern Irish students studying in England or Wales can claim these.

---

# 6. Social work students

## England

### Undergraduate support

**Note:** the bursary system changed for new students from 2013/14, although students who started before 1 September 2013 remain on the old system.

Students studying an undergraduate diploma or degree in social work in England may be eligible for a non-means-tested bursary from the Department of Health. The NHS Business Services Authority (BSA) administers these bursaries on its behalf.

If you are a full-time undergraduate studying at an institution in England, you may be eligible to receive this bursary in addition to the Department for Business, Innovation and Skills student support package (see Chapter 2), which includes a tuition fee loan, as the bursary is not intended to cover tuition fees for undergraduates.

New undergraduate students who started their course on 1 September 2013 or later no longer receive a social work bursary in their first year of study. Once students move into their second and third years of study bursaries are payable, but these are limited in number and, therefore, not all students receive a bursary. Higher education institutions are expected to allocate bursaries in a way that produces 'high-quality' graduates, so while the exact allocation criteria varies, factors such as assessments and previous experience before the course are expected to be used in making decisions. You should ask what criteria your institution uses to allocate bursaries, ideally before you start your course. In 2015/16 about 2,600 bursaries were available for those students who started their courses in the 2014/15 academic year.

Students who started their course before 1 September 2013 will have received a bursary in their first year and continue to do so for the remainder of their course.

### Basic bursary

If you are allocated a bursary, the amount you receive depends on where you study. The bursary paid includes a contribution of £862.50 to cover the costs of travel to placements.

If you started your course on or after 1 September 2013 and you are awarded a bursary, you can get £4,862.50 if you are studying at an institution outside London, or £5,262.50 if you are studying at a university or college in London or at the University of London. Essentially, if Student Finance England deems you eligible for the London rate of loan, you are eligible for the London rate of bursary. The bursary is paid for 52 weeks and is taken into account as income for benefit purposes, except for the element paid for travelling expenses, which is disregarded.[5] However, this is not usually specifically identified and can be taken into account by mistake. Check your calculation if this might apply to you.

If you started your course before 1 September 2013, the bursary rates are £4,575 outside London and £4,975 inside London. This is inclusive of £575 towards placement costs.

### Part-time students

If you are a part-time undergraduate student, you can receive the bursary pro rata over the length of your course. As with full-time undergraduates, new part-time undergraduates do not receive a bursary in the first year of the course, and numbers are capped thereafter. All students are also eligible for help with placement costs. You are not entitled to any other forms of support.

### Placement expenses

If you do not receive a bursary allocation but incur placement expenses, you can claim a contribution towards your placement costs of £862.50 (pro rata if you are a part-time student) from the BSA.

## Postgraduate support

In addition to the undergraduate bursary, the BSA also administers support for students studying a postgraduate-level course, such as the Masters in Social Work, or for students studying an undergraduate degree or diploma who already have a first degree.

Changes have been introduced for new students starting on 1 September 2013 or later. As for undergraduates, the number of bursaries has been capped, although it is expected that most postgraduate students will receive support. There are around 1,500 bursaries available across England. Bursaries are allocated to support 'high-quality' applicants (eg, those with relevant previous experience), with the institution making the final decision. You should ask your institution what criteria it intends to use to allocate bursaries. If you do not receive a bursary, you can still get help with placement costs (see p94).

If you qualify for a bursary, it helps with your extra study and living costs, and there is additional money available if you have children or a disability.

### Tuition fees

If you receive a bursary, you also receive a grant of up to £4,052 towards your tuition fees. This grant is paid by the BSA, directly to the institution. The grants are not means tested. You should check how much your institution intends to charge for tuition as, in some cases, it may exceed the tuition fee grant available.

### Basic grant

Eligible postgraduate students can receive a basic non-means-tested grant from the NHS if they get a bursary. You can get £3,362.50 if you are studying at an institution outside London, or £3,762.50 if you are studying at a university or college in London or at the University of London. This includes a placement travel expenses allowance of £862.50. Postgraduate students are not eligible for student support from Student Finance England.

### Additional maintenance grant

This is a means-tested grant paid in addition to the basic grant for those who secure a bursary allocation. Up to £4,201 is available to students studying in London or at the University of London, with up to £2,721 available to those studying elsewhere.

The grant is means tested on your unearned income and any taxable income of a partner, if you have one.

### Students with dependants

If you have a child and/or an adult who is financially dependent on you, you can apply for an **adult dependants' grant**, the **parents' learning allowance** and the **childcare grant**. These broadly mirror the same grants that undergraduates can apply for from Student Finance England (see p33).

### Disabled students' allowance

Postgraduate social work students can apply for a disabled students' allowance from the NHS BSA at the same rates as for undergraduates (see p34). If you do not receive a bursary allocation, you may still be able to claim a postgraduate disabled students' allowance from Student Finance England (see p72).

### Part-time students

Part-time postgraduate students who secure a bursary allocation have their tuition fees paid by the NHS BSA. They can receive the 'incentive to train' bursary at half the rate for full-time study, plus help with placement costs. They are not eligible for other forms of support.

### Placement expenses

If you do not receive a bursary allocation but incur placement expenses, you can still claim a contribution towards your placement costs of £862.50 (pro rata if you are a part-time student) from the NHS BSA.

## How to apply

If you are an undergraduate, you should first apply to Student Finance England for student support. When it has assessed your application and you have received notification of this (sometimes known as an 'award notification'), contact the NHS BSA for an application form for the bursary. Postgraduates should apply directly to the NHS BSA. There is a deadline for applications: for 2015/16 applications, this is 30 November 2015 for courses starting in autumn 2015 and 14 February 2016 for course starting in January 2016.

Application forms are available at www.nhsbsa.nhs.uk/students.

## Wales

Students in Wales studying for qualifications in social work may qualify for financial help from the Care Council for Wales. The number of bursaries is restricted: there are 224 available in Wales in 2015/16. Higher education institutions nominate which students should receive support, subject to these students meeting standard eligibility criteria in relation to residency and their personal circumstances.

## Undergraduate support

If you are studying for an undergraduate degree or diploma in social work, first apply for student support through your local authority, as for other undergraduate students (see Chapter 3).

If you are nominated for a bursary and meet the eligibility criteria, you receive a non-means-tested bursary to help cover your living costs of £2,500 in 2015/16. If you are studying part time, the bursary is calculated on a pro rata basis.

In addition, a **practice learning opportunity allowance** is paid to help cover the costs of attending placements. This is paid at £7.50 per day of placement. If your travel costs to placements are more than the initial payment, you can apply to the Care Council for Wales for reimbursement of these extra costs, subject to a daily maximum. Keep all receipts, as you may be asked to submit these as proof of expenditure.

Students who started their course before 2012/13 may be eligible for additional help towards their tuition fees. Contact the Care Council for Wales if you are uncertain.

To apply, contact the Care Council for Wales for an application form or see www.ccwales.org.uk.

## Postgraduate support

If you are on a postgraduate diploma or Masters course in Wales, you may get an additional non-means-tested graduate bursary of £6,640 in 2015/16. This includes a contribution of £3,390 towards tuition fees. You can apply for the adult dependants' grant, the parents' learning allowance and the childcare grant at the same time as the additional graduate bursary, although these are means tested. You can also get a practice learning opportunities allowance, as for undergraduates (see above).

If you have a disability, you may be eligible for extra help through the postgraduate disabled students' allowance (see p72).

## Northern Ireland

If you are studying for a degree in social work in Northern Ireland, you can apply for an additional incentive grant from the Department of Health, Social Services and Public Safety. Non-means-tested grants of £4,000, plus a further £500 towards placement expenses, are available for each year of the course.

You must pay tuition fees, but the funding is in addition to any money to which you are entitled through Student Finance NI as part of the main undergraduate support system, including loans for fees.

Students in receipt of the incentive grant can now apply to the discretionary support funds for extra help (see p68).

**Note:** the Northern Ireland Executive intends to review the bursary for future years and it is possible changes will be introduced from 2016/17.

# 7. **Dance and drama awards**

The Department for Education has set up a scholarship programme to ensure that talented dance and drama students can attend courses at the leading dance and drama institutions in England, in cases where fees and living costs would otherwise be prohibitively expensive. Dance and drama awards fund Trinity College level five and six diploma courses in dance, drama and musical theatre. Funding is available through selected, approved specialist schools for between one and three years of study. You must be aged 16 and over for dance courses, or 18 and over for drama-related courses. There are a limited number of awards made each year and they are generally issued to those who show exceptional talent in an audition.

The residency rules for other higher education support apply (see p21) and students from England and Wales can apply for full support, while students from Northern Ireland can apply for help with fees only. A separate scheme operates in Northern Ireland for help with other costs (see below).

You cannot receive any support if your household income exceeds £90,000 a year (£70,000 if you started before 2015/16). **Note:** the scheme changed in 2013/14, but students who started in previous years continue under the old arrangements.

If you are a new student in 2015/16, receive an award and your household income is below £30,000, your fees are paid in full. If your household income is between £30,000 and £90,000 (£70,000 if you started before 2015/16), you can receive a contribution towards your fees on a sliding scale, with a higher contribution expected the higher your family income.

The award may also provide support for your living costs, depending on your circumstances. The maximum available is £5,185 for those living in London, and £4,550 for those living elsewhere. If you live at home with your parents, the maximum is £1,417. If you have a household income of more than £30,000, you are not eligible for maintenance support.

Dance and drama award recipients cannot access student loans and grants through Student Finance England.

Other allowances may be available if you have extra costs associated with a disability or childcare expenses.

More information on the awards is available through the participating dance and drama schools or from www.dadainfo.org.uk (where a list of the participating schools can also be found).

## **Northern Ireland**

The dance and drama (Northern Ireland) awards form part of the Northern Ireland further education awards scheme (see p17). They provide assistance for courses at one of the 21 accredited providers in the rest of the UK (as there is no provision in Northern Ireland). If a student receives a main dance and drama award which pays for the majority of the fees charged, s/he can also apply to the western regional office of the Northern Ireland Education Authority for a dance and drama (Northern Ireland) award for help with the remainder of the fee and maintenance.

As in the rest of the UK, the amounts available depend on where you study. The maximum available is £5,460 for those living in lodgings in London, and £4,823 for those living elsewhere. If your family income exceeds £33,000 per year, you are not entitled to any support.

For more information, contact Student Finance NI.

## 8. **Alternative sources of finance**

### Professional and career development loan

The Department for Business, Innovation and Skills, in participation with two major banks (Barclays and the Co-operative) operates a deferred repayment loan system.[6] You can borrow between £300 and £10,000 towards your fees and other expenses if you are on a vocational full-time, part-time or distance learning course lasting up to two years (and including up to one year's practical work experience if it is part of your course). Degree and postgraduate courses are included, and the loans are available across the UK.

The interest charged varies, depending on the bank, when you apply and the length of repayment, but currently is typically 9.9 per cent a year. You should, however, check with the bank. Throughout your period of study and up to one month after completing or leaving the course, the Skills Funding Agency (which administers the scheme) pays the interest on the loan for you. Repayments are fixed and can be spread between one and five years. If you are registered unemployed at the end of the first month of completing your course, you may apply to the bank to have your repayments deferred for up to five months initially, and for two further extensions of six months each.

More information on professional and career development loans can be found at www.gov.uk/career-development-loans.

### Armed forces bereavement scholarship scheme

The armed forces bereavement scholarship scheme provides additional support for children of servicemen/women killed on active duty since 1990. The scheme offers fee support of up to £9,000 per year to help pay for fees if you are liable and a maintenance grant of £4,950 for the length of the course.

To qualify, your parent must have died while in service with the UK armed forces and her/his death must be attributable to that service.

---

*Parent*

A person counts as your '**parent**' if s/he was your biological or adoptive parent, or you were the subject of a special guardianship order, or if s/he was your step-parent and had financial responsibility for you. A foster parent does not count.

---

If your parent dies while you are in higher education, support can be backdated to the start of the current term, or it starts from the next term if s/he dies during a vacation.

Support is not means tested. You must study at an institution in the UK, although you do not have to be resident in the UK. If you are on a further education course, you can also receive help from the scheme (see p6). You can download an application form and get further information at www.gov.uk/government/publications/afbss-form-1.

## Charities

It is unlikely that a course lasting more than one year could be financed entirely by trust fund help. Educational charities and trusts can, however, provide supplementary help to students who may be without funding for part of their course or who, for various reasons, need help over and above that provided by public funds.

Educational charities and trusts often have specific, even unusual, terms of reference. For example, thay may be restricted to helping only students:
* on certain courses of study; *or*
* above or below a certain age (often 21 or 25); *or*
* from particular parts of Britain or the world; *or*
* in defined occupations, professions or industries, or who have a parent working in one of these.

A student does not usually receive more than a few hundred pounds from any one charity, although higher amounts are not unknown. Charities usually make single, rather than ongoing, payments. Payments tend to be:
* for particular items – eg, tools or equipment; *or*
* for a specific purpose – eg, childcare; *or*
* those which the charity or trust believes might make the difference between completion and non-completion of the course.

Charities are more sympathetic to students whose need for assistance is as a result of sickness or unforeseen circumstances than to students who have mismanaged their money or who have started a course knowing they had insufficient funds.

Many charities only give assistance to first-time students. Assistance is more difficult to find if you are a postgraduate or taking a second undergraduate course. Applications often take some time to process, so it is wise to apply for support well in advance of the course start date.

### Further information

There are a number of publications that contain details of charities and trusts. See Appendix 1 for details.

Students in need should also consult their local authority, students' union, careers service, local Citizens Advice Bureau, town hall and local clergy as they may know of other trusts. In addition to awarding scholarships and prizes in specific subjects, colleges may have funds available for students in financial difficulties and unable to apply to the discretionary hardship/support funds, so it may be useful to consult your institution's student services.

# Notes

1. **Healthcare students in England and Wales**
   1 This is not necessarily the first day of your course.
   2 This is not necessarily the first day of your course.

3. **Initial teacher training in England**
   3 Reg 4 and Sch 2 E(SS) Regs

4. **Initial teacher training in Wales**
   4 E(WMTTIS) Regs

6. **Social work students**
   5 **IS** Reg 62(2)(h) IS Regs
   **HB** Reg 59(2)(g) HB Regs
   **UC** Reg 70 UC Regs
   See also para 30122 DMG

8. **Alternative sources of finance**
   6 s2 ETA 1973

# Part 2

## Benefits and tax credits

# Chapter 7

# Carer's allowance

**This chapter covers:**
1. What is carer's allowance (below)
2. Who is eligible (below)
3. Amount of benefit (p105)
4. Claiming carer's allowance (p105)
5. Challenging a decision (p105)
6. Other benefits and tax credits (p105)

*Basic facts*
– Carer's allowance is paid to people who care for someone with a severe disability.
– Part-time students are eligible to claim.
– Full-time students cannot claim.
– Carer's allowance is not means tested, but you cannot get it if you work and earn more than £110 a week.
– Getting carer's allowance qualifies you for a carer premium in your income support, income-based jobseeker's allowance, income-related employment and support allowance and housing benefit, or a carer element in universal credit.

## 1. What is carer's allowance

Carer's allowance (CA) is for people who spend at least 35 hours a week looking after a disabled person (an adult or child). The disabled person must be getting attendance allowance, the middle or highest rate of disability living allowance care component or the daily living component of personal independence payment. The amount of CA you get is not means tested and your student loan, grant or other income does not affect it. Part-time students can get CA, but full-time students are not eligible.

## 2. Who is eligible

You are eligible if you are a part-time student and you satisfy the basic rules on p104. You are not eligible if you are in full-time education.

## Full-time education

You are in full-time education if an overall consideration of your course requirements, and your performance against these, suggests this. If you are on a full-time course of education, you are normally taken to be in full-time education for the purpose of carer's allowance (CA).[1] If you think that, given your circumstances, you are not in full-time education, you may be able to argue that you are a part-time student.[2]

You are also treated as being in full-time education if you 'attend a course' (see below) at a university, college or other educational establishment for 21 hours or more a week.[3] These 21 hours include not just classes, lectures and seminars, but also individual study for course work. Meal breaks and unsupervised study are ignored. However, you are regarded as studying under supervision if you are doing course work, whether at home or at college, alone or in the presence of a supervisor.[4] Unsupervised study is work beyond the requirements of the course.

If your college or university says that it expects students to spend 21 hours or more a week in supervised study and classes, the DWP usually assumes that you are in full-time education.

In practice, if you want to show that you spend fewer hours on course work than the college or university expects, you need to provide detailed evidence and be prepared to appeal. If your particular circumstances mean that you are not expected to satisfy the normal requirements of the course (eg, because you are exempt from certain subjects), you may be able to argue that your hours of study are fewer than those expected of other students on the course.[5]

## Temporary absences

'Attending' a course means being enrolled on and pursuing a course.[6] You are treated as still being in full-time education during short and long vacations, and until the course ends or you abandon it or are dismissed from it. You are still regarded as being in full-time education during temporary interruptions.[7] If you have to take time out to care for someone, you cannot get CA unless you have finally abandoned your course (see p291).

## Basic rules

As well as being a student who is eligible to claim, to qualify for CA you must satisfy all of the following conditions.[8]
* You are aged 16 or over.
* You spend at least 35 hours a week caring for someone.
* The person for whom you care gets the middle or highest rate of disability living allowance care component, the daily living component of personal independence payment, attendance allowance or constant attendance allowance.
* You are not working and earning more than £110 a week.

- You satisfy certain rules on residence and presence in the UK and are not a 'person subject to immigration control'. See CPAG's *Welfare Benefits and Tax Credits Handbook* for details.

# 3. Amount of benefit

You get £62.10 a week (April 2015 rate).

# 4. Claiming carer's allowance

You claim carer's allowance on Form DS700, available from local Jobcentre Plus offices or by phoning the Carer's Allowance Unit on 0345 608 4321. You can also claim online at www.gov.uk/carers-allowance. Your claim can be backdated for up to three months if you qualified during that earlier period.

Benefit is usually paid directly into a bank account.

# 5. Challenging a decision

If you think a decision about your carer's allowance is wrong, you can ask the DWP to look at it again. This process is known as a 'reconsideration' (the law refers to it as a 'revision'). Provided you ask within the time limit (usually one month), the DWP notifies you of the decision in a 'mandatory reconsideration notice'. If you are still not happy when you get this notice, you can appeal to the independent First-tier Tribunal. If it was not possible to ask the DWP to reconsider the decision within a month, you can ask for a late revision (within 13 months), explaining why it is late. You can also ask the DWP to look at a decision again at any time if certain grounds are met – eg, there has been an official error.

# 6. Other benefits and tax credits

Carer's allowance (CA) is taken into account when calculating whether the benefit cap applies (see p154 and p208).

### The disabled person's benefit

Your entitlement to CA depends on the person for whom you care continuing to get her/his disability benefit. If her/his benefit stops, your benefit should also stop. To avoid being overpaid, make sure you tell the Carer's Allowance Unit if the disabled person's attendance allowance, disability living allowance or personal independence payment stops being paid.

It is not always financially prudent to claim CA. Although it may mean more money for you, it may result in the person for whom you care losing some income support (IS), income-related employment and support allowance (ESA), pension credit or housing benefit (HB). If s/he lives alone, s/he may be getting a severe disability premium included in the assessment of these benefits. S/he cannot continue to get this premium if you get CA for her/him. See CPAG's *Welfare Benefits and Tax Credits Handbook* for details.

## Overlapping benefits

Although CA is not means tested, you cannot receive it at the same time as incapacity benefit, maternity allowance, severe disablement allowance, bereavement benefits, retirement pension, contribution-based jobseeker's allowance (JSA) or contributory ESA. If you are eligible for more than one benefit, you get whichever is worth the most.

## Getting a carer premium or element

If you are a part-time student, getting CA may mean you become eligible for IS. Carers are not expected to look for work and are eligible for IS instead of JSA. An extra carer premium is included in IS, income-based JSA, income-related ESA and HB, even if your CA is not being paid because you are getting another benefit that overlaps with it. If you are getting CA and claiming universal credit (UC), you are eligible for a carer element in your UC and you are not expected to look for work.

## Working tax credit

If you have a child(ren) and a partner and you get CA, you are eligible for working tax credit if your partner works at least 16 hours a week, rather than the usual 24.

# Notes

**2. Who is eligible**
  1  *SSWP v Deane* [2010] EWCA Civ 699
  2  CG/1154/2010
  3  Reg 5 SS(ICA) Regs

  4  *Flemming v SSWP* [2002] EWCA Civ 641;
     *Bronwyn Wright-Turner v Department for
     Social Development* [2002] NICA 2
  5  CG/3189/2004
  6  *Flemming v SSWP* [2002] EWCA Civ 641
  7  Reg 5(3) SS(ICA) Regs
  8  s70 SSCBA 1992

# Chapter 8

## Child benefit

**This chapter covers:**

*Basic facts*

– Child benefit is paid to people who are responsible for a child or a 'qualifying young person'.

– Both full-time and part-time students can claim child benefit.

– If you are under 20, someone else may be able to claim child benefit for you if you are studying.

– Child benefit is not means tested.

## 1. **What is child benefit**

Child benefit is paid to people who are responsible for a child or 'qualifying young person'. You do not have to have paid national insurance contributions to qualify for child benefit. It is not means tested, so the amount you get is not affected by your student loan, grant or other income. If you earn over £50,000 and you or your partner get child benefit, you may have extra income tax to pay (known as the 'high income child benefit charge').

## 2. **Who is eligible**

You qualify for child benefit if:[1]

● you are responsible for a child or 'qualifying young person' – ie:
   – s/he lives with you; *or*

– you contribute to the cost of supporting her/him at a rate of at least the amount of child benefit for her/him; *and*

• you have priority over other potential claimants. Only one person can get child benefit for a particular child. There is an order of priority for who receives it where two or more people would otherwise be entitled; *and*

• you are 'present and ordinarily resident' in Britain, not a 'person subject to immigration control' and have a 'right to reside'. These terms are explained in CPAG's *Welfare Benefits and Tax Credits Handbook*.

You do not have to be the child's parent to claim child benefit for her/him.

Being a student, whether full or part time, does not affect your entitlement to child benefit.

If you are a 'qualifying young person' (see below), your parent or someone else who is responsible for you may be able to claim child benefit. You cannot, however, claim child benefit for yourself.

If a qualifying young person gets income support, income-based jobseeker's allowance, employment and support allowance, universal credit, working tax credit or child tax credit in her/his own right, any child benefit paid for the young person stops.

If a young person lives with a partner, or is married or in a civil partnership, you can get child benefit for her/him if s/he lives with you or you still contribute to her/his support, but only if her/his partner is in 'relevant education' (see p157) or approved training. The young person's partner cannot be the claimant.

In some circumstances, special rules apply – eg, if your child is being looked after by a local authority or is in prison or a young offenders' institution.

## Who counts as a child

Anyone aged under 16 counts as a **'child'** for child benefit purposes, whether or not s/he goes to school. Provided you meet the other qualifying conditions, child benefit can be paid for her/him.[2] Child benefit can also be paid for a child after s/he reaches 16 until at least 31 August after her/his 16th birthday, and then for as long as s/he continues to count as a 'qualifying young person'.

## Who counts as a qualifying young person

A **'qualifying young person'** is someone who:[3]

• is aged 16 and has left full-time non-advanced education (see p109) or training. This only applies up to 31 August after her/his 16th birthday (but see p109); *or*

• is aged 16 or 17, has left education or training and satisfies the extension period rule (see p110); *or*

• is aged 16 or over but under 20 and is on a course of full-time non-advanced education (see p109) not provided as a result of her/his employment, or approved training not provided under a contract of employment – ie, Foundation Learning or Access to Apprenticeships in England, Traineeships or Foundation Apprenticeships in Wales or Training for Success (including Programme-led Apprenticeships) in Northern Ireland.[4] The young person must have started the course or training before reaching 19, or have been accepted or enrolled to undertake it before that age; *or*

• is aged 16 or over but under 20 and has finished a course of full-time non-advanced education not provided as a result of her/his employment or approved training not provided under a contract of employment, but is accepted or enrolled on another such course. **Note:** if the course s/he has finished is an approved training course, this only applies if the following course is also approved training. Although someone must have started, or been accepted or enrolled on, the training or education when s/he was under 19 to be a qualifying young person once the course begins, the rules do not specify this for the gap between courses.[5] If the young person was accepted or enrolled after reaching age 19, you can argue that s/he is a qualifying young person from the end of the course until the next course begins; *or*

• is aged 16 or over but under 20 and has left full-time non-advanced education (see below) or approved training but has not passed her/his terminal date (see p110).

---

*Full-time non-advanced education*
**'Full time'** is more than 12 hours a week of classes and supervised study during term time. **'Non-advanced education'** is anything below degree, Higher National Certificate or Higher National Diploma level, and includes school-level courses, National Vocational Qualification levels 1–3, GCSEs, AS and A levels.

---

If your child counts as a qualifying young person on more than one of the above grounds, s/he counts as a qualifying young person until the last day that applies.[6]

If you stop being entitled to child benefit for your child because s/he no longer counts as a qualifying young person, but s/he later satisfies one of the above conditions again and so counts as a qualifying young person once more, child benefit can again become payable for her/him. **Note:** in some cases, you can continue to claim during such an interruption – eg, if the young person is ill or the gap is less than six months. In both cases, the interruption must be accepted as being reasonable.[7]

**Note:** in the rest of this chapter, the term 'child' is used to mean both children under 16 and qualifying young people aged 16 or over.

## The extension period

If your child is aged 16 or 17, s/he continues to count as a qualifying young person, and so child benefit can continue to be paid for her/him, during an 'extension period' if:[8]

- s/he has left education or training; *and*
- s/he is registered as available for work, education or training with the National Careers Service or a specified body; *and*
- s/he is not in remunerative work – ie, work of 24 hours a week or more for payment or in expectation of payment; *and*
- you were entitled to child benefit for her/him immediately before the extension period started; *and*
- you apply in writing or by phone within three months of the date your child's education or training having finished.

In this context, 'education' and 'training' are not defined and so may mean any kind of education or training.

The extension period starts from the Monday after your child's course of education or training ends and lasts for 20 weeks from that date. If your child reaches 18 during the extension period, unless s/he counts as a qualifying young person on another ground (see p108), your child benefit for her/him ends from the first child benefit payday on or after s/he reaches 18.[9]

## The terminal date

If your child leaves full-time, non-advanced education (see p109) or approved training before reaching 20, s/he continues to count as a qualifying young person until either:[10]

- the 'terminal date' (see below); *or*
- her/his 20th birthday, if this falls before the terminal date.

The general rule means that unless s/he continues to count as a qualifying young person on another ground or is returning to sit an exam (see p111), you stop receiving child benefit for her/him on that date.

*The terminal date*

Your child's **'terminal date'** is the first of the following dates that falls after the date her/his full-time, non-advanced education or approved training finishes:

– the last day in February;
– the last day in May;
– the last day in August;
– the last day in November.

A child who returns to sit an external examination in connection with her/his course of relevant education is treated as still being in relevant education until the date of the last exam.[11]

# 3. Amount of benefit

*Weekly rate from April 2015*

| | |
|---|---|
| Eldest eligible child | £20.70 |
| Other children (each) | £13.70 |

**Note:** the government plans to freeze child benefit rates for the next four years.[12]

# 4. Claiming child benefit

Child benefit is administered by HM Revenue and Customs (HMRC). You claim child benefit on Form CH2, which you can get from the Child Benefit Office on 0300 200 3100,www.gov.uk/child-benefit/how-to-claim or from Jobcentre Plus offices.

You should make a claim within three months of becoming eligible. This is because your claim can usually only be backdated for up to three months. You do not have to show any reasons why your claim was late.

## Getting paid

Child benefit is usually paid directly into your bank (or similar) account. Which account it goes into is up to you. If you do not want your benefit to go into an account that is overdrawn, give HMRC details of an alternative account if you have access to, or can open, one.

# 5. Challenging a decision

If you think a decision about your child benefit is wrong, you can ask HM Revenue and Customs (HMRC) to look at it again. This process is known as a 'reconsideration' (the law refers to it as a 'revision'). Provided you ask within the time limit (usually one month), HMRC notifies you of the decision in a 'mandatory reconsideration notice'. If you are still not happy when you get this notice, you can appeal to the independent First-tier Tribunal. If it was not possible to ask HMRC to reconsider the decision within a month, you can ask for a late revision (within 13 months), explaining why it is late. You can also ask HMRC to look at a decision again at any time if certain grounds are met – eg, there has been an official error.

## 6. **Other benefits and tax credits**

If you get child benefit, you count as being responsible for a child for income support (IS) and income-based jobseeker's allowance (JSA), and usually for housing benefit (HB). This can help you qualify for these benefits in some circumstances while you are a full-time student (see Chapters 12, 13 and 14).

Child benefit is ignored as income for IS and income-based JSA if you are getting child tax credit. However, if you have been getting IS or income-based JSA since before 6 April 2004 which includes amounts for your child(ren), child benefit is taken into account as income. Child benefit is ignored as income for income-related employment and support allowance, HB and universal credit.

Child benefit is taken into account when calculating whether the benefit cap applies (see p154 and p208).

## **Notes**

### 2. **Who is eligible**
1 ss141-47 SSCBA 1992
2 s142(1) SSCBA 1992; reg 4 CB Regs
3 s142(2) SSCBA 1992; regs 2-8 CB Regs
4 Reg 1(3) CB Regs
5 Reg 3 CB Regs
6 Reg 2(2) CB Regs
7 Reg 6 CB Regs
8 Reg 5 CB Regs
9 Reg 14 CBGA(A) Regs; reg 5(3) CB Regs
10 Reg 7 CB Regs
11 Reg 7(2) case 2.1 CB Regs

### 3. **Amount of benefit**
12 clause 9(2) Welfare Reform and Work Bill 2015

# Chapter 9

# Disability living allowance

This chapter covers:
1. What is disability living allowance (below)
2. Who is eligible (p114)
3. Amount of benefit (p117)
4. Claiming disability living allowance (p117)
5. Challenging a decision (p118)
6. Other benefits and tax credits (p118)

*Basic facts*

– Disability living allowance is paid to disabled people who need personal care or who have mobility difficulties.
– You must be under 16 to make a new claim.
– Getting disability living allowance allows you to claim income-related employment and support allowance as a full-time student. You may also be able to claim housing benefit as a full-time student and you may get a disability premium.
– Getting disability living allowance allows you to claim universal credit as a full-time student, provided you satisfy certain other conditions.
– Disability living allowance is not means tested.

## 1. What is disability living allowance

Disability living allowance (DLA) is a benefit for disabled people who need help with personal care or who have mobility difficulties. Unless you are under 16 or claiming in Northern Ireland, you cannot make a new claim for DLA and must claim personal independence payment (PIP) instead (see p191). **Note:** at the time of writing, the legislation introducing PIP was still being considered in Northern Ireland, and new claims for DLA are expected to continue for the time being.

DLA has two components:
- care component, paid at either the lowest, middle or highest rate;
- mobility component, paid at either the lower or higher rate.

You can get either or both components.

Students already getting DLA can continue to do so, but are expected to claim PIP instead by the end of 2017. Starting college or university does not usually lead the DWP to reassess your entitlement to DLA.

The amount you get is not means tested, and so is not reduced because of student support or other income.

If you are a full-time student and get DLA, you are eligible for income-related employment and support allowance. You may also be eligible for housing benefit. If you are a full-time student getting DLA and you satisfy certain other conditions, you are eligible for universal credit (see p199).

## 2. **Who is eligible**

Full-time and part-time students can continue to get disability living allowance (DLA). In England and Wales, you cannot make a new claim unless you are under 16, but should claim personal independence payment (PIP) instead if you think you may be entitled.

If you get DLA and your condition changes which means you should qualify for a different rate of DLA (see below), or your DLA award is due to end, or you turn 16, you must claim PIP instead. Otherwise, at some point you will be reassessed for PIP, with everyone expected to be reassessed by the end of 2017. In Northern Ireland, you should continue to claim DLA until PIP is introduced.

### Care component

To get the care component, you must have a physical or mental disability that means you need the following kinds of care from another person. What is important is the help you need rather than the help you actually get.

You get paid either the lowest, middle or highest rate.

### Lowest rate
You get the lowest rate if you meet either (or both) of these two conditions.
- You need attention in connection with your bodily functions (see p115) for a significant portion of the day. This attention might be given all at once or be spread out. It should normally add up to about an hour or more, or be made up of several brief periods.
- You cannot prepare a cooked meal for yourself if you have the ingredients. This is a test of whether you can manage all the tasks involved in preparing a main meal for one on a traditional cooker – eg, planning the meal, reading labels, chopping vegetables, carrying pans and using the cooker.

## Middle rate

This is for people who need care either during the day or during the night, but not both. You get the middle rate if you meet one (or both) of the day care conditions *or* one (or both) of the night care conditions.

### Care during the day

- You need frequent attention throughout the day in connection with your bodily functions (see below). This means you may qualify if you need help several times, not just once or twice, spread out throughout the day. If you need help just in the mornings and evenings, for instance, you might get the lowest rate instead.
- You need continual supervision throughout the day in order to avoid substantial danger to yourself or others. The supervision must be frequent or regular, but need not be continuous.

### Care at night

- You need prolonged or repeated attention at night in connection with your bodily functions (see below). You should qualify if you need help once in the night for 20 minutes or more. You should also qualify if you need help twice in the night (or more often), however long it takes.
- In order to avoid substantial danger to yourself or others, you need another person to be awake at night for a prolonged period (20 minutes) or at frequent intervals (three times or more) to watch over you.

## Highest rate

This is for people who need care both day and night. You get the highest rate if you meet one (or both) of the above day care conditions and one (or both) of the above night care conditions. You also get the highest rate if you are terminally ill – ie, you have a progressive disease and could reasonably be expected to die within six months.

## Attention with bodily functions

This is help from someone else to do personal things you cannot do entirely by yourself. 'Bodily functions' are things like breathing, hearing, seeing, eating, drinking, walking, sitting, sleeping, getting in or out of bed, dressing, undressing, and using the toilet. However, any help in connection with an impaired bodily function can count if it involves personal contact (physical or verbal in your presence) and it is reasonably required.

For example, a blind student might need the help of a notetaker or reader, or a guide around campus or around town. A deaf student might need an interpreter. A student with arthritis might need help getting in and out of chairs.

You must need the help of another person to qualify for DLA. If you only need artificial aids, you will not get DLA.

You cannot count help with domestic chores, unless someone is helping you to do them for yourself.

If you have dyslexia, you could argue that you qualify for DLA, but only if you need someone to be with you to help you read and write – ie, someone sitting beside you reading to you or helping you develop reading skills.[1] This could count as attention with the bodily function of seeing or of the brain.[2]

### Having a social life

The kind of help you need must be reasonably required. This means that you need it to enable you as far as reasonably possible to live a normal life. You can include help needed to take part in social activities, sport, recreation, cultural or political activities, provided the help required is in connection with a bodily function.

## Mobility component

There are two rates of the mobility component.

### Lower rate

This is for people who can walk, but need guidance or supervision. You qualify if you are able to walk but, because of your disability, you cannot walk outdoors without guidance or supervision from someone else most of the time.

You can still qualify if you are able to manage on familiar routes. If you cannot manage without guidance or supervision on unfamiliar routes or you cannot manage anywhere, you should qualify. For example, someone with learning disabilities may qualify even if s/he has learned the route to and from home and college if s/he still needs guidance in other places.

### Higher rate

This is for people who cannot walk or have great difficulty walking because of a physical disability. You qualify if:

- you are unable to walk; *or*
- you have no legs or feet; *or*
- you are virtually unable to walk. This takes account of the distance you can walk before you experience severe discomfort. There is no set distance at which you pass or fail the test. Some people have passed who can walk 100 metres. Others have failed who can walk only 50 metres. The speed at which you walk and how you walk also count; *or*
- the exertion required to walk would be dangerous or could cause a serious deterioration in your health; *or*
- you are deaf and blind; *or*
- you have a severe visual impairment.

Someone who is severely mentally impaired may also qualify if s/he gets the highest rate care component and meets other conditions.

## Claiming for children

You can claim DLA for a disabled child. There is no lower age limit for the care component, but the cooked meal condition for the lowest rate does not apply to children under age 16. You can claim the higher rate mobility component for your child from age three and the lower rate mobility component from age five.

Because all children need care or supervision to some extent, there is an extra test. As well as passing the disability test, children under 16 must have needs substantially in excess of the normal requirements of other children their age to qualify for the care component. For the lower rate mobility component, children under 16 must need substantially more guidance or supervision than other children of their age.

## 3. Amount of benefit

*Weekly rate from April 2015*
**Care component**

| | |
|---|---|
| Lowest rate | £21.80 |
| Middle rate | £55.10 |
| Highest rate | £82.30 |

**Mobility component**

| | |
|---|---|
| Lower rate | £21.80 |
| Higher rate | £57.45 |

## 4. Claiming disability living allowance

You cannot make a new claim for disability living allowance (DLA) unless you are under 16; you must claim personal independence payment (PIP) instead (see p191).

If you still get DLA, you will be reassessed for PIP at some point. The reassessment process is expected to be completed by the end of 2017.

In Northern Ireland, you can claim DLA by requesting an application form from your local Jobcentre Plus office, or by phoning 0800 220 674 (or textphone 028 9031 1092).

DLA is usually paid directly into your bank account, and usually paid every four weeks in arrears.

## 5. **Challenging a decision**

If you think a decision about your disability living allowance is wrong, you can ask the DWP to look at it again. This process is known as a 'reconsideration' (the law refers to it as a 'revision'). Provided you ask within the time limit (usually one month), the DWP notifies you of the decision in a 'mandatory reconsideration notice'. If you are still not happy when you get this notice, you can appeal to the independent First-tier Tribunal. If it was not possible to ask the DWP to reconsider the decision within a month, you can ask for a late revision (within 13 months), explaining why it is late. You can also ask the DWP to look at a decision again at any time if certain grounds are met – eg, there has been an official error.

## 6. **Other benefits and tax credits**

If you are a full-time student and get disability living allowance (DLA), you are eligible for income-related employment and support allowance (ESA). You may also be eligible for housing benefit (HB). If you meet certain other conditions and are a full-time student getting DLA, you are eligible for universal credit (UC – see p199).

DLA is paid in addition to income support (IS), UC and HB and may qualify you for an additional premium in IS and HB.

If you claim other benefits or tax credits, make sure the office dealing with your claim knows you get DLA. Similarly, inform the local authority office dealing with your HB. Also notify the local authority or Tax Credit Office if your child gets DLA (or the DWP if you are getting UC).

If you, your partner or a child for whom you are responsible get DLA, you are exempt from the benefit cap (see p154 and p208).

## **Notes**

**2. Who is eligible**
1  CDLA/1983/2006; CDLA/3204/2006
2  *KM v SSWP (DLA)* [2013] UKUT 159
    (AAC), reported as [2014] AACR 2

# Chapter 10

# Employment and support allowance

### This chapter covers:

*Basic facts*

– Employment and support allowance is for people who are assessed as having limited capability for work because of their health or disability.
– There is an income-related and a contributory employment and support allowance.
– Part-time students who have limited capability for work and full-time students who get disability living allowance or personal independence payment are eligible for income-related employment and support allowance.
– Part-time and full-time students can claim contributory employment and support allowance if they have paid sufficient national insurance contributions.

## 1. What is employment and support allowance

Employment and support allowance (ESA) is for people who have limited capability for work because of illness or disability.[1] People already claiming incapacity benefit or income support on incapacity or disability grounds when ESA was introduced continue to receive these benefits, although they are being transferred to ESA.

There is a contributory and an income-related ESA. **Contributory ESA** is for people who have paid national insurance contributions. **Income-related ESA** is means tested and is for people who have limited capability for work and who are on a low income. It is possible to receive one or both types of ESA.

## 2. **Who is eligible**

To qualify for employment and support allowance (ESA), you must meet all the basic conditions.[2]

- You have limited capability for work (see p122).
- You are aged 16 or over and under pension age.
- You are in Great Britain (although some absences are allowed – see CPAG's *Welfare Benefits and Tax Credits Handbook* for more details).
- You satisfy the rules for contributory ESA (see below) or income-related ESA (see below).
- You are not working, although some 'permitted work' is allowed. See CPAG's *Welfare Benefits and Tax Credits Handbook* for more details.

### Contributory employment and support allowance

Contributory ESA is not means tested. To qualify, you must meet the basic conditions on p120 and have paid sufficient national insurance contributions.[3] See CPAG's *Welfare Benefits and Tax Credits Handbook* for details on this. There are no special rules for students.

### Income-related employment and support allowance

Income-related ESA is means tested. You are eligible if you are a part-time student and have limited capability for work. If you are a full-time student, you are usually only eligible if you get disability living allowance (DLA) or personal independence payment (PIP).

To qualify for income-related ESA while studying, you must satisfy the basic conditions on p120 and all the following conditions.[4]

- You are either a full-time student (see p121) who is entitled to DLA (either component, paid at any rate – see pp114–16) or PIP, or you are a part-time student.[5] However, if you are a full-time student who has been transferred to ESA from income support, which you were receiving because you were a disabled student, you do not have to get DLA or PIP to qualify for income-related ESA.[6]
- Your income is less than the set amount the law says you need to live on (known as your 'applicable amount') – see p125.
- You have no more than £16,000 capital.
- Your partner (if you have one) is not working 24 hours or more a week.
- You are in Great Britain, satisfy the 'habitual residence' and the 'right to reside' tests, and are not a 'person subject to immigration control'. These terms are

explained in CPAG's *Welfare Benefits and Tax Credits Handbook*. Further advice is available from UKCISA (see Appendix 2).

## Full-time student

You are a full-time student if you are:[7]
- under 20 and a 'qualifying young person' (see below); *or*
- 19 or over and a full-time student, unless you are aged 19 and count as being a qualifying young person (see below); *or*
- under 19 in full-time, advanced education (see p122).

### Under 20 and a qualifying young person

You are a 'qualifying young person' if you are 19 or under and attending a full-time course of non-advanced education which you were accepted on, enrolled on or started when you were under 19. If you are accepted on, enrol on or start the course on or after your 19th birthday, you are not a qualifying young person (see below). 'Non-advanced education' is anything below degree, Higher National Certificate or Higher National Diploma level and includes school-level courses. Your course is classed as 'full time' for income-related ESA if it is for more than 12 hours a week during term time. These 12 hours include classes and supervised study, but not meal breaks or unsupervised study either at home or at college. You may count as a qualifying young person in a gap between courses or for a period after you have finished a course (see p108).

### 19 or over and a full-time student

You count as a full-time student if you are undertaking a full-time course of study at an educational establishment. There are two definitions of 'full time' that apply: the first covers mostly courses of advanced education; the second covers most courses of non-advanced education.

- Your course is full time if it is classed as full time by the institution. If the institution describes the course as full time, you need convincing evidence to persuade the DWP otherwise, bearing in mind that what matters is the course itself rather than the hours you attend. This definition covers all courses of advanced education and any courses of non-advanced education not funded in whole or in part by the government at a further education (FE) college.
- Your course is full time if it involves more than 16 guided learning hours a week. What matters is the number of hours specified in a document signed by the college. This is often called a 'learning agreement', but your college may refer to it by some other name. This definition applies if you are at an FE college, not undertaking a higher education course, and your course is fully or partly funded by the government. In Northern Ireland, whether or not your course is full time depends on the institution's definition. When applying for ESA, a letter from the institution stating that your course is part time should be sufficient.

**Under 19 in full-time advanced education**

If you are under 19 and in full-time advanced education rather than in non-advanced education, the rules on when you count as full time are the same as for those aged 19 or over (see p121).

## 3. **Limited capability for work**

One of the basic rules of entitlement to employment and support allowance (ESA) is that you must be assessed as having 'limited capability for work'. This means that your mental or physical condition makes it unreasonable to require you to work. You are normally assessed at a medical, known as the 'work capability assessment'. This also assesses whether you have 'limited capability for work-related activity'. If you are assessed as having both limited capability for work and limited capability for work-related activity, your ESA includes an amount called a 'support component', which is paid to the most disabled people. If you are assessed as only having limited capability for work, your ESA includes a 'work-related activity component' and you are expected to attend work-focused interviews and may be required to undertake work-related activity. If you do not do so, your benefit may be reduced. If you are assessed as having neither, you are not entitled to ESA. However, you can appeal (see p128).

Full-time students who get disability living allowance (DLA) or personal independence payment (PIP) and who are claiming income-related ESA are treated as having limited capability for work and do not have to satisfy this part of the test.[8] However, this does not apply to all full-time students. You must still satisfy the test if:

- you are a qualifying young person under 20; *or*
- you are claiming contributory ESA.

All students, unless they get the support component, must take part in work-focused interviews and may have to undertake work-related activity as a condition of getting full benefit.[9]

If you are required to undertake full-time study as part of your work-related activity, you can continue to get ESA, whether or not you get DLA or PIP.[10]

Starting to study may prompt the DWP to call you for a reassessment, although this should not happen routinely. At the next assessment, your ability to perform the set activities is considered in the context of what you can do in a typical day, including your college or university routines. For example, you may be asked questions about your ability to get around campus, your ability to get to and from lectures, how long you can sit comfortably to study, or your ability to hold a pen to take notes or write essays.

The questions you are asked depend on which of the set activities (such as standing and sitting, manual dexterity and understanding communication) are relevant to your condition.

See CPAG's *Welfare Benefits and Tax Credits Handbook* for advice on medical examinations and what to do if you do not pass the assessment.

*Example*
Rachel is 29 and getting contributory ESA that includes a support component. She starts a full-time course of study in August 2015. She continues to be eligible for contributory ESA, but is called for a medical reassessment. Her condition is still the same, she passes the assessment and her contributory ESA continues.

## 4. Amount of benefit

Employment and support allowance (ESA) is payable after seven 'waiting days'. You are paid a limited amount of ESA during an initial 'assessment phase'. In most cases, this is expected to last 13 weeks. After this, you are then paid more in the 'main phase' that follows.

The exact amount of ESA you are paid depends on:
- whether you are claiming contributory ESA or income-related ESA;
- whether you are in the assessment or the main phase;
- which of the two possible additional components you get after the assessment phase. These are a support component of £36.20 a week and a work-related activity component of £29.05 a week.

ESA is worked out as follows.

In the assessment phase, you get a basic allowance of contributory ESA. The amount of income-related ESA you get depends on your needs (your applicable amount) and how much income you have.

In the main phase, either the work-related activity component or the support component is added. In income-related ESA, it is added to your applicable amount and, as in the assessment phase, your income is subtracted from your applicable amount. In contributory ESA, it is added to the basic allowance.

### Contributory employment and support allowance

*Weekly rate from April 2015* [11]

| | |
|---|---|
| Assessment phase, basic allowance (under 25) | £57.90 |
| Assessment phase, basic allowance (25 or over) | £73.10 |
| Main phase, basic allowance (16 or over) | £73.10 |

| Main phase, support component | £36.20 |
|---|---|
| Main phase, work-related activity component | £29.05 |

Contributory ESA is paid for up to a year if you get the work-related activity component, or indefinitely if you get the support component.

## Income-related employment and support allowance

The amount of income-related ESA you get depends on your circumstances and the circumstances of your partner.[12] The amount also depends on your income and capital. Go through the following steps to work out the amount of ESA to which you are entitled.

### Step one: capital

If your capital is over £16,000, you cannot get income-related ESA (see p120). Some kinds of capital are ignored. For details, see CPAG's *Welfare Benefits and Tax Credits Handbook*.

### Step two: work out your applicable amount

This is an amount for basic weekly needs. It is made up of:[13]

- personal allowances (see p125);
- premiums (see p126);
- work-related activity or support component (see p127);
- housing costs (see p127).

### Step three: work out your weekly income

Chapter 21 explains how your loan, grant or other income is taken into account for ESA and how to work out your weekly income.

### Step four: deduct weekly income from applicable amount

If your income is *less* than your applicable amount, your ESA equals the difference between the two.

If your income is *the same as or more than* your applicable amount, you cannot get ESA. You can claim again if your income decreases – eg, during the long vacation.

Income-related ESA tops up contributory ESA if you are entitled to both and the income-related amount is higher.

*Example*
Doreen is 19 and has cerebral palsy. She gets the standard rate daily living component of personal independence payment (PIP) and lives with her parents. In August 2015 she starts a full-time National Certificate course. She claims ESA. She is eligible for income-related ESA.

Assessment phase:

**Step one:**

Doreen has no savings or capital.

**Step two:**

Her applicable amount is:

Basic allowance for herself = £57.90

**Step three:**

Her weekly income is:

£0 (PIP is disregarded).

**Step four:**

She gets income-related ESA of £57.90.

Main phase:

Doreen is assessed as having limited capability for work and as being in the work-related activity group.

**Step two:**

Her applicable amount is:

Basic allowance for herself (£73.10) and work-related activity component (£29.05) = £102.15

**Step three:**

Her weekly income is:

£0 (PIP is disregarded).

**Step four:**

She gets income-related ESA of £102.15.

## Applicable amount

Your applicable amount is worked out by adding together your personal allowances, premiums, the component that applies to you in the main phase and any eligible housing costs. **Note:** benefit rates are usually uprated in April each year, although the government plans to freeze many amounts for the next four years.[14] It is usually possible to find out what the new rates will be from the beginning of December. Check the DWP website at www.gov.uk/dwp for a press release on social security uprating. The rates below are from April 2015.

### Personal allowance

Your personal allowance is paid at either the single, lone parent or couple rate depending on your situation. The amount depends on your age and whether you are in the assessment phase or the main phase (see p123).

| | Assessment phase £ | Main phase £ |
|---|---|---|
| **Single** | | |
| Under 25 | 57.90 | 73.10 |
| 25 or over | 73.10 | 73.10 |
| **Lone parent** | | |
| Under 18 | 57.90 | 73.10 |
| 18 or over | 73.10 | 73.10 |
| **Couple** | | |
| Both under 18 (higher rate) | 87.50 | 114.85 |
| Both under 18 (not eligible for higher rate) | 57.90 | 73.10 |
| One under 18, one 18 or over (higher rate) | 114.85 | 114.85 |
| One under 18, one 18–24 (not eligible for higher rate) | 57.90 | 73.10 |
| One under 18, one 25 or over (not eligible for higher rate) | 73.10 | 73.10 |
| Both 18 or over | 114.85 | 114.85 |

If you are both under 18, you get the higher rate if:
- one of you is responsible for a child; *or*
- you and your partner would both be eligible to claim income-related ESA if you were single; *or*
- your partner would qualify for income support (IS) if s/he were single; *or*
- your partner would qualify for income-based jobseeker's allowance (JSA) or severe hardship payments of JSA.

If one of you is under 18 and the other is 18 or over, you get the higher rate if the younger partner would:
- qualify for IS or income-related ESA if s/he were single; *or*
- qualify for income-based JSA or severe hardship payments of JSA.

**Premiums**
Qualifying for premiums depends on your circumstances. You can qualify for the following.
- **Pensioner premium.** You or your partner must have reached the qualifying age for pension credit (see p143). If you are single, you get £78.10; if you are a couple, you get £116.00. In the main phase, these amounts are reduced by the amount of the work-related activity component or support component for which you qualify.
- **Carer premium** of £34.60. The qualifying conditions are the same as for IS (see p168).
- **Enhanced disability premium**. You qualify for this if you or your partner get the highest rate of the disability living allowance (DLA) care component, the

enhanced rate of the daily living component of PIP or if you get the support component of ESA. You get £15.75 or £22.60 if you are a couple.

* **Severe disability premium.** This is for severely disabled people who live alone, or can be treated as living alone. You qualify if you get the middle or highest rate of the DLA care component or the daily living component of PIP paid at either rate, and no one gets carer's allowance for looking after you. You do not get the premium if you live with another person aged 18 or over (eg, a friend or parent), unless s/he is separately liable for rent, you only share a bathroom or hallway, or in some other circumstances. See CPAG's *Welfare Benefits and Tax Credits Handbook* for details. If you have a partner, you do not qualify unless s/he also qualifies in her/his own right or is certified as severely sight impaired or blind. If you both qualify, you get two premiums. The rate of the premium is £61.85.

### Components

In the main phase (see p123), you receive either the work-related activity or support components (see p123). The work-related activity component is £29.05. The support component is £36.20.

### Housing costs

If you own your own home, income-related ESA can help with the cost of mortgage interest payments once you have been getting it for 13 weeks. You must claim housing benefit for help with your rent (see Chapter 12). For an outline of the rules, see p169 and for full details, see CPAG's *Welfare Benefits and Tax Credits Handbook*.

---

## 5. Claiming employment and support allowance

You start your claim by phoning a Jobcentre Plus contact centre on 0800 055 6688 (textphone 0800 023 4888), or in Northern Ireland 0800 085 6318 (textphone 0800 328 3419). You can also claim on Form ESA1 which you can download from www.gov.uk/employment-support-allowance/how-to-claim.

Either member of a couple can make a claim for income-related employment and support allowance (ESA) for both, but whoever claims must be eligible in her/his own right. You claim contributory ESA for yourself only.

You are usually interviewed after you claim. You must provide medical certificates from your GP until you are assessed under the work capability assessment.

Claims for ESA can be backdated for up to three months.

# 6. **Challenging a decision**

If you think a decision about your employment and support allowance is wrong, you can ask the DWP to look at it again. This process is known as a 'reconsideration' (the law refers to it as a 'revision'). Provided you ask within the time limit (usually one month), the DWP notifies you of the decision in a 'mandatory reconsideration notice'. If you are still not happy when you get this notice, you can appeal to the independent First-tier Tribunal. If it was not possible to ask the DWP to reconsider the decision within a month, you can ask for a late revision (within 13 months), explaining why it is late. You can also ask the DWP to look at a decision again at any time if certain grounds are met – eg, there has been an official error.

# 7. **Other benefits and tax credits**

You cannot get employment and support allowance (ESA) if you are getting statutory sick pay (SSP) from an employer.[15] SSP runs out after 28 weeks, after which you can claim ESA.

You cannot get ESA if you are getting income support (IS) or jobseeker's allowance (JSA). You can claim contributory ESA if your partner is getting IS or JSA. You are excluded if you get joint-claim JSA.[16] You cannot get income-related ESA if your partner gets IS, income-based JSA, universal credit or pension credit.

Income-related ESA passports you to maximum housing benefit, free school lunches and social fund payments. It also passports you to free dental treatment, free prescriptions, free NHS sight tests and vouchers for glasses, and to Healthy Start vouchers and free vitamins if you are pregnant (see Chapter 11).

If you have a child(ren) and a partner and you get contributory ESA, you may be eligible for working tax credit if your partner works 16 hours or more a week, rather than the usual 24 hours.

ESA is taken into account when calculating whether the benefit cap applies, unless you or your partner get a support component in your ESA. If this is the case, you are exempt from the benefit cap (see p154 and p208).

## Incapacity benefit and severe disablement allowance

Incapacity benefit (IB) was abolished for most new claims from 27 October 2008. If you got IB before this date, you can continue to get it until you are transferred to ESA.

The long-term rate of IB is £105.35 from April 2015, with an additional age addition of £11.15 if you were under 35, or £6.20 if you were under 45, at the start of your incapacity.

Severe disablement allowance (SDA) was abolished for new claims from 6 April 2001. Provided you continued to meet the conditions for SDA after this date, you can continue to receive it until you are transferred to ESA.

The basic rate of SDA from April 2015 is £74.65, with an age addition if you first qualified when you were under 40 (£11.15), 40–49 (£6.20) or 50–59 (£6.20).

Studying part time or full time should have no effect on IB or SDA.

# Notes

### 1. What is employment and support allowance
1 Reg 1 ESA Regs

### 2. Who is eligible
2 s1 WRA 2007
3 s1 WRA 2007
4 Sch 1 para 6 WRA 2007
5 Reg 18 ESA Regs
6 Sch 1 para 2 The Employment and Support Allowance (Transitional Provisions, Housing Benefit and Council Tax Benefit) (Existing Awards) (No.2) Regulations 2010, No.1907
7 Regs 14-16 ESA Regs

### 3. Limited capability for work
8 Reg 33(2) ESA Regs
9 Regs 54 and 63(1) ESA Regs
10 Reg 14(2A) ESA Regs

### 4. Amount of benefit
11 s2 WRA 2007; reg 67(2) and (3) ESA Regs
12 s4 WRA 2007; reg 67(1) and (3) ESA Regs
13 Reg 67 and Sch 4 ESA Regs
14 clause 9 Welfare Reform and Work Bill 2015

### 7. Other benefits and tax credits
15 s20 WRA 2007
16 s1(3)(f) WRA 2007

# Chapter 11

. . . . . . . . . . . . . . . . . . . . . . . . . . . . . . . . . . . . . . . . . . . . . . . .

# Health benefits

**This chapter covers:**

. . . . . . . . . . . . . . . . . . . . . . . . . . . . . . . . . . . . . . . . . . . . . . . .

*Basic facts*

– People under 19 and in full-time education can get free prescriptions, sight tests, vouchers for glasses and dental treatment.

– Prescriptions are free in Wales. In addition, you can get a free dental examination if you are under 25, or are 60 or over. Prescriptions in Northern Ireland are also free.

– Other students can get help if they are on a low income or in certain other circumstances.

. . . . . . . . . . . . . . . . . . . . . . . . . . . . . . . . . . . . . . . . . . . . . . . .

## 1. What are health benefits

This chapter gives an outline of the rules on health benefits and focuses on issues relevant to students. For more detailed information, see CPAG's *Welfare Benefits and Tax Credits Handbook*.

Although most health treatment is free under the NHS for UK residents, there are fixed charges for some NHS services and treatments. These include:

- prescriptions;
- sight tests;
- glasses or contact lenses;
- dental treatment;
- wigs and fabric supports; *and*
- fares to hospital.

You are exempt from the charges in specified circumstances, or if your income is sufficiently low. As a student, you are not automatically exempt from paying these charges unless you fall into one of the categories listed on p131. Otherwise, you can apply for a 'remission certificate' under the low income scheme (see p134). If you get a remission certificate, part or all of the charges are waived, depending on how much income you have. For information about claims, see p137.

**Note:** you may also qualify for vouchers for Healthy Start food and for free vitamins. See p134 for further information.

## 2. **Who is eligible**

You are exempt from NHS charges if:[1]
- you or a member of your family receive income support (IS), income-based jobseeker's allowance (JSA), income-related employment and support allowance (ESA) or the guarantee credit of pension credit (PC);
- in England, you or a member of your family receive universal credit (UC) and either have no earnings or your earnings are no more than £435 a month (£935 if you have a child or a limited capability for work or limited capability for work-related activity element included in your UC);
- in Wales, you or a member of your family receive UC. This is an interim arrangement and these rules may change after March 2016. At time of writing, details of any changes were unavailable; or
- you or a member of your family receive:
    - child tax credit (CTC); or
    - CTC and working tax credit (WTC); or
    - WTC including a disabled worker or severe disability element and your gross annual income is £15,276 or less a year.

There are other categories of people who are exempt from NHS charges – eg, if you are a permanent resident in a care home, a hospital inpatient, an asylum seeker (see p138), aged 16 or 17 and being financially maintained by a local authority, a war disablement pensioner and you need the item or service because of your war disability, or if you are in prison or a young offenders' institution.

You may also be exempt from some charges because of your age or a specific health condition – see the individual types of charges on pp132–34.

If you are not exempt on any of the grounds listed above or below, you may be entitled to a full or partial remission of charges on grounds of low income (see p134).

### If you are exempt because you receive tax credits

If you are exempt from NHS charges because you receive tax credits, you should automatically be sent an NHS tax credits exemption certificate. This could be up to six weeks after you are awarded tax credits. If you have a tax credits award, but have not yet been sent your certificate, you can sign the relevant treatment forms to say you do not have to pay. You can use your award letter as evidence of this. If this is not accepted and you are charged, keep your receipts so you can claim a refund (see p138). Seek advice if there is a delay in getting your exemption certificate.

If you are getting CTC but are exempt from charges because you are getting IS, income-based JSA, income-related ESA or the guarantee credit of PC, you do not get an NHS tax credits exemption certificate. However, if you stop getting IS, income-based JSA, income-related ESA or the guarantee credit of PC because of, for example, your student income, you need a certificate. You should let HM Revenue and Customs know about your change in circumstances as soon as possible. It notifies the NHS Business Services Authority (BSA) in Newcastle upon Tyne, which issues you with a certificate.

## Free prescriptions

The cost of a prescription in England is £8.20 (April 2015). Prescriptions are free if you live in Wales or Northern Ireland.

In England, you qualify for free prescriptions if:[2]

- you are in one of the exempt groups listed on p131; *or*
- you are aged under 16, or under 19 and in full-time education (see below); *or*
- you are aged 60 or over; *or*
- you are pregnant or have given birth within the last 12 months; *or*
- you have one or more of the following specific medical conditions:
  - a continuing physical disability which prevents you from leaving home except with the help of another person;
  - epilepsy requiring continuous anticonvulsive therapy;
  - a permanent fistula, including caecostomy, ileostomy, laryngostomy or colostomy, needing continuous surgical dressing or an appliance;
  - one of the following conditions: diabetes mellitus (except where treatment is by diet alone), myxoedema, hypoparathyroidism, diabetes insipidus and other forms of hypopituitarism, forms of hypoadrenalism (including Addison's disease) for which specific substitution therapy is essential, or myasthenia gravis; *or*
- your income is low enough (see p134).

*Full-time education*

'**Full-time education**' is full-time instruction at a recognised educational establishment – eg, a school, college or university. If you are studying elsewhere, or you have finished your A levels and are waiting to start college or university, check whether you are exempt because you are on a low income.

## Prepayment certificates

Prepayment certificates are available in England and can save you money if you are likely to need a lot of prescriptions, but are not exempt from paying for them. You do not have to pay any further charges for prescriptions for the duration of the certificate, regardless of how many are required.[3]

A three-month certificate saves money if you need four or more items in the three-month period, while a 12-month certificate saves money if you require more than 12 prescriptions in a year. Apply by post on Form FP95, available from chemists, some doctors' surgeries and relevant health bodies. Applications can also be made by telephone on 0300 330 1341 or online at www.nhsbsa.nhs.uk and at registered pharmacies. The cost of 12-month certificates can be split over 10 direct debit instalments.

## Free sight tests

You qualify for a free NHS sight test if:[4]
- you are in one of the exempt groups listed on p131; *or*
- you are under 16, or under 19 and in full-time education (see p132); *or*
- you are aged 60 or over; *or*
- you are registered as blind or partially sighted; *or*
- you have been prescribed complex or powerful lenses; *or*
- you have diabetes or glaucoma or are at risk of getting glaucoma; *or*
- you are 40 or over and are the parent, sibling or child of someone who has glaucoma; *or*
- you are a patient of the Hospital Eye Service; *or*
- in England, if you are on leave from prison or a young offenders' institution; *or*
- your income is low enough (see p134).

**Note:** you may also qualify for a voucher towards the cost of buying or repairing glasses or contact lenses.[5]

## Free dental treatment and dentures

If you live in Wales and are under 25 or are 60 or over, you qualify for free dental examinations.[6] Otherwise, you qualify for free dental treatment (including check-ups) and appliances (including dentures) if:[7]
- you are in one of the exempt groups listed on p131; *or*
- you are aged under 18, or are under 19 and in full-time education (see p132); *or*
- you are pregnant or have given birth within the last 12 months; *or*
- you are a patient of the Community Dental Service; *or*
- your income is low enough (see p134).

## Free wigs and fabric supports

In Wales, wigs and fabric supports are free. In England and Northern Ireland, you qualify for free wigs and fabric supports if:[8]
- you are in one of the exempt groups listed on p131; *or*
- you are under 16, or under 19 and in full-time education (see p132); *or*
- you are a hospital inpatient when the wig or fabric support is provided; *or*
- your income is low enough (see below).

## Fares to hospital

You qualify for help with the costs of travel to hospital or any other establishment for NHS treatment or services if:[9]
- you are in one of the exempt groups listed on p131; *or*
- you live on the Isles of Scilly; *or*
- your income is low enough (see below).

**Note:** in some cases, you can get help with the costs of travel to obtain NHS treatment abroad.

## Healthy Start food and vitamins

You can get free Healthy Start food vouchers and vitamins if:[10]
- you are aged 18 or over and pregnant and you or your partner get IS, income-based JSA or income-related ESA, or get CTC (but not WTC, except during the four-week run-on) and have an income for tax credit purposes of £16,190 or less; *or*
- you are aged under 18 and pregnant, whether or not you get any of the above benefits; *or*
- you have a child under four and get IS or income-based JSA, or get CTC (but not WTC, except during the four-week run-on) and have an income for tax credit purposes of £16,190 or less; *or*
- you are 18 or over and pregnant or have a child under four, and get UC. **Note:** the rules are not yet finalised, but it is likely that if you get UC and your income is under a certain level, you will qualify. In the meantime, the DWP says that it will make discretionary payments for Healthy Start vouchers and vitamins for people on UC, if applicable.

## The low income scheme

You may be entitled for help with NHS charges if you have a low income. The NHS BSA has a means test to determine whether you qualify for either full or partial remission. The means test is roughly based on the applicable amounts for IS (see Chapter 13), but there are some differences.

See p137 for how to apply.

## Calculating your entitlement

To qualify for help, you must have less than £16,000 capital (£23,250 if you are in a care home in England or, £24,000 in Wales).[11]

If your weekly income (see below) does not exceed your requirements (see below) by more than 50 per cent of the cost of a prescription (currently 50 per cent of £8.20, so £4.10), you receive a full remission certificate (an HC2 in England and Northern Ireland; HC2W in Wales).[12] If your income exceeds your requirements by more than this amount, you receive a partial remission certificate (an HC3 in England and Northern Ireland; HC3W in Wales). Depending on the level of excess, you may get:[13]

- a remission of dental charges and charges for wigs and fabric supports which are higher than three times your excess income;
- a voucher for glasses or lenses, reduced by an amount equal to twice your excess income;
- a reduction in the cost of a sight test to the amount of your excess income, if lower, plus the amount by which the cost exceeds the NHS sight test fee;
- a reduction by the amount of your excess income in the amount you can get for hospital fares.

If you qualify for a remission certificate, it is normally valid for 12 months. If you are a full-time student, your certificate is normally valid until the end of your course or the start of the next academic year. You should make a repeat claim shortly before the expiry date. Remember that if you qualify for IS or income-based JSA over the summer vacation, you are automatically exempt from NHS charges during that period.

### Calculating your income

Income is calculated in the same way as for IS, with some modifications.[14] Your and your partner's income is taken into account. Your parents' income is not taken into account. However, any money given to you by your parents may be taken into account when assessing your eligibility. See Chapter 24 for how your income is calculated and how student income is treated.

### Calculating your requirements

Your requirements are based on those used for calculating the applicable amount for IS.[15] This is an amount for your basic weekly needs. See Chapter 13 for more details.

Your requirements are made up of:

- **personal allowance**
  - single person aged under 25, £57.90;
  - single person under 25 entitled to an ESA component, or incapable of work for 28 weeks since 27 October 2008, £73.10;
  - single person aged 25–59, £73.10;

- single person aged 60 or over, £151.20;
- lone parent aged under 60, £73.10;
- lone parent aged 60 or over, £151.20;
- couple aged under 60, £114.85;
- couple aged 60 or over, £230.85;
- **premiums**
  - carer premium (as for IS);
  - disability premium (as for IS, except that you can include a disability premium after 28 weeks of incapacity for work, rather than 52 weeks). You can also get a disability premium if you or your partner are under 60 and get ESA with a work-related activity or support component, or have been getting ESA for at least 28 weeks, or have been incapable of work for at least 28 weeks and have had the incapacity since 27 October 2008. The amount of the disability premium increases to £36.20 if you are single or a lone parent and *either* get ESA with the support component *or* get disability living allowance middle or highest rate care component or personal independence payment and have been getting ESA or have been incapable of work, for 28 weeks since 27 October 2008 and your incapacity did not start before that date;
  - enhanced disability premium for an adult (as for IS);
  - severe disability premium (as for IS);
- **weekly rent** less any housing benefit (HB) and non-dependant deductions. **Note:** at the time of writing, it was not yet clear how UC will be treated if it covers an amount for rent;
- **weekly council tax;**
- **mortgage interest**, endowment payments and capital repayments on your home, as well as on loans to adapt a home for a disabled person, deducting any non-dependant deductions.

If your income is £4.10 or less (half the cost of a prescription in England) higher than your needs, you are entitled to health benefits. If your income is more than £4.10 higher than your needs, you do not get free prescriptions, but you might get partial help with other charges.

*Examples*
Oliver is 21, and a third-year full-time undergraduate in Wales. His income is assessed to be £110.06 a week.
His requirements are calculated as his personal allowance (£57.90) plus his weekly rent (£110). This gives a total of £167.90. This is more than his income, so he receives full help with health costs. As a Welsh-domiciled student, however, Oliver already qualifies for free prescriptions and, as he is under 25, free dental examinations.

Louisa is 24, and a second-year full-time undergraduate in London. Her income is assessed to be £187.20 a week.

Her requirements are calculated as her personal allowance (£57.90) plus her weekly rent (£150). This gives a total of £207.90. This is more than her income, so she receives full help with health costs.

---

# 3. **Claiming health benefits and refunds**

How and where you claim help with NHS charges depends on your circumstances.

## Under 19 and in full-time education

- To claim an exemption from NHS prescription charges, you must sign the declaration form on the back of the prescription.
- To claim a free sight test, you must sign the optician's form before your test.
- To claim free dental treatment, you must tell the receptionist before your treatment that you think you are exempt from charges and complete a form at this point. Remember, in Wales, if you are under 25 you qualify for free dental examinations.

## Pregnant women and women who have recently given birth

- To claim free dental treatment and prescriptions, you must apply for a maternity exemption certificate on Form MATB1, available from your midwife, health visitor or doctor.
- You must claim Healthy Start food and vitamins in writing. Complete Form HS01 in the Healthy Start application leaflet, available from maternity clinics and some doctors' surgeries or from 0345 607 6823. A downloadable claim form is also available at www.healthystart.nhs.uk. Your claim form must be countersigned by a health professional (eg, a midwife or health visitor), certifying that you have been given appropriate advice about healthy eating and breastfeeding.

## Prescribed medical condition

To claim free prescriptions because you have a prescribed medical condition, you must apply for an exemption certificate on a form available from your doctor, hospital or pharmacist.

## The low income scheme

Applications for help under the low income scheme should be made to the NHS Business Services Authority on Form HC1 (HC1W in Wales), available from

Jobcentre Plus offices, NHS hospitals, some doctors' surgeries, some chemists, many students' union advice centres or at www.nhsbsa.nhs.uk.

## Refunds

If you pay for an item or service that you could have got free of charge or at a reduced cost, you can apply for a refund. You must apply within three months of payment, although the time limit can be extended if you can show a good cause for applying late – eg, you were ill.[16]

For a refund of prescription charges, use Form FP57, which you must get when you pay for the prescription at the pharmacy or dispensing chemist.

For other items and services, use Form HC5 (HC5W in Wales), available from post offices, Jobcentre Plus offices, NHS hospitals and some doctors' surgeries.

If you wish to have your costs refunded on the basis of low income, but do not already have an HC2 or an HC3 remission certificate (see p135), send a completed Form HC1 with Form HC5.

## 4. **Challenging a decision**

If you think a decision about your health benefits is wrong, you can ask for a review. Write to the Service Improvement Team, NHS Help with Health Costs, Bridge House, 152 Pilgrim Street, Newcastle upon Tyne NE1 6SN. You can also request a review at www.nhsbsa.nhs.uk.

If you think a decision is wrong because it was based on your circumstances at the time you applied for a remission certificate and these have now changed, consider making a fresh claim, or reporting the change, if you think you would now be entitled to more help with NHS charges.

If there are delays in obtaining a certificate, you can complain to the customer services manager. If necessary, you could pay for the treatment or items you need, then apply for a refund (see above).

## 5. **Overseas students**

Many overseas students can get certain type of treatment free from the NHS. However, the UK government has implemented a series of charges for non-European Economic Area (EEA) students since April 2015 (see p139).

### Asylum seekers

If you are an asylum seeker or a dependant of an asylum seeker and receiving support from either the Home Office or a local authority, you are exempt from

NHS charges. If you are getting asylum support, you should be sent an HC2 certificate with your first support payment. If you are not supported by the Home Office or a local authority, apply using Form HC1.

## European Economic Area students and Swiss nationals

If you are a student from any part of the EEA or Switzerland, you can get NHS treatment during a temporary stay in the UK on the same basis as UK residents, provided you have a European health insurance card (EHIC). You can also get help with NHS charges on the same basis as UK residents. Following the introduction of charges for non-EEA international students, if you are an EEA or Swiss student, it is essential to have an EHIC to avoid charges.

## Other overseas students

Since April 2015, non-EEA international students are subject to charges for some types of treatment, and may have to make a payment towards health costs as part of any visa application. Whether you are required to make this payment, or whether a specific treatment is free or a charge applies, depends on several factors. These include your specific immigration status, your length of stay in the UK, your country of origin and the type of treatment. It can also depend on whether you are living in England, Wales or Northern Ireland. Detailed information is available at www.ukcisa.org.uk.

All overseas students can get emergency treatment, treatment for certain communicable diseases and compulsory psychiatric treatment free of charge through the NHS. Nevertheless, you are strongly advised to take out adequate medical insurance for the duration of your stay in the UK.

# Notes

**2. Who is eligible**
1  Regs 3-5 NHS(TERC) Regs; regs 3-5 NHS(TERC)(W) Regs
2  Regs 3-6 NHS(CDA) Regs; regs 4 and 5 NHS(TERC) Regs; NHS(CDA) Regs; NHS(FP&CDA)(W) Regs
3  Reg 9 NHS(CDA) Regs
4  Reg 13 NHS(GOS) Regs; reg 3 NHS(OCP) Regs
5  Regs 9 and 15 NHS(OCP) Regs
6  Reg 3 NHS(DC)(W) Regs
7  Regs 4 and 5 NHS(TERC) Regs; regs 4 and 5 NHS(TERC)(W) Regs; Sch 2 and 3 NHS(DC) Regs; reg 9 and Sch 5 NHS(DC)(W) Regs
8  Regs 4 and 5 NHS(TERC) Regs; NHS(CDA) Regs; NHS(FP&CDA)(W) Regs
9  Regs 3, 5 and 9 NHS(TERC) Regs; regs 3 and 5 NHS(TERC)(W) Regs

10  Reg 3 HSS&WF(A) Regs
11  Sch 1 NHS(TERC) Regs; Sch 1
     NHS(TERC)(W) Regs
12  Reg 5 NHS(TERC) Regs; reg 5
     NHS(TERC)(W) Regs
13  Reg 6 NHS(TERC) Regs; reg 6
     NHS(TERC)(W) Regs
14  Reg 16 and Sch 1 NHS(TERC) Regs; reg
     15 and Sch 1 NHS(TERC)(W) Regs
15  Reg 17 and Sch 1 NHS(TERC) Regs; reg
     16 and Sch 1 NHS(TERC)(W) Regs

3. **Claiming health benefits and refunds**
16  Reg 11 NHS(TERC) Regs; reg 10
     NHS(TERC)(W) Regs; reg 10 NHS(CDA)
     Regs; Sch 1 para 1 NHS(FP&CDA)(W)
     Regs; regs 6 and 20 NHS(OCP) Regs; reg
     10 NHS(DC) Regs; reg 10 NHS(DC)(W)
     Regs

# Chapter 12

# Housing benefit

**This chapter covers:**

*Basic facts*

– Housing benefit helps with your rent. In Northern Ireland, it also helps with your rates.
– It is administered by local authorities.
– Full-time students are eligible if they are on a non-advanced course and are under 21 (or are 21 and turned 21 on their course).
– Other full-time students can claim if they get income support, income-based jobseeker's allowance or income-related employment and support allowance, or if they are a lone parent, disabled or over the qualifying age for pension credit.
– Couples with a child can claim throughout the year, whether one or both are students.
– There are limits to the rent covered by housing benefit.
– Housing benefit is means tested and the amount you get depends on your grant, loan and other income.

# 1. **What is housing benefit**

Housing benefit (HB) helps with your rent. In Northern Ireland, it also helps with your rates. Most full-time students cannot claim, but part-time students can. You can get help with rent in private accommodation, but not if you live with your parents. There are limits to the level of rent that HB covers. HB is means tested, so your grant, loan and other income affect the amount you get.

**Note:** some people in some areas cannot make a new claim for HB and must claim universal credit (UC) instead (see Chapter 18). The government expects that UC will be available across England and Wales by early 2017, but you should check for updates. In Northern Ireland, the introduction of UC is still under debate and, at the time of writing, the Bill to introduce it had not been passed. In the meantime, new claims for HB continue.

## 2. **Who is eligible**

To qualify for housing benefit (HB), you must be a student who is eligible to claim (see below), your accommodation must be eligible for HB (see p146) and you must satisfy the basic HB rules (see p144).

### Full-time students

If you are a full-time student 'attending or undertaking a full-time course of study', you cannot normally claim HB.[1] However, there are exceptions that allow some students to claim.

You start being a student from the first day you attend or undertake the course. You stop being a student after the last day of the final academic term in which you are enrolled, or from the day you finally abandon your course or are dismissed from it.[2]

#### Who counts as a full-time student

In most cases, you are treated as a full-time student if your college or university says your course is full time.

If you are at a further education (FE) college, not on a higher education course, and your course is government funded, a learning agreement from the college shows how many hours are involved in the course and a 16-hour rule determines whether it is full or part time.[3] The rules on whether or not you count as a full-time student are the same as for income support (IS), except that there is no 12-hour rule if you are claiming HB and are aged under 20 and in relevant education. In this case, the 16-hour rule applies (see p160).

Guidance states that postgraduates stop being treated as full-time students for HB purposes when their course ends. If you go on to do further research or write up a thesis, whether or not you are regarded as full time depends on how much work you are doing at the time, not on whether the course is full time.[4]

#### Who can claim housing benefit

You can claim HB as a full-time student if you are in one of the following groups.[5]

- You are under 21 on a full-time course of non-advanced education (see p157) (benefit can continue if you turn 21 on your course, but stops once you turn 22), or you are a child or qualifying young person for child benefit purposes (see Chapter 8), even if no one gets child benefit for you.[6] If HB stops because you are no longer in this group, check below to see whether you are in one of the other groups of people who can claim HB. If not, ask your college if there is discretionary financial assistance available. **Note:** if you are a care leaver and are aged 16 or 17, you cannot get HB, even if you come into one of the groups below, because the local authority should be supporting you.

- You are on IS, income-based jobseeker's allowance (JSA) or income-related employment and support allowance (ESA).
- You are a lone parent of a child under 16, or under 20 if s/he is still a qualifying young person (see p108). Lone parents can only usually get IS until their youngest child's fifth birthday (see p161). If your IS stops, make sure you tell the local authority that pays your HB.
- You or your partner have reached the qualifying age for pension credit (PC). Entitlement to PC for both men and women is linked to the minimum age at which a woman can receive state retirement pension. Starting in April 2010, this began to rise gradually from age 60 and is planned to reach 65 in November 2018. For more details, see *CPAG's Welfare Benefits and Tax Credits Handbook*.
- You qualify for a disability premium or severe disability premium with your HB – eg, you get disability living allowance (DLA), personal independence payment or long-term incapacity benefit (IB), or are certified as severely sight impaired or blind. See p168 for details. **Note:** you cannot qualify for a disability premium if you have limited capability for work.[7]
- You have been incapable of work for the last 28 weeks. Since 27 October 2008, new claimants are assessed under the limited capability for work test (see below). However, the previous incapacity for work test may still apply to you if you are already getting IB, or IS on the basis of disability.
- You have had limited capability for work for the last 28 weeks. You should claim ESA to have your limited capability for work acknowledged (although you do not have to get any ESA to qualify). You can add together weeks of limited capability for work on either side of a gap of up to 12 weeks.
- You get a disabled students' allowance because of deafness. You are eligible for HB from the date you apply for the allowance.[8] However, if you are still waiting to hear about the allowance, the local authority may put off making a decision on your HB claim, but should then fully backdate your benefit.[9]
- You are in a couple, your partner is also a full-time student and you have a dependent child under 16, or under 20 if s/he is a qualifying young person (see p108). Unlike IS and JSA, which you can only claim in the summer vacation, you can claim HB throughout the academic year. If you are claiming IS or income-based JSA, remember that if these benefits stop at the end of the summer vacation, you must tell the local authority so it can reassess your HB. If your partner is not a student, s/he can claim HB for both of you, whether or not you have a child.

• You are single and caring for a child placed with you by the social services department.

### Studying part time

You can claim HB throughout your studies. You must pass all the basic rules below, including being liable for rent and being in eligible accommodation. You are a part-time student if you do not count as a full-time student under the definition on p157. The rules on who counts as full time are the same as those for IS, with one exception. If you are under 20 and in 'relevant education', there is no 12-hour rule. The 16-hour rule applies to you if you are on a non-advanced course, whatever your age.

## 3. **Basic rules**

As well as being a student who is eligible to claim housing benefit (HB – see p142), you must also meet all the following conditions to qualify.
• You are liable to pay rent (see below).
• You pay rent for the home in which you normally live (see p145).
• Your accommodation is eligible for HB (see p146).
• You satisfy the 'habitual residence' and 'right to reside' tests, and are not a 'person subject to immigration control'. These terms are explained in CPAG's *Welfare Benefits and Tax Credits Handbook*. Overseas students can get further advice from UKCISA (see Appendix 2).
• You have no more than £16,000 capital. There is no capital limit if you are getting pension credit (PC) guarantee credit.
• Your income is sufficiently low (see Chapter 21).

What follows is a brief outline of the basic HB rules, including those that refer specifically to students. For more details, see CPAG's *Welfare Benefits and Tax Credits Handbook*.

### Liable for rent

You must be liable for rent. If you are jointly liable for the rent with others (eg, you have each signed the tenancy agreement), the amount of HB you get is based on your share of the rent (although, less commonly, it may not be an equal share if that seems reasonable to the local authority).

If you are part of a couple, it does not matter whose name is on the rent agreement; either of you can claim. So if you are a student who is eligible for HB, you can claim for both of you, or if you are not eligible for HB, your non-student partner can claim for both of you.

There are some circumstances in which a local authority has the discretion to treat you as liable for the rent even when you are not legally liable – eg, if you have taken over paying the rent from someone else.

## Your normal home

Usually, you can only get HB for one home, and that is the place where you normally live. If you are away from your normal home, in some cases your HB may stop. In other cases, you can get HB for two homes at the same time.

### You are away from your term-time home

In the summer vacation, you cannot get HB for any weeks you are away from your term-time home, unless you would live there even if you were not studying. To continue to get HB for weeks of absence, you need to argue that your main purpose for living there is not simply to make it easier to attend the course – eg, you were settled there before the course or you are independent of, or estranged from, your parents.[10] However, if your grant or loan covers the summer vacation, your HB does not stop during any weeks of absence.[11] HB does not stop if you have to go into hospital.

If you leave your home during the academic year (or at any time if you live there not just to facilitate attending your course), your HB does not stop, provided you intend to return, you do not sublet, and you are not likely to be away for more than 52 weeks.[12] You cannot use this provision if you can get HB under the 'two homes rule' described below. The two homes rule is, however, more generous because it does not have a time limit.

*Examples*
John flatshares in Sheffield while attending university. He gets HB as a disabled student. During the summer vacation, he goes home to his parents in Leicester for seven weeks. His HB stops for these seven weeks. He should give the local authority the dates he intends to be away.

Donna has always lived in Cardiff and is attending her local college. She is a lone parent and gets HB. She regularly visits her family in Aberystwyth during vacations. Her HB continues during her absence.

### You have two homes

If you live in one home so that you can attend your course and in another home at other times, but you are only liable for rent on one, you can get HB for that place even while you are not there. This rule applies to lone parents and single students eligible for HB. It does not help you if you pay rent at one place and a mortgage on the other.[13]

*Example*
Emily's normal home is in Bristol where she lives with her 18-year-old daughter who is at college. She has to pay rent for her Bristol home. Emily is studying at Leeds University and lives with a cousin rent free while in Leeds. Emily is eligible to claim HB for her Bristol home throughout the year. Whether any HB is payable, and at what times, depends on the amount of her grant and loan.

A couple (one of whom is a student eligible for HB) who have to live in two separate homes can get HB on both if the local authority decides that this is reasonable.[14]

## Eligible accommodation

You can get HB to help pay the rent – eg, to a private landlord, local authority, housing association or co-operative. It is not essential for you to have a written tenancy agreement; it could be verbal. In some circumstances you cannot get HB – eg, if:[15]

- you live with and pay rent to your parents, a sister or brother, or a son or daughter (including in-laws, partners and step-relatives);
- you pay rent to someone (who might be a relative or friend), but your tenancy is not on a commercial basis. This rule often prevents people getting HB if they live in a property owned by their parents. It is possible, however, to get HB in these circumstances if the tenancy is a commercial one. If this applies to you, seek advice;
- your tenancy was contrived in order to try to get HB;
- you pay rent to an ex-partner with whom you used to share the home in which you now live.

## Halls of residence

You can get HB for rent in a student hall of residence.[16] You must be a full-time student who is eligible to claim HB (see p142). You cannot get HB in a hall if you are claiming while waiting to return to your course after taking time out because of disability, illness or caring responsibilities.

Part-time students can also get HB in a hall of residence if, had they been full time, they would have been eligible to claim HB as:

- an under-22-year-old in non-advanced education;
- a lone parent;
- a disabled student;
- someone with a child and a full-time student partner; *or*
- someone who has reached the qualifying age for PC (see p142).

If you get income support (IS), income-based jobseeker's allowance (JSA) or income-related employment and support allowance (ESA) as a part-time student, you can only get HB in a hall of residence if you are also one of the above. Although you can claim HB, it might not cover the whole cost (see below).

Full-time students waiting to return to their course after a period of illness or caring, and part-time students on IS, income-based JSA or income-related ESA, and not in another category cannot get HB in a hall of residence during term time or short vacations unless the educational establishment does not own the hall, does not have a long-term lease on the building or does not rent it from the education authority.[17] For example, if the university leases flats on a short-term lease from a private landlord and rents these to students, you can get HB. During the summer vacation, you can get HB if you remain in the hall, unless your student support covers the summer vacation.

# 4. **Amount of benefit**

The amount of housing benefit (HB) you get depends on the maximum rent the local authority is prepared to pay, and on your income compared with the amount the law says you need to live on. The amount you get may be reduced if your total income from benefits and tax credits is above a certain level (see p154). To work out your HB, go through the following steps.

### Step one: capital
If your capital is over £16,000, you cannot get HB unless you are over 60 and get pension credit (PC) guarantee credit (see p241). Some kinds of capital are ignored. For details, see CPAG's *Welfare Benefits and Tax Credits Handbook*.

### Step two: maximum rent
This is the maximum rent the local authority is prepared to pay. This might be less than the actual amount of rent you pay – eg, if you pay service charges that are not covered by HB, or if your rent for HB purposes is reduced because you have a spare bedroom (see p148).

HB does not cover some items included in rent, such as charges for:
* water or sewerage;
* fuel. Either the actual charge specified in the rental agreement or a fixed rate is deducted;
* meals. If these are included in your rent, the local authority may deduct a fixed rate;
* services. Some are included (eg, cleaning communal areas, provision of a laundry room and TV signal relay, including free-to-view TV but not an individual satellite dish or set-top box) and others are not – eg, sports facilities and TV rental.

See CPAG's *Welfare Benefits and Tax Credits Handbook* for details of the deductions.

If you rent from a private landlord (including a hall of residence) and you claimed HB or moved home on or after 7 April 2008, the 'local housing allowance' rules apply. If this is the case, HB is based on the standard local housing allowance for the size of property that applies to you, even if your rent is higher than this amount. If your rent is lower, HB is based on the amount of your actual rent. Each local authority has its own rates for properties of different sizes. Check your local authority's rates at http://lha-direct.voa.gov.uk/search.aspx.

Generally, unless you are a single person aged under 35, you are allowed one bedroom for:

- an adult couple;
- another single adult aged 16 or over;
- two children under 16 of the same sex;
- two children under 10;
- any other child.

You are allowed a maximum of four bedrooms. If you are a single person under 35, you usually only get the lower, shared-accommodation rate. If you are disabled and need overnight care, you may qualify for an additional bedroom for a carer.

See CPAG's *Welfare Benefits and Tax Credits Handbook* for details. If the local housing allowance rules do not apply, your case is usually referred to a rent officer to decide how much help with rent you should get, based on other local rents. For details of these 'local reference rent' rules, see CPAG's *Welfare Benefits and Tax Credits Handbook*.

If you rent from a local authority or housing association, your maximum rent is usually the same as the weekly rent due, less any of the above ineligible charges. However, your HB is reduced if you are considered to have a spare bedroom (known as the 'bedroom tax'). The rules about how many bedrooms you can have is similar to the local housing allowance rules, but see CPAG's *Welfare Benefits and Tax Credits Handbook* for more information. If you are considered to have one spare bedroom, your maximum rent is reduced by 14 per cent, and by 25 per cent if you have two spare bedrooms. If your HB is reduced in this way, you should apply for a discretionary housing payment from the local authority (see below).

### Discretionary housing payments

If your HB does not cover your rent, you may be able to get a discretionary housing payment from your local authority. These can be paid if you get HB and need additional help with your housing costs – eg, to make up the shortfall in rent due to HB being reduced because you have a spare bedroom. They are usually awarded for a temporary period, beyond which you have to reapply.

## Step three: deductions for non-dependants

An amount is deducted from your maximum rent if you have a 'non-dependant' living with you.

A 'non-dependant' is someone, usually a friend or adult relative, who lives with you but not on a commercial basis. A deduction is made to reflect an assumed contribution from her/him to the household, whether or not s/he pays anything. There is no deduction for:[18]

- a full-time student during the academic year (whether or not s/he works);
- a full-time student during the summer vacation (but there is a deduction if s/he starts working 16 hours or more a week, unless her/his student support covers the summer vacation);
- a full-time student at any time if you or your partner are 65 or over;
- a joint occupier or joint tenant;
- a resident landlord;
- a sub-tenant;
- your partner or dependent child;
- anyone under 18;
- anyone under 25 if s/he gets income support (IS), income-based jobseeker's allowance (JSA), income-related employment and support allowance (ESA) without a work-related activity component or support component (this usually only applies in the first 13 weeks of an ESA claim) or universal credit (UC), provided s/he does not have any earned income for UC purposes;
- someone who gets a youth training allowance;
- someone who normally lives elsewhere;
- someone in hospital for more than 52 weeks or in prison;
- a live-in paid carer from a voluntary organisation;
- someone on PC.

No deductions are made for your non-dependants if you or your partner are registered blind, get disability living allowance care component, personal independence payment daily living component or attendance allowance.

For anyone else, fixed deductions are made based on the non-dependant's income. See CPAG's *Welfare Benefits and Tax Credits Handbook* for details and amounts. **Note:** if your non-dependant is working, you should provide the local authority with evidence of her/his gross income. If you do not, the local authority may make the highest deduction.

If you or your partner are 65 or over, the deduction is not made until 26 weeks after the non-dependant moves in with you or her/his income goes up, increasing the deduction.

## Step four: getting a means-tested benefit

If you get IS, income-based JSA, income-related ESA or PC, HB is the amount worked out at Step three – ie, your maximum rent less any amount for non-dependants. In this case, you do not need to continue with the rest of these steps.

## Step five: not getting a means-tested benefit

If you do not get IS, income-based JSA, income-related ESA or PC, you must compare your income with your weekly needs.

## Step six: work out your applicable amount

This is an amount for your basic weekly needs. It is made up of:

- personal allowances;
- premiums;
- a work-related activity or support component if you have limited capability for work.

The applicable amount includes amounts for yourself and for your partner, if you have one. It also includes amounts for any dependent children. The amounts for HB are the same as for IS (see p166), but with the following differences.

- **Personal allowance:**
  - the child allowance is included in HB;
  - single people under 25 and lone parents under 18 who are entitled to main phase ESA get £73.10;
  - young couples get £114.85, unless both are under 18 and the claimant is not entitled to main phase ESA (see p123), in which case they get £87.50;
  - single people have a personal allowance of £151.20 if they are under 65 but have reached the qualifying age for PC (see p142) or £166.05 if aged 65 or over;
  - couples get £230.85 if at least one is under 65 but has reached the qualifying age for PC (see p142), and £248.30 if one or both are 65 or over.
- **Premiums:**
  - family premium, disabled child premium and enhanced disability premium for a child are included in HB;
  - you do not get a disability premium if you have been assessed as having limited capability for work for ESA and you (ie, not your partner) are the HB claimant.
- **Components:**
  - instead of a disability premium, add a work-related activity component of £29.05 if you have claimed ESA and have limited capability for work, or a support component of £36.20 if you have limited capability for work-related activity (see p127).

## Step seven: work out your weekly income

Chapter 21 explains how your loan, grant or other income is taken into account and how to work out your weekly income.

## Step eight: calculate your housing benefit

If your income is *less than or the same as* your applicable amount, HB is the amount worked out at Step three – ie, your maximum rent less any amounts for non-dependants.

If your income is *more than* your applicable amount, work out 65 per cent of the difference. Your HB is the amount worked out at Step three (ie, your maximum rent less any amounts for non-dependants) minus 65 per cent of the difference between your income and applicable amount.

*Examples*

Maria is 18 and studying full time for a national diploma in animal husbandry. She shares a private rented flat with a friend. They each pay £70 a week rent. Maria has received payments from the 16–19 bursary fund totalling £500. The rent officer uses the local housing allowance amount for a single room rent in Maria's area (£60 a week) to calculate her entitlement.

|  | £ |
|---|---|
| Eligible rent | 60.00 |
| Applicable amount | 57.90 |
| Income | 0 |
| (16–19 bursary fund payment disregarded) | |
| **Weekly HB** | **60.00** |

Craig is a lone parent with two children aged three and six. He is a second-year student. He is also a joint tenant with his friend Karl, who is not a student. Craig's share of the rent is £95. His income is his student support (including a maintenance loan, a special support grant and a parents' learning allowance), child tax credit (CTC) and child benefit. He makes a claim for HB at the start of the academic year.

**Craig's HB entitlement from September 2015 is calculated as follows:**

|  | £ |
|---|---|
| Eligible rent | 95.00 |
| Applicable amount: | |
| Personal allowance | 73.10 |
| Allowances for two children | 133.80 |
| Family premium | 17.45 |
| **Total applicable amount** | **224.35** |
| Income: | |
| Student loan | 5,740 |

| | |
|---|---|
| *Less* travel | 303 |
| *Less* books £390 = | 5,047 |
| Divided by 42 weeks = | |
| (7 September 2015 to 26 June 2016) | 120.16 |
| *Less* £10 disregard = | 110.16 |
| (Special support grant disregarded in full) | |
| (Parents' learning allowance disregarded in full) | |
| CTC | 116.83 |
| **Total income** | **226.99** |

Craig's HB is worked out as follows:

| | |
|---|---|
| Income | 226.99 |

Craig's income (£226.99) is more than his applicable amount (£224.35) by £2.64. He must contribute 65 per cent of this (£1.71) to his rent, with the remainder **£93.29 met by HB.**

**Summer 2016**
Craig's student loan is only treated as income between 7 September 2015 and 26 June 2016. If Craig has no other income at this point, he is entitled to claim IS and will receive full help with his rent – ie, **£95 HB a week**. If he has income from, for example, a summer job, this may reduce his HB. **Note:** if Craig lives in an area in which UC has been introduced, at some point he may need to claim UC instead.

**Northern Ireland**
If Craig were living in Northern Ireland, his HB for rent would be calculated in exactly the same way. If, in addition to his rent, he were liable to pay rates of £15 a week, he would receive this in full as his income is below his applicable amount. If, however, he had, for example, £26 more weekly income than his applicable amount, his HB for rates would be calculated as follows:

| | £ |
|---|---|
| Income less applicable amount | 26.00 |
| 20% x £26 = | 5.20 |
| 12% x £26 = | 3.12 |

| | |
|---|---|
| HB for rates: | |
| Maximum rates (£15) – £5.20 = | 9.80 |
| Rate relief: | |
| Maximum rates (£15) – £9.80 = | 5.20 |
| Remaining rate liability (£5.20) – £3.12 = | 2.08 |

Craig would be entitled to **£78.10 HB** for rent (his rent less 65% excess income) and **£9.80** for rates, plus rate relief of **£2.08.**

# 5. Claiming housing benefit

You can get a claim form from your local authority housing benefit (HB) office. When you return it, ask for a receipt. If you return it by post, keep a copy, as claim forms are often lost. If you need to fill in another form, the local authority can backdate it if you can show the date of your original claim.

If you are also claiming income support (IS), income-based jobseeker's allowance (JSA), incapacity benefit, employment and support allowance (ESA) or pension credit (PC), you can claim HB at the same time. The DWP should either take your claim over the phone or give you a form, usually Form HCTB1.

## When your housing benefit starts

Your HB starts from when you make your claim. It can be backdated for up to six months if you ask for this and you have continuous 'good cause' for not claiming throughout the whole period. When deciding whether there is good cause to backdate a claim, a local authority must take into account how a reasonable person of your age, experience and state of health would have acted or failed to act in the same circumstances.[19] If you have reached the qualifying age for PC (see p142) and are not on IS, income-based JSA or income-related ESA, HB can be backdated for up to three months whatever the reason for the delay. **Note:** the government plans to reduce backdating to a maximum of four weeks from April 2016.[20]

HB is usually paid directly into your rent account if you are a council tenant; otherwise, it is either paid to you or directly to your landlord.

By law, local authorities are supposed to pay you within 14 days of receiving your completed claim form or as soon as possible after that. However, in many areas there are long delays. If you are a private tenant, ask for a **'payment on account'** until your claim can be properly assessed. Local authorities are legally obliged to give you an interim payment of a reasonable amount, unless it is obvious that you will not be entitled to HB or you have not supplied information that has been requested.

# 6. Challenging a decision

If you think a decision about your housing benefit is wrong (eg, because the decision maker got the facts or law wrong), there are a number of ways you can try to get the decision changed.

- You can ask for a revision or a supersession of the decision. In some cases, you must show specific grounds. In others, you must apply within a strict time limit, usually one month.

- You can appeal to the independent First-tier Tribunal. There are strict time limits for appealing – usually one month from the date you are sent the decision. You can make a late appeal in limited circumstances.

If you are considering challenging a decision, seek advice as soon as possible.

# 7. **Other benefits and tax credits**

Child tax credit (CTC) counts in full as income when housing benefit (HB) is worked out. It is the actual amount you are paid that counts. If your CTC award is reduced because an overpayment of tax credit is being recovered, it is the reduced amount that counts for HB. If you are underpaid CTC and get a lump-sum repayment, this is treated as capital for HB, so it only affects your HB if it takes your savings above the capital limit. The rules are the same for working tax credit (WTC).

Child benefit is disregarded as income for HB.

Bear in mind that you should tell the local authority about any changes in income when they occur, including benefit and tax credit changes. Do not assume that the DWP or HM Revenue and Customs passes on the information for you.

## The benefit cap

Your HB is reduced if your total income from benefits is over the maximum amount that you or your partner can receive. The amount is £500 a week if you are a lone parent or member of a couple, and £350 if you are a single person. **Note:** the government plans to reduce the caps to around £384 and £257 a week respectively.[21]

Most benefits count towards the cap, including income support, jobseeker's allowance, employment and support allowance (ESA), child benefit, CTC, carer's allowance and HB. The cap also applies to universal credit (see p208).

If you or your partner are working, or if you are disabled or a war widow/er, you are exempt from the cap. To count as working, you must get WTC. You are exempt from the cap because of disability if you or your partner get certain disability benefits, including disability living allowance (DLA), personal independence payment (PIP) and ESA with a support component. You are also exempt if a child or young person for whom you are responsible gets DLA or PIP.

There is protection for nine months before the cap applies if you are no longer working but were working at least 16 hours a week for the last year.

# Notes

### 2. **Who is eligible**
1 Regs 53(1), definition of 'full-time student', and 56(1) HB Regs
2 Reg 53(1), definition of 'last day of the course', and (2)(b) HB Regs
3 Reg 53(1), definition of 'full-time course of study', HB Regs
4 para 2.354 C2 GM
5 Reg 56(2) HB Regs
6 Reg 56(2)(h) HB Regs
7 Sch 3 paras 12 and 13(9) HB Regs
8 Reg 56(2)(i) HB Regs
9 para 2.30 C2 GM

### 3. **Basic rules**
10 Reg 55 HB Regs
11 Regs 53(1), definition of 'period of study', and 55 HB Regs
12 Reg 7(16)(c)(viii) HB Regs
13 Reg 7(3) HB Regs
14 Reg 7(6)(b) HB Regs
15 Reg 9 HB Regs
16 Reg 57(4) HB Regs
17 Reg 57(2) HB Regs

### 4. **Amount of benefit**
18 Regs 3 and 74 HB Regs

### 5. **Claiming housing benefit**
19 Reg 83(12) HB Regs; R(S) 2/63(T)
20 Summer Budget 2015, para 2.110

### 7. **Other benefits and tax credits**
21 clause 7 Welfare Reform and Work Bill 2015

# Chapter 13

# Income support

**This chapter covers:**
1. What is income support (below)
2. Who is eligible (p157)
3. Basic rules (p164)
4. Amount of benefit (p165)
5. Claiming income support (p170)
6. Challenging a decision (p171)
7. Other benefits and tax credits (p171)

*Basic facts*
- Income support provides basic financial support for people who are not expected to 'sign on' for work.
- It can include amounts for mortgage interest.
- Part-time students can claim if they are a lone parent with a child under five, a carer, pregnant (and sick or nearly due), and in some other circumstances.
- Full-time students aged under 19/20 (sometimes 22) on non-advanced courses can claim if they are a parent, an orphan, or estranged or separated from their parents, and in some other circumstances.
- Other full-time students can claim if they are a lone parent with a child under five, and in some other circumstances.
- The amount is usually affected by any grant, loan or other income you may have.

## 1. **What is income support**

Income support (IS) provides basic financial support for people under the qualifying age for pension credit (see p164) who are not expected to 'sign on' as available for work. Students who are lone parents with a child under five may be able to claim IS, as may some younger students on non-advanced courses who are estranged from their parents or are parents themselves. Most other full-time students are not eligible. See p157 for which students can claim IS.

The amount you get is based on your circumstances – eg, whether you have a partner or whether you (or your partner) have a disability or care for someone with a disability. IS can include help with mortgage payments. The amount you get is usually affected by any grant, loan or other income you have.

You do not get amounts for children in your IS. Instead, you claim child tax credit (CTC) and child benefit. Only people who have been getting IS since before April 2004 and have not claimed CTC continue to get amounts for children in their IS.

## 2. **Who is eligible**

To qualify for income support (IS), you must be in one of the groups eligible to claim and you must satisfy all the basic rules described on p164.

Only certain groups of students are eligible for IS, depending on your age and your course – ie, whether you are:
- under 20 and in 'relevant education' (see below); *or*
- 19 or over and a full-time student, unless you are aged 19 and count as being in relevant education (see p160); *or*
- under 19 in full-time advanced education (see p163); *or*
- studying part time (see p163).

### Under 20 in relevant education

Generally, you cannot claim IS if you are under 20 and in 'relevant education', but there are exceptions.[1]

### What is relevant education

You count as being in relevant education if you are a 'qualifying young person' for child benefit purposes (see p108) – ie, you are 19 or under and attending a full-time course of non-advanced education or an approved training course which you were accepted on, enrolled on or started when you were under 19.[2] If you are accepted on, enrol on or start a full-time course of non-advanced education on or after your 19th birthday, you are not in relevant education. The rules on p160 apply to you instead.

*Full-time non-advanced education*
Your course is classed as **'full time'** for IS purposes if it is for more than 12 hours a week during term time. These 12 hours include classes and supervised study, but not meal breaks or unsupervised study either at home or at college.[3]
**'Non-advanced education'** is anything below degree, Higher National Certificate (HNC) or Higher National Diploma (HND) level, and includes school-level courses.

| Non-advanced courses | Advanced courses |
|---|---|
| Standard grades | BTEC HNC or HND |
| National Vocational Qualification (NVQ) levels 1–3 | Diploma of higher education |
| GCSEs | Degree level |
| AS and A levels | Postgraduate degree |

You may still count as being in relevant education for a period after your course ends (see p159).

## Who can claim income support

If you are aged 16, 17, 18 (or, in some cases, 19 – see p157), and in relevant education, you are eligible for IS if you are in one of the following groups.[4]

- You are an orphan and no one is acting in place of your parent. You do not qualify if, for example, you are living with a foster parent or being looked after by the local authority.
- You must live away from your parents or anyone acting in their place because you are estranged from them. Decision makers should believe you if you say you are estranged unless there is valid evidence of doubt.[5] If they are in doubt, they may, with your permission, seek further evidence.[6] It is possible to be estranged from a parent even if you do not both feel the same way about it.[7]
- You must live away from your parents because there is a serious risk to your physical or mental health, or because you are in physical or moral danger. Decision makers are advised to accept your own evidence of physical or moral danger unless there is stronger evidence to the contrary.[8]
- You are living away from your parents and anyone acting in their place, they cannot support you financially, and:
  - they are chronically sick or physically or mentally disabled; *or*
  - they are in prison; *or*
  - they are not allowed to enter Britain.
- You are a parent and your child lives with you.
- You are a refugee learning English in certain circumstances (see p162).
- You have left local authority care and you have to live away from your parents or anyone acting in their place. However, if you are aged 16 or 17 and are a care leaver, you should normally get financial support from the local authority social services department, and you cannot get IS in relevant education unless you are a lone parent.[9]

### Examples
Pete is 17 and studying cookery full time leading to an NVQ level 2. His father is in prison and his mother is chronically ill. Neither of them can support him financially and he does not live with them. He is eligible for IS.

Ginny is 18 and studying information technology for a BTEC. She is the mother of a two-year-old child and they both live with Ginny's parents. She is eligible for IS.

Ahmed is 18 and studying full time for his A levels. He is a refugee whose parents live in Somalia. It would be dangerous for him to return home. Ahmed is eligible for IS.

Kelly is 16 and studying full time for A levels. She has lived on her own since her father told her to leave home. She is estranged from both her parents. She is eligible for IS.

Laurie is 17 and has left local authority care. She is undertaking a full-time NVQ in beauty therapy. She is a lone parent and is therefore not excluded from IS as a 16/17-year-old care leaver.

Once you reach your 20th birthday, you are no longer classed as being in 'relevant education' and cannot get IS under these rules. You may be able to continue to get IS as a full-time or part-time student, but only if you are in one of those groups who can claim (see p161 and p163).

In particular, your claim for IS may be able to continue if you are under 22 on a non-advanced course and without parental support – ie, you are in one of the first four groups in the list above.

Alternatively, you may be able to 'sign on' for jobseeker's allowance (JSA) as a part-time student (see p177). Otherwise, you may need to contact your college for discretionary financial assistance.

## Parents claiming for you

If you are in relevant education but are not in any of the above groups, you cannot get IS. Your parents may be able to claim child benefit and child tax credit (CTC) for you (see Chapters 8 and 19).

If you get IS for yourself, the amount of your parents' benefit may reduce, as:
- any child benefit or CTC they get for you stops;
- any IS or income-based JSA they get for you stops;[10]
- any working tax credit they get stops, unless there are other dependent children in the family or they qualify in another way.

## When a course ends

You count as being in relevant education if you have finished a course of non-advanced education and are enrolled or accepted on another such course.[11] This means you are still in relevant education during the summer vacation between courses. Otherwise, you still count as being in relevant education when you finish a course until the latest of the following dates, or until you turn 20 if that is earlier:
- 31 August after your 16th birthday;[12]
- for 16/17-year-olds, at the end of your 'extension period' for child benefit (see p110). **Note:** if you are an orphan, estranged from your parents, living away from your parents because of a risk to your health or because they cannot support you financially, or a care leaver, the requirement that someone must

have received child benefit for you immediately before the period started does not apply;[13]

- the last day in February, May, August or November following the date the course ends.[14]

## 19 or over and a full-time student

If you are a full-time student aged 19 or over, whether in non-advanced or advanced education, you cannot usually claim IS during your 'period of study', but there are exceptions.[15] If you are aged 19 and in relevant education, you come under the rules above.

*Period of study*

The **'period of study'** starts on the first day of the course and ends on the last day of the course – ie, the last day of the final academic year.[16] It only ends earlier than this if you abandon your course or are dismissed from it, in which case it ends on the day that happens. You are within your period of study during all vacations and, for sandwich courses, during periods of work placements. In your first year, you do not count as a student at all until you first start attending or undertaking the course.[17] So if the course has already begun, you are not excluded from IS as a student until the day you actually start.

### Who counts as a full-time student

You count as a **'full-time student'** if you are 'attending or undertaking a full-time course of study at an educational establishment'.[18] There are two definitions of 'full time' that apply: the first covers mostly courses of advanced education; the second covers most courses of non-advanced education.

- **Advanced education.** Your course is full time if it is classed as full time by the institution. If the institution describes the course as full time, you need convincing evidence to persuade the DWP otherwise, bearing in mind that what matters is the course itself rather than the hours you attend.[19] This definition covers all courses of advanced education, and any courses of non-advanced education that are not wholly or partly funded by the government at a further education (FE) college.
- **Non-advanced education.** Your course is full time if it involves more than 16 hours a week classroom or workshop learning under the direct guidance of teaching staff.[20] The benefits office will usually use the number of hours specified in a particular document signed by the college. This is often called a 'learning agreement', but your college may refer to it by some other name. This definition applies if you are at an FE college, not undertaking a higher education course and your course is fully or partly funded by the government.

## Sandwich courses

You count as a full-time student if you are on a sandwich course. A **'sandwich course'** is made up of alternate periods of work experience and full-time study at college or university, where the study periods add up to at least 18 weeks in the year.[21]

Work experience includes periods of employment abroad for modern language students whose course is at least half composed of modern language study.

Initial teacher training courses are not treated as sandwich courses.

## Modular courses

A **'modular course'** is one that is made up of two or more modules and you are required to do a certain number to complete the course.[22] If you are attending or undertaking part of a modular course that is full time according to the rules described above, you are regarded as being a full-time student for the duration of that module, from the day it begins until the last day of registration on the module (or earlier if you abandon the course or are dismissed from it). This includes all vacations during the module on which you are registered and, except for the final module, the vacation immediately following it. It also includes periods when you are attending the course to do re-sits. If the modular course allows you to undertake some modules on a part-time basis, you are not excluded from IS while you are studying part time.

## Postgraduates

If you are a postgraduate, the law is not clear on whether you still count as a student during the period at the end of your course when you are writing up your thesis. DWP guidance says someone is 'not a full-time student during the period after the end of the course when they are expected to complete any course work'.[23] If you are refused IS, consider appealing. You could try arguing that you are no longer attending or undertaking a course.

# Who can claim income support

You can claim IS if you are:[24]

- a lone parent (see below);
- a single foster parent (see p162);
- in a couple, your partner is also a full-time student and you have a child (but you can only get IS in the long vacation – see p162);
- a refugee learning English (see p162);
- on a non-advanced course, under 22 and without parental support (see p162).

## Lone parents

To qualify as a lone parent, your youngest child must normally be under age five (you can also qualify if you are under 18, regardless of your youngest child's age).[25] Once your youngest child reaches her/his fifth birthday, you no longer count as a lone parent and your IS stops.

You may be required to attend work-focused interviews if your youngest child is aged one to four, and to undertake work-related activity if your youngest child is aged three or four.

If you are a lone parent and your child is above the age at which you count as a lone parent for IS, but is under 20 and a qualifying young person (see p108), in certain circumstances you can get IS during the summer vacation. You must be in one of the other groups of people who are eligible for IS, such as a carer (see p163). If you are not in one of these groups, you can claim JSA in the summer vacation instead (see p177).

### Single foster parents

You are eligible if you are a single foster parent with a child under 16.

### Couples

If you have a child and your partner (of either sex) is also a full-time student, you are not excluded from IS in the summer vacation.[26] To be eligible, you must be in one of the groups of people who can get IS (eg, a carer), listed under 'studying part time' on p163. Your child must be under 16, or under 20 and still a qualifying young person (see p108). During term time and short vacations, you are not eligible for IS.

If your partner is not a full-time student or is a part-time student, s/he is not excluded from IS and can claim for you as well as for her/himself whether or not you have a child. S/he can claim IS throughout the year, not just in the long vacation. To be eligible, s/he must be in one of the groups of people who can get IS listed on p163. If s/he is not in one of these groups, s/he cannot get IS but may be able to claim JSA for both of you.

### Refugees

Your English course must be more than 15 hours a week and aimed at helping you get work. You must have refugee status and you must have been in Britain for a year or less when your course starts. Payment of IS is limited to nine months.[27]

### Under 22 without parental support

To qualify, you must be on a full-time course of non-advanced education on which you were accepted, enrolled or started before you turned 21.[28] If you turn 21 on your course, you continue to be eligible. In addition, you must:

- be an orphan, and no one is acting in place of your parent; *or*
- live away from your parents, or anyone acting in their place, because you are estranged from them; *or*
- live away from your parents because there is a serious risk or danger to you; *or*

- live away from your parents. They must be unable to support you financially and be sick or disabled, in prison or not allowed to enter Britain.

For more details, see the first four groups who can claim IS in relevant education listed on p158.

*Examples*

Julie is studying full time for a degree in chemistry. She is a lone parent with a three-year-old child. She is eligible for IS.

Emma is studying full-time for an HND in social care. She is single and fosters a 13-year-old boy. She is eligible for IS.

Anne is a lone parent with a 14-year-old daughter who has a disability. Anne is a full-time student on a four-year degree course. She is not eligible for IS as a lone parent, but is eligible as a carer in the summer vacation only.

## Under 19 in full-time advanced education

If you are under 19 and in full-time advanced education rather than in non-advanced education, the rules are the same as for those aged 19 or over. You count as a full-time student if you are 'attending or undertaking a full-time course of advanced education'.[29] What is or is not a full-time course is the same as for over-19-year-olds (see p160). Only some students can claim IS. The groups who can claim are the same as for full-time students aged 19 or over (see p160).

## Studying part time

Part-time students can claim IS under the usual rules without restriction. You must satisfy all the basic rules (see p164) and you must be in one of the groups of people who are eligible for IS. In brief, these are:
- lone parents under age 18 (regardless of the child's age) or lone parents with a child under five;
- some young people up to age 25 on youth training schemes;
- carers who get carer's allowance or care for someone who gets attendance allowance, the middle or highest rate of the disability living allowance care component, or the daily living component of personal independence payment;
- pregnant women from 11 weeks before to 15 weeks after the birth (or earlier if they are incapable of work because of pregnancy);
- single foster parents of children under 16 or with a child placed for adoption, or people looking after a child while their partner is abroad or if the parents are temporarily ill, or away temporarily;
- some people on unpaid paternity or parental leave;
- people caring for a family member who is temporarily ill;

- refugees on English courses in their first year in Britain;
- people entitled to statutory sick pay;
- people appealing against a decision that they are not incapable of work;
- people who are incapable of work, but only if they already get incapacity benefit (IB);[30]
- people who are registered or certified as blind, but only if they already get IB.

For more details of all the groups of people who are eligible for IS, see CPAG's *Welfare Benefits and Tax Credits Handbook*.

## What counts as part time

You are regarded as a part-time student if you are not a full-time student. If you are under 20 and in relevant education, see p157 for who counts as full time. If you are in advanced education at any age, or you are 19 or over and in non-advanced education (and not a 19-year-old in relevant education), see p160 for who counts as full time.

If you are at an FE college studying a non-advanced course (see Chapter 1), the DWP may ask you for a learning agreement to show that the course is part time – ie, no more than 16 classroom hours. Your college can provide you with this.

*Example*
Betty is a carer for her disabled mother, and has been getting IS on this basis for two years. She starts studying at college 12 hours a week towards a NVQ. She continues to be eligible for IS.

---

## 3. **Basic rules**

As well as being a student who is eligible to claim, to qualify for income support (IS) you must satisfy all the following conditions.[31]
- You are aged 16 or over.
- You have not reached the qualifying age for pension credit (PC). If you have reached this age, you may be eligible for PC instead. Entitlement to PC for both men and women is linked to the minimum age at which a woman can receive state retirement pension. This is rising gradually from 60 from April 2010. It is currently just over 62 and a half. See CPAG's *Welfare Benefits and Tax Credits Handbook* for more details.
- You are not working 16 hours or more a week. If you are working 16 hours or more, you may be eligible for working tax credit instead (see p217).
- Your partner is not working 24 hours or more a week.
- You are present in Great Britain, satisfy the 'habitual residence' and 'right to reside' tests, and are not a 'person subject to immigration control'. (You can

sometimes be paid IS for the first four or eight weeks you are outside Britain.) These terms are explained in CPAG's *Welfare Benefits and Tax Credits Handbook*. Further advice is available from UKCISA (see Appendix 2).

- You have no more than £16,000 capital.
- Your income is less than the set amount the law says you need to live on (known as your 'applicable amount' – see p166).

# 4. **Amount of benefit**

The amount of income support (IS) you get depends on your and your partner's circumstances. The amount also depends on your income and capital. Go through the following steps to work out the amount of IS to which you are entitled.

### Step one: capital
If your capital is over £16,000, you cannot get IS (see p241). Some kinds of capital are ignored. For details, see CPAG's *Welfare Benefits and Tax Credits Handbook*.

### Step two: work out your applicable amount
This is an amount for basic weekly needs. It is made up of:
- personal allowances (see p167);
- premiums (see p168);
- housing costs (see p169).

### Step three: work out your weekly income
Chapter 21 explains how your loan, grant or other income is taken into account and how to work out your weekly income.

### Step four: deduct weekly income from applicable amount
If your income is *less* than your applicable amount, IS equals the difference between the two.

If your income is *the same as or more than* your applicable amount, you cannot get IS. You can claim again if your income goes down – eg, during the long vacation.

*Example*

Karen is 23 and a full-time, second-year undergraduate student and a lone parent of Penny, aged two. She gets a tuition fee loan of £9,000, plus a full special support grant of £3,387 a year, a full student loan for living costs of £5,740, a parents' learning allowance of £1,523 a year and £80 a week childcare grant. Her only other income is child benefit of £20.70 a week and child tax credit (CTC) of £63.63 a week.

**During the academic year September 2015 to June 2016:**

Step one     Karen has no savings or capital.

Step two     Her applicable amount is:

Personal allowance for herself       £73.10

Step three     Her weekly income is:

Loan       £107.37

The loan for tuition fees, special support grant, parents' learning allowance, childcare grant, child benefit and CTC are disregarded. See Chapter 21 for details of how the student loan for living costs is taken into account.

Step four     Her income is above her applicable amount, so she cannot get IS.

**During the long vacation from June 2016 to September 2016:**

Step two     At 2015/16 rates, Karen's applicable amount is :

Personal allowance for herself       £73.10

Step three     Her weekly income for IS purposes from the end of June 2016 to the beginning of September 2016 is nil. This is because her loan only counts as income during the academic year. Child benefit and CTC are disregarded.

Step four     From the end of June 2016 to the beginning of September 2016, her weekly IS is:       £73.10

Karen should reclaim IS from the end of June.

**Note:** as universal credit (UC) is rolled out, Karen may have to claim UC instead.

## Applicable amount

Work out your applicable amount by adding together your personal allowances, premiums and eligible housing costs. Note that benefit rates are uprated in April each year, although the government plans to freeze most rates for the next four years.[32] It is usually possible to find out the new rates from the beginning of December. Check the DWP website at www.gov.uk/dwp for a press release on social security uprating. The amounts in this *Handbook* are from April 2015.

## Claiming for children

From 6 April 2004, IS personal allowances for children and premiums for children were abolished for all new claims and for anyone claiming CTC. Amounts for children are paid through CTC and child benefit instead. If you were already getting IS with amounts for children included before 6 April 2004 and have not claimed CTC, your IS continues to include amounts for children. You can claim CTC earlier than this if you think you will be better off. If you have a grant or loan, you may be better off claiming CTC. Ask your local Jobcentre Plus for a better-off calculation.

## Personal allowance

Your personal allowance is made up of the following.[33]

- One personal allowance at either the single, lone parent or couple rate depending on your situation. The amount depends on your age.
- If you still get IS with amounts for children but do not yet have an award of CTC, add one personal allowance of £66.90 for each dependent child under 16, or under 20 if s/he is still a qualifying young person. For new claims from 6 April 2004, do not include any personal allowance for children.

| Circumstances | £ per week | Conditions |
| --- | --- | --- |
| **Single** | | |
| Under 25 | 57.90 | No special conditions. |
| 25 or over | 73.10 | No special conditions. |
| **Lone parent** | | |
| Under 18 | 57.90 | No special conditions. |
| 18 or over | 73.10 | No special conditions. |
| **Couple** | | |
| Both aged 16–17 (certain cases) | 87.50 | You get this rate if:<br>– you or your partner are responsible for a child; or<br>– you and your partner would be eligible to claim IS or income-related employment and support allowance (ESA) if you were single; or<br>– your partner is eligible for income-based jobseeker's allowance (JSA) or severe hardship payments of JSA. |
| Both aged 16–17 (everyone else) | 57.90 | For everyone else who cannot get the higher rate. |
| One aged 16–17, one 18 or over | 114.85 | The younger partner:<br>– is eligible to claim IS or income-related ESA or would be if s/he were single; or<br>– is eligible for income-based JSA; or<br>– is entitled to severe hardship payments of JSA. |
| One aged 16–17, one 18–24 | 57.90 | For those who are not eligible for the rate above. |
| One aged 16–17, one 25 or over | 73.10 | For those who are not eligible for the rate above. |
| Both aged 18 or over | 114.85 | No special conditions. |

## Premiums

Qualifying for premiums depends on your circumstances.

You can qualify for either one, but not both, of the following.

- **Disability premium** of £32.25 (£45.95 for a couple). You get a disability premium if you get:[34]
  - disability living allowance (DLA);
  - personal independence payment (PIP);
  - long-term incapacity benefit (IB);
  - severe disablement allowance;
  - working tax credit with a disability or severe disability element;
  - war pensioner's mobility supplement;
  - constant attendance allowance;
  - exceptionally severe disablement allowance.

  You also qualify if:
  - you are certified as severely sight impaired or blind, and for 28 weeks after coming off the register; *or*
  - you are terminally ill and have been entitled to statutory sick pay (SSP) for at least 196 days.

  Since the introduction of ESA in October 2008, it is usually no longer possible to have a disability premium added to your IS because of incapacity for work. If you already get a disability premium because of incapacity for work, you continue to get this.

  If you are the IS claimant and you have a partner, you get the disability premium if s/he gets any of the qualifying benefits or is blind.

- **Pensioner premium** of £116 for couples. People who have reached the qualifying age for pension credit (PC – see p164) claim PC rather than IS. However, you get a pensioner premium if you are under this age and claiming IS and you have a partner who has reached this age.[35]

In addition, you can qualify for any, or all, of the following.[36]

- **Carer premium** of £34.60. You get a carer premium if you are entitled to carer's allowance (CA – see p103). If you are entitled to CA but not paid it because it overlaps with another benefit (eg, IB), you still qualify for a carer premium. You get two carer premiums if both you and your partner qualify.
- **Enhanced disability premium** for an adult of £15.75 (£22.60 for a couple). You get this premium if you get the highest rate of the DLA care component or the enhanced rate of the PIP daily living component.[37]
- **Severe disability premium** of £61.85. This is a premium for severely disabled people who live alone, or can be treated as living alone. You qualify for this premium if you get the middle or highest rate of the DLA care component, or the standard or enhanced rate of the PIP daily living component, and no one gets CA for looking after you. You do not get it if you live with another person aged 18 or over (eg, a friend or parent), unless s/he is separately liable for rent,

or you only share a bathroom or hallway, or in some other circumstances.[38] See CPAG's *Welfare Benefits and Tax Credits Handbook* for details. If you have a partner, you do not qualify unless s/he also qualifies in her/his own right or is severely sight impaired or blind. If you both qualify, you get two premiums.

If your IS was awarded before 2004 and you do not get CTC, it may also include:
- family premium of £17.45;
- disabled child premium of £60.06 for each qualifying child;
- enhanced disability premium for each qualifying child of £24.43.

## Housing costs

If you own your own home, IS can help with the cost of mortgage interest payments.[39] You can usually get help once you have been getting IS for 13 weeks (sometimes up to 39 weeks). This is the 'waiting period'.

You must claim housing benefit (HB – see Chapter 12) for help with your rent.

For more details, see CPAG's *Welfare Benefits and Tax Credits Handbook*.

The amount you get is based on a standard interest rate, so it could be higher or lower than the mortgage interest you pay.

IS can also include amounts for certain service charges and interest on loans for certain types of repairs or improvements in the home. IS does *not* include amounts for any capital repayments or endowment premiums.

Payment is usually made directly to your mortgage lender.

IS can include interest on up to £200,000 of the loan if the 13-week waiting period applies, and £100,000 if the 39-week waiting period applies (there are very limited exceptions). You may also find that the amount paid is reduced if the DWP decides that your costs are excessive – eg, if your home is bigger than you need, or if you have a 'non-dependant' (eg, a friend or parent) living with you. **Note:** the government plans to increase the waiting period to 39 weeks and limit the interest covered to £200,000, from April 2016.[40]

### Buying a house on income support

You cannot usually get your housing costs paid if you buy a house while you are on IS unless you are replacing one mortgage with another and, even then, IS does not cover any extra amount of loan. However, if you were getting HB and you buy a house to live in, you can get up to the level of your previous HB paid by IS, even if you took out the mortgage while you were getting IS. There are exceptions for people who need to move somewhere more suitable because of their disability and for people who need a bigger house to give separate bedrooms to a son and daughter over age 10.

### The waiting period

Your student income may mean that you cannot get IS until your housing costs are included in your applicable amount because your income is higher than your personal allowances and premiums. In this case, there are special rules that allow some people to serve the waiting period before they go onto IS.

Lone parents can serve the waiting period in this way if they claim IS first and get refused, then claim again once the waiting period has expired. Similarly, part-time students who are eligible for IS as carers can get IS with housing costs in this way. You can also serve the waiting period while you are getting IB, SSP, contributory ESA, contribution-based JSA or national insurance credits for unemployment, limited capability for work or incapacity.[41]

### Living away from home

Normally you have to live in the home you own to get IS for mortgage costs, but there are exceptions for full-time students (and some others). You can still get IS towards the mortgage if you have moved elsewhere to study but are not paying rent or mortgage at your term-time address. If you pay for both places, you can get IS for both if you are a couple and it is unavoidable that you live in two separate homes. Otherwise, you can get IS towards the mortgage if you are away from your home temporarily and have not let it out and are not likely to be away for more than 52 weeks.

---

## 5. **Claiming income support**

If you think you might be entitled to income support (IS), claim as soon as you can. There are only very limited situations in which backdating is allowed.

To start your claim, contact the Jobcentre Plus contact centre national number on 0800 055 6688 (textphone 0800 023 4888).

When you call, details of your claim are taken and a date for a work-focused interview is arranged (unless it is agreed that you do not need to attend one). A call-back can be arranged if a single call is not appropriate – eg, if you have language or hearing difficulties. You are sent a statement to check and sign, and you are told what evidence and information you should take to your interview or forward to the DWP. The work-focused interview is intended to help you into full-time work, even if you have no intention of working until you finish your studies, but you are under no obligation to look for work.

If you cannot, or do not want to, use the telephone to start your claim, you should still be able to claim in other ways. A claim form should still be accepted, which you can get from Jobcentre Plus, or you may be able to start a claim online at www.gov.uk/income-support. It is important to let your Jobcentre Plus office know you want to claim IS, as otherwise you might lose benefit. You should return the form within one month of your initial contact.

Either member of a couple can make the claim for both, but whoever claims must be eligible in her/his own right.

## Getting paid

Payment is usually made directly into your bank or building society. Which account it goes into is up to you. If you do not want your benefit to go into an account that is already overdrawn, give the DWP details of an alternative account if you have access to, or can open, one. If you do not have an account, you are usually expected to open one with a bank, building society or the Post Office.

## If your claim is refused

Your claim may be unsuccessful for a variety of reasons, including if your student income is too high to qualify. You might find that you should qualify in the long vacation because of the way your grant and loan are divided up through the year. So if you are turned down, claim again as soon as you think you might qualify.

# 6. Challenging a decision

If you think a decision about your income support is wrong, you can ask the DWP to look at it again. This process is known as a 'reconsideration' (the law refers to it as a 'revision'). Provided you ask within the time limit (usually one month), the DWP notifies you of the decision in a 'mandatory reconsideration notice'. If you are still not happy when you get this notice, you can appeal to the independent First-tier Tribunal. If it was not possible to ask the DWP to reconsider the decision within a month, you can ask for a late revision (within 13 months), explaining why it is late. You can also ask the DWP to look at a decision again at any time if certain grounds are met – eg, there has been an official error.

# 7. Other benefits and tax credits

Income support (IS) tops up other income you have to the level of your basic requirements (your 'applicable amount'). Most other benefits you get are therefore taken into account as income when working out your IS. This means they reduce your IS pound for pound. Disability living allowance, personal independence payment and housing benefit (HB) are, however, always disregarded as income.

If you have children and get child tax credit (CTC), both CTC and child benefit are disregarded as income for IS. If you do not yet have a CTC award and have had amounts for children in your IS since before 6 April 2004, child benefit is taken into account for IS.

Even though getting another benefit may reduce your IS, it may still be worth claiming. Getting another benefit might mean you qualify for a premium with your IS (eg, getting carer's allowance means you qualify for a carer premium), so you could be better off overall (although in this case, the person you care for could get less benefit – see p105).

If you get IS and you pay rent, you are eligible as a student for HB (unless you are a care leaver aged 16 or 17).

IS is taken into account when calculating whether the benefit cap applies (see p154 and p208).

## Passported benefits

Provided you meet any other conditions, getting IS entitles you to:
- free dental treatment;
- free prescriptions in England;
- free NHS sight tests;
- vouchers for glasses;
- Healthy Start vouchers and free vitamins;
- social fund payments;
- free school lunches from the local authority.

See Chapters 11 and 17 for details.

## Notes

**2. Who is eligible**

1  s124(1)(d) SSCBA 1992
2  Reg 12 IS Regs; s142 SSCBA 1992
3  Reg 1(3) CB Regs
4  Reg 13(2) and Sch 1B para 15 IS Regs
5  paras 7 and 28 'Making a Severe Hardship Decision' (DWP guidance at www.gov.uk). This guidance is for JSA but should apply equally for IS.
6  para 20686 vol 4 DMG
7  CIS/4096/2005
8  para 20693 vol 4 DMG
9  Reg 2 C(LC)SSB Regs
10 Reg 14(2) IS Regs; reg 76(2) JSA Regs
11 Reg 3(2)(b) CB Regs
12 Reg 4 CB Regs
13 Reg 13(2A)(b) IS Regs; reg 5 CB Regs
14 Reg 7 CB Regs
15 Reg 4ZA(2) IS Regs

16 Regs 2(1), definition of 'period of study', and 61(1), definition of 'last day of the course', IS Regs
17 Reg 61(2)(b) IS Regs
18 Reg 61(1), definition of 'full-time student', IS Regs
19 R(SB) 40/83; R(SB) 41/83
20 Reg 61(1)(c), definition of 'full-time course of study', IS Regs
21 Reg 61(1), definition of 'sandwich course', IS Regs; reg 2(10) E(SS) Regs
22 Reg 61(4) IS Regs
23 para 30238 vol 6 DMG
24 Reg 4ZA(3) IS Regs
25 Sch 1B para 1 IS Regs; s137 SSCBA 1992
26 Reg 4ZA(3)(c) IS Regs
27 Sch 1B para 18 IS Regs
28 Sch 1B para 15A IS Regs
29 Reg 61(1), definition of 'full-time student', IS Regs
30 Regs 1(4) and 2(1) ESA(TP) Regs

**3. Basic rules**
  31  s124 SSCBA 1992

**4. Amount of benefit**
  32  clause 9 Welfare Reform and Work Bill
      2015
  33  Sch 2 para 1 IS Regs
  34  Sch 2 paras 11 and 12 IS Regs
  35  Sch 2 paras 9, 9A and 10 IS Regs
  36  Sch 2 para 6 IS Regs
  37  Sch 2 paras 13A and 15(8) IS Regs
  38  Sch 2 para 13 IS Regs
  39  Sch 3 IS Regs
  40  Summer Budget 2015, para 2.114
  41  Sch 3 para 14(4)-(5B) IS Regs

# Chapter 14

· · · · · · · · · · · · · · · · · · · · · · · · · · · · · · · · · · · · · · · · · · · · · · · ·

# Jobseeker's allowance

**This chapter covers:**
1. What is jobseeker's allowance (below)
2. Who is eligible (p175)
3. Basic rules (p180)
4. Amount of benefit (p181)
5. Claiming jobseeker's allowance (p183)
6. Challenging a decision (p184)
7. Other benefits and tax credits (p184)

· · · · · · · · · · · · · · · · · · · · · · · · · · · · · · · · · · · · · · · · · · · · · · ·

*Basic facts*

– Jobseeker's allowance is basic financial support for people who are expected to 'sign on' for work.
– Full-time students cannot normally claim.
– Student couples with children can claim in the long vacation.
– Lone parents can claim in the long vacation if they are not eligible for income support.
– Part-time students can claim if they are available for work.
– You do not need to have paid national insurance contributions to qualify, but you might get more money if you have.
– The amount is usually affected by any grant, loan or other income you may have.

· · · · · · · · · · · · · · · · · · · · · · · · · · · · · · · · · · · · · · · · · · · · · · ·

## 1. **What is jobseeker's allowance**

Jobseeker's allowance (JSA) provides basic financial support for people of working age who are not working full time and who are expected to 'sign on' as available for work.

Full-time students are normally excluded from JSA, but there are exceptions. Part-time students can claim if they are available for work.

If you have paid sufficient national insurance contributions, you get contribution-based JSA for the first six months. This is paid on top of any student or other income you might have. Otherwise, you may get income-based JSA. This is means tested, so most of your student income and most other income are taken into account when working out how much benefit you get. Chapter 21 explains how your income affects your benefit.

Depending on where you live, you may have to claim universal credit (UC) instead of JSA (see Chapter 18).

**Note:** the following rules for full-time students and young people in relevant education do not apply to contribution-based JSA if you are claiming this and come under the UC system (see p199). If this is the case, you can only get contribution-based JSA and study full time if you took time out of your course because of illness or caring responsibilities, you have now recovered or the caring responsibilities have ended, and you are waiting to rejoin your course.[1]

## 2. **Who is eligible**

To qualify for jobseeker's allowance (JSA), you must not be excluded as a student, and you must satisfy the basic rules. See below for details of students who can claim. The basic rules are covered on p180. If you are claiming contribution-based JSA and come under the universal credit (UC) system, see the note above.

### Under 20 in relevant education

You cannot get JSA while in 'relevant education'.[2]

**Relevant education**

You are in **'relevant education'** if:
- your course is non-advanced (ie, school level or below degree, Higher National Certificate or Higher National Diploma level) of more than 12 hours a week;[3] *and*
- you are under 19, or aged 19 and were accepted on, enrolled on or started your course before you turned 19.

This is the same definition as that used for child benefit and similar to that for child tax credit (CTC). So, although you cannot get JSA for yourself, your parents may still be able to get child benefit and CTC for you.

A special rule allows part-time students who have been on benefit for some months to study and claim JSA at the same time, even though their course is over 12 hours a week. This applies if your course is not full time according to the rules below that apply to most students over 19, and you got JSA, employment and support allowance (ESA), or were on an apprenticeship or other similar training:
- during the last three months before the start of the course; *or*
- for three out of the last six months before the course if you were working the rest of the time.

## 19 or over and a full-time student

You cannot usually get JSA as a full-time student aged 19 or over (and not in relevant education – see p175), whether in advanced or non-advanced education, at any time during your 'period of study'.[4]

*Period of study*

Your '**period of study**' is the whole of your course from the first day you attend or undertake the course to the last day – ie, the last day of the final academic year, including short and long vacations.[5] It includes a period of study in connection with the course after you have stopped doing the course itself. It does not include freshers' week, unless your course actually starts that week.[6]

You are not a student in between courses. For example, you can claim JSA in the summer between completing an undergraduate degree and starting a postgraduate course.

Postgraduates writing up their thesis at the end of a course may be regarded by the DWP as being in 'a period of study undertaken by the student in connection with the course'. However, guidance for decision makers says someone is 'not a full-time student during the period after the end of the course when they are expected to complete any course work'.[7] If you do claim, remember that to get JSA, you must be both available, and actively looking, for work. If you say you are not prepared to fit your thesis writing around a job should one come up, the DWP will decide you are not available for work.

### What counts as full time

In most cases, the college or university defines whether the course is full or part time. However, for some further education (FE) students, there is a 16-hour study rule. The JSA rules are the same as those for income support (IS – see p160).

### Who can claim jobseeker's allowance

You can get JSA in the following circumstances. If you are claiming contribution-based JSA and come under the UC system, see the note on p175.

- If you are in a couple, both of you are full-time students and you have a dependent child aged under 16, or aged under 20 and a qualifying young person (see p108), you can get JSA during the summer vacation only. The person who claims must be available for work and meet all the other basic rules for JSA.[8]

- If you are a single person with a dependent child aged under 16, or aged under 20 and a qualifying young person (see p108), you can get JSA during the summer vacation only. You must be available for work and meet all the other basic rules for JSA. Check whether you can claim IS instead. This depends on the age of your youngest child and whether you meet the usual IS rules (see p161).[9]

- If you are on a course regarded by an employment officer at the Jobcentre Plus office as a qualifying course, you must be aged 25 or over and have been getting JSA for at least two years before the course starts. During term time you are not expected to sign on or look for work, although you may be required to provide evidence of your attendance and progress on the course. During vacations, you are expected to look for casual work.[10]

- If you are on a full-time employment-related course approved by an employment officer at the Jobcentre Plus office, you can claim JSA for just two weeks.[11]

*Example*
Kiera and Mike are a couple and are both studying full time on degree courses. They have a seven-year-old son. Kiera signs on for JSA during the summer, claiming benefit for herself and Mike, who is not working. They also get CTC and child benefit throughout the year.

## Under 19 and in full-time advanced education

You cannot usually get JSA if you are under 19 and studying full time in advanced education. The rules are the same for you as they are for full-time students aged 19 or over (see p176).

## Studying part time

You can claim JSA while studying part time. You must continue to pass all the basic rules for JSA, including being available for work and actively looking for work.

### What counts as part time

Generally, your college or university determines whether you count as a part-time or full-time student, rather than the number of hours you study or attend lectures.[12] The rules are the same as for IS (see p163).

However, if you are under age 20 and in relevant education (see p175), there is a 12-hour rule. Your course is full time if it is more than 12 hours a week of classes and supervised study in term time.

If you are aged 19 or over (and not a 19-year-old in relevant education) at an FE college but not on a higher education course, there is a 16-hour rule for courses funded or partly funded by the government. A part-time course is up to 16 hours a week classroom or workshop-guided learning, under the direct guidance of teaching staff.[13] This is set out in a learning agreement provided by your college.

### Examples

Shona is 20 and attending an FE college, studying for A levels. She has 10 hours a week of classes and 10 hours a week of timetabled independent study. She is classed as a part-time student.

Gwyneth is 24 and at an FE college on an NVQ level two course. She has classes for 18 hours a week and three hours of timetabled study. She is classed as a full-time student.

Russell is 18 and studying for a BTEC. He has 15 hours of classes a week. He is classed as full time.

Saleem is 19 and studying for a degree. He has 15 hours of lectures a week. The university regards his course as full time. He is classed as a full-time student for JSA.

## Studying and availability for work

When you claim JSA, you may have agreed which hours of the day and which days of the week you are available for work. This 'pattern of availability' is set out in your 'claimant commitment' (a new form of jobseeker's agreement). You are allowed to do this provided the hours you choose still give you a reasonable chance of getting work and do not considerably reduce your prospects of getting work.

If the hours you study are completely different to the hours you have agreed to be available for work, you should have no problem. If, however, there is some overlap, or if you have agreed to be available for work at any time of day and on any day of the week, the DWP must be satisfied that you are available for work despite your course. It expects you to:

- rearrange the hours of your course to fit round a job or be prepared to give up the course if a job comes up; *and*
- be ready to take time off the course to attend a job interview; *and*
- be ready to start work immediately.

Guidance tells DWP decision makers to look at various factors when deciding whether you are genuinely available for work, such as:[14]

- what you are doing to look for work;
- whether your course will help you get work. Bear in mind that if you say the course is necessary to get the kind of job you want, the DWP may assume you are not prepared to give it up to do another kind of job and, therefore, decide you are not available for work;
- whether you can be contacted about a possible job if you are studying away from home;
- whether you gave up work or training to do the course;
- your hours of attendance on the course;

- whether it is possible to change the hours if necessary;
- whether you could still complete the course if you missed some classes;
- how much you paid for the course and whether any fees could be refunded if you gave up the course. The DWP is likely to assume that you are not prepared to give up the course to take a job if you have paid a significant amount in course fees;
- whether any grant would need to be repaid if you gave up your course.

At the Jobcentre Plus office you are given a student questionnaire, Form ES567S *Attending a Training or Education Course*, to complete.

However, under a special rule applying to some people who have already been on certain benefits for some months, the DWP does not need to know about any of the above factors. This rule applies if you got JSA, incapacity benefit, IS on incapacity for work grounds or ESA, or were on an apprenticeship or similar training:

- during the last three months before the start of the course; *or*
- for three out of the last six months before the course if you were working the rest of the time.

If this applies to you and your course hours overlap with your pattern of availability but you are willing and able to rearrange them in order to take up employment, no other questions about your course are relevant to your availability for work.[15] You need only complete Part 1 of the student questionnaire and sign Part 3.

Once you have qualified for JSA, you must continue to be available for work and actively look for work. When you 'sign on', you must show what steps you have taken to look for work – eg, checked job adverts or applied for jobs. If you do not look for work each week, or you turn down a job or interview, you could lose your JSA under a sanction, which could be for up to three years. If this happens, you can appeal. You might be able to reduce the sanction or have it overturned (seek advice about this) and ask for a hardship payment in the meantime.

Open University students can attend a residential course for up to a week and keep their JSA. You are not expected to be available for, or to look for, work during that week.[16]

## 16/17-year-olds

Normally, you can only get JSA if you are aged 18 or over. If you are under 18, you can get income-based JSA in the following circumstances, provided you meet all the other entitlement conditions.

- You are in severe hardship. All your circumstances should be considered. Payments are discretionary and usually for just eight weeks at a time.
- You come within one of the groups of people who can claim IS. These are the same groups as for part-time students who can claim IS (see p163).

- You are a couple with a child.
- You are married or in a civil partnership and your partner is aged 18 or over. JSA is paid for a limited period after you leave full-time education.
- You are married or in a civil partnership and your partner is under 18 and registered for work or training, or long-term sick or disabled, or a student who can claim IS, or a carer who can claim IS. JSA is paid for a limited period after you leave full-time education.
- You are leaving local authority care and are a lone parent.[17] JSA is usually paid for just eight weeks. **Note:** your local authority social services department may give financial support if you have been in care.

## 3. **Basic rules**

As well as being a student who is eligible to claim jobseeker's allowance (JSA), you must satisfy all of the basic rules.[18]

- You are available for work. You must be willing and able to take up work immediately (although some people are allowed notice). You must be prepared to work at least 40 hours a week. People with caring responsibilities and disabled people can restrict themselves to fewer than 40 hours. During your child's school holidays, you are not expected to be available for work if there is no childcare reasonable for you to arrange, but this provision does not apply if you are a full-time student.[19]
- You are actively seeking work.
- You have a 'claimant commitment' (a new form of jobseeker's agreement). This sets out, for instance, the hours you have agreed to work, the type of work you are looking for and any restrictions on travel and pay.
- If you are doing any work, it is for less than 16 hours a week. You can get contribution-based JSA if your partner is working, but not income-based JSA unless s/he works less than 24 hours a week.
- You are capable of work (although you can continue to get JSA for up to 13 weeks while sick).
- You are under pension age (rising from 60 for women from April 2010; 65 for men).
- You are in Great Britain, although JSA can be paid in other countries in some circumstances. See CPAG's *Welfare Benefits and Tax Credits Handbook* for details.
- You pass the conditions for either contribution-based JSA or income-based JSA (see p181). If you pass the conditions for both, you get contribution-based JSA topped up by income-based JSA.

## Contribution-based jobseeker's allowance

You must have paid sufficient national insurance contributions to qualify for contribution-based JSA, as well as meeting all the basic rules above.[20]

You must have paid Class 1 contributions on earnings of at least the lower earnings limit in 26 weeks which need not be consecutive in one of the two complete tax years (6 April to 5 April) before the start of the benefit year (which runs from the first Sunday in January) in which you claim. You also must have paid or been credited with Class 1 contributions on earnings of 50 times the lower earnings limit in these years.

For example, you qualify if you claim JSA in 2015 and you paid contributions on earnings of £5,350 in the tax year April 2012 to April 2013 and £5,450 in the tax year April 2013 to April 2014, earning in the first year £107 a week or more, or in the second year £109 a week or more, for at least 26 weeks.

## Income-based jobseeker's allowance

As well as satisfying all the basic rules above, to get income-based JSA you must meet the following conditions.[21]

- You are aged 18 or over. You can still get income-based JSA if you are aged 16 or 17 but there are extra rules (see p179).
- You satisfy the 'habitual residence' and 'right to reside' tests, and are not a 'person subject to immigration control'. These terms are explained in CPAG's *Welfare Benefits and Tax Credits Handbook*. Further advice for overseas students is available from UKCISA (see Appendix 2).
- Your income is below the amount set for your basic living needs (known as your 'applicable amount').
- You have no more than £16,000 capital. See Chapter 21 for how your income and capital affect your benefits.
- You do not get pension credit.

## 4. **Amount of benefit**

Jobseeker's allowance (JSA) is payable after seven 'waiting days'. You may get contribution-based JSA and/or income-based JSA, depending on your circumstances.

## Contribution-based jobseeker's allowance

Contribution-based JSA is paid at different weekly rates depending on your age. **Note:** the government plans to freeze these rates for the next four years.[22]

*Weekly rate from April 2015*

| | |
|---|---|
| Under 25 | £57.90 |
| 25 or over | £73.10 |

You may get less than this if you have part-time earnings or an occupational or personal pension, but the amount is not affected by a student loan or grant. Contribution-based JSA is only paid for up to 26 weeks. After that, you can claim income-based JSA if your income is low enough. Unlike income-based JSA, you only get amounts for yourself, not for a partner.

## Income-based jobseeker's allowance

Income-based JSA is worked out in the same way as income support (IS). The amount you get is made up of:
- personal allowances;
- premiums;
- housing costs – ie, mortgage interest payments.

The total of these is called your 'applicable amount'. If you have no other income (the student loan and some grants count as income), you are paid your full applicable amount. Otherwise, any income you have is topped up with income-based JSA to the level of your applicable amount. If your weekly income is above your applicable amount, you are not entitled to income-based JSA. See Chapter 21 for how to work out your weekly income. See Chapter 13 for how to work out your applicable amount. The rules are almost the same as for IS, with the following differences.
- For couples, if only one of you is under 18, you get the higher £114.85 personal allowance if the younger partner is responsible for a child or is eligible for income-based JSA, severe hardship payments, IS (or would be if not a member of a couple) or income-related employment and support allowance (ESA).
- For couples, if both of you are under 18, you get the higher £87.50 personal allowance if:
  - you or your partner are responsible for a child;
  - both of you would be eligible for income-based JSA, or your partner would be eligible for IS or income-related ESA, if you were both single;
  - you are both eligible for severe hardship payments, or one of you is while the other is eligible for income-based JSA, IS or income-related ESA;

- you are married or civil partners and one of you is registered with the National Careers Service in England, Careers Wales in Wales or your local Jobs and Benefits office in Northern Ireland, or both of you are eligible for income-based JSA.
- Joint-claim couples can get a disability premium (at the couple rate) if one has had limited capability for work for 364 days (196 days if terminally ill). You must claim ESA to establish limited capability for work, even if you might not get it.
- Claimants who are entitled to housing costs after 13 weeks only have these included in their applicable amount for two years.

## 5. **Claiming jobseeker's allowance**

You should claim jobseeker's allowance (JSA) by phoning the Jobcentre Plus contact centre national number (0800 055 6688). You are given an appointment for an interview. Claim as soon as you can, as JSA can only be backdated in very limited circumstances. If you are under 18, you should register with the National Careers Service in England, Careers Wales in Wales or your local Jobs and Benefits office in Northern Ireland first.

At the interview, you are asked to complete Form ES2, *Helping You Back to Work,* which has questions about looking for work. When filling in this form, remember that even though you are a student, you are expected to be available for work and actively looking for work. Make sure your answers do not cast doubt on your willingness to work. Part-time students are also given the student questionnaire to complete and are asked for a learning agreement from their college to show that they are studying part time.

### Couples

If you are a full-time student or in relevant education but your partner is not, s/he can get JSA for both of you if s/he is eligible for JSA.[23] You both need to claim, but only your partner must continue to sign on and look for work. Similarly, your partner can get JSA for both of you if you are not yet a full-time student, but you have applied for or been accepted on a course.

Most other couples, including if one or both of you are part-time students, need to claim income-based JSA jointly. This means that both of you must make the claim, be eligible for JSA, sign on and look for work.

Some people need not claim jointly. Only the person who makes the claim for the couple must be eligible and sign on if:
- you have dependent children; *or*
- you are both under 18; *or*
- you were both born before 28 October 1947.

## 6. **Challenging a decision**

If you think a decision about your jobseeker's allowance is wrong, you can ask the DWP to look at it again. This process is known as a 'reconsideration' (the law refers to it as a 'revision'). Provided you ask within the time limit (usually one month), the DWP notifies you of the decision in a 'mandatory reconsideration notice'. If you are still not happy when you get this notice, you can appeal to the independent First-tier Tribunal. If it was not possible to ask the DWP to reconsider the decision within a month, you can ask for a late revision (within 13 months), explaining why it is late. You can also ask the DWP to look at a decision again at any time if certain grounds are met – eg, there has been an official error.

## 7. **Other benefits and tax credits**

You cannot get income support (IS) and jobseeker's allowance (JSA) at the same time, so if you are eligible for both, you must choose which to claim. In general, the amounts of income-based JSA and IS are the same, but you are not expected to sign on for work for IS.

Child tax credit (CTC) and, except for some existing claimants, child benefit are ignored as income when JSA is assessed. If you have been getting income-based JSA since before 6 April 2004 and still have amounts for children included in JSA, child benefit is taken into account as income.

If you get income-based JSA, you are also eligible as a student for housing benefit, provided you meet the other rules of entitlement.

JSA is taken into account when calculating whether the benefit cap applies (see p154 and p208).

### Passported benefits

Provided you meet any other conditions, getting income-based JSA entitles you to:
- free dental treatment;
- free prescriptions in England;
- free NHS sight tests;
- vouchers for glasses;
- Healthy Start vouchers and free vitamins;
- social fund payments;
- free school lunches from the local authority.

Contribution-based JSA does not give you automatic access to these benefits, but you may qualify for health benefits on low income grounds. See Chapter 11 for details.

# Notes

### 1. What is jobseeker's allowance
1　Reg 45(6) JSA Regs 2013

### 2. Who is eligible
2　s1(2)(g) JSA 1995
3　Reg 54 JSA Regs
4　Reg 15(1)(a) JSA Regs
5　Regs 4 and 130 JSA Regs
6　para 30221 vol 6 DMG
7　para 30238 vol 6 DMG
8　Reg 15(2) and (3) JSA Regs
9　Reg 15(2) and (3) JSA Regs
10　Regs 17A and 21A JSA Regs
11　Reg 14(1)(a) JSA Regs
12　Reg 1(b)(i), definition of 'full-time student', JSA Regs
13　Reg 1(b)(iii), definition of 'full-time student', JSA Regs
14　para 21242 vol 4 DMG
15　Reg 11 JSA Regs
16　Regs 14(1)(f) and 19(1)(f) JSA Regs
17　C(LC)SSB Regs

### 3. Basic rules
18　s1 JSA 1995
19　Reg 15(4) JSA Regs
20　s2 JSA 1995
21　ss3 and 13 JSA 1995

### 4. Amount of benefit
22　clause 9 Welfare Reform and Work Bill 2015

### 5. Claiming jobseeker's allowance
23　Sch A1 JSA Regs; para 30245 vol 6 DMG

# Chapter 15

· · · · · · · · · · · · · · · · · · · · · · · · · · · · · · · · · · · · · · · · · · · · · · · · · · · · · · ·

# Maternity, paternity and adoption benefits

**This chapter covers:**
1. What are maternity, paternity and adoption benefits (below)
2. Who is eligible (p187)
3. Amount of benefit (p189)
4. Claiming maternity, paternity and adoption benefits (p189)
5. Challenging a decision (p189)
6. Other benefits and tax credits (p190)

· · · · · · · · · · · · · · · · · · · · · · · · · · · · · · · · · · · · · · · · · · · · · · · · · · · · · · ·

*Basic facts*

– Women having a baby can claim statutory maternity pay if they have an employer, or maternity allowance if they have recently worked.
– The mother's partner can claim statutory paternity pay.
– Parents adopting a child can claim statutory adoption pay and statutory paternity pay.
– Either partner can claim statutory shared parental pay instead of statutory maternity, paternity or adoption pay.
– Part-time and full-time students are eligible for these benefits.

· · · · · · · · · · · · · · · · · · · · · · · · · · · · · · · · · · · · · · · · · · · · · · · · · · · · · · ·

## 1. **What are maternity, paternity and adoption benefits**

### Statutory maternity pay

You can get statutory maternity pay (SMP) for 39 weeks if you are pregnant or have just had a baby, have an employer and earn at least £112 a week (April 2015 rate).

### Maternity allowance

If you cannot get SMP but you have recently worked, either employed or self-employed, you may be able to get maternity allowance (MA) for 39 weeks. You may also qualify if you have helped your partner with her/his self-employment. See CPAG's *Welfare Benefits and Tax Credits Handbook* for details.

## Statutory paternity pay

You can get ordinary statutory paternity pay (SPP) for two weeks if your partner is having a baby and you are taking leave from work to care for her or for the child. You can also get additional SPP or statutory shared parental pay (SSPP) in some circumstances. See CPAG's *Welfare Benefits and Tax Credits Handbook* for details. Unmarried partners, including same-sex partners, can claim SPP.

## Statutory adoption pay

You can get statutory adoption pay (SAP) for 39 weeks if you are adopting a child and are earning at least £112 a week from employment (April 2015 rate). If a couple (including same-sex couples) are adopting a child, one can claim SAP and the other can claim SPP for two weeks (and additional SPP, or SSPP, in some circumstances).

## Statutory shared parental pay

You or your partner can get SSPP if your baby was due on or after 12 April 2015 (if your baby was due before this date, your partner can get additional SPP). SSPP can be paid instead of SMP, MA or SAP in certain circumstances.

---

# 2. **Who is eligible**

Students are eligible for maternity, paternity and adoption benefits if they pass the basic rules for these. See CPAG's *Welfare Benefits and Tax Credits Handbook* for details. What follows is a brief outline of the qualifying conditions.

## Statutory maternity pay

You can get statutory maternity pay (SMP) if:
- you are pregnant or have recently had a baby;
- you have worked for the same employer for 26 weeks ending with the 15th week before your expected week of birth;
- your average gross earnings are at least £112 a week (April 2015 rate); *and*
- you give your employer the correct notice.

## Maternity allowance

You can get maternity allowance (MA) if you cannot get SMP and:
- you are pregnant or have recently had a baby;

- you have worked, either as an employee or self-employed, for at least 26 weeks out of the 66 weeks before the expected week of birth; *and*
- your average earnings are at least £30 a week.

## Statutory paternity pay

You can get ordinary statutory paternity pay (SPP) if:
- you are the child's father or partner of the child's mother and you will be caring for the child or supporting the mother;
- you have worked for the same employer for 41 weeks before the baby is born;
- your average gross earnings are at least £112 a week (April 2015 rate); *and*
- you give your employer the correct notice.

If the baby was due before the week beginning 5 April 2015, you may get additional SPP for up to 20 weeks if the mother returns to work before she has had her full entitlement of SMP or MA. If the baby was due on or after week beginning 5 April 2015, you may get statutory shared parental pay (SSPP) instead. You can also get SPP if you are adopting a child. You cannot get both SPP (adoption) and statutory adoption pay (SAP) at the same time, although one member of a couple can claim SAP while the other claims SPP (adoption).

## Statutory adoption pay

You can get SAP if:
- you are adopting a child;
- you have worked for the same employer for 26 weeks ending with the week in which you are told you have been matched with a child for adoption;
- your average gross earnings are at least £112 a week (April 2015 rate); *and*
- you give your employer the correct notice.

## Statutory shared parental pay

You can get SSPP if:
- you are caring for a child; *and either*
- you are the mother of the child or have adopted the child, and you have reduced your MA, SMP or SAP period; *or*
- you are the father of the child or the partner of the mother/adopter and your partner has reduced her/his MA, SMP or SAP period.

Your partner must also meet employment and earnings tests. See CPAG's *Welfare Benefits and Tax Credits Handbook* for more details.

# 3. **Amount of benefit**

*Weekly rate from April 2015*

| | | |
|---|---|---|
| Statutory maternity pay (SMP) | for the first six weeks | 90% of average weekly earnings |
| | for the following 33 weeks | £139.58 (or 90% of earnings if less) |
| Statutory paternity pay (SPP) | for two weeks (ordinary) | £139.58 (or 90% of earnings if less) |
| Statutory adoption pay (SAP) | for 39 weeks | £139.58 (or 90% of earnings if less) |
| Statutory shared parental pay (SSPP) | for 37 weeks | £139.58 (or 90% of earnings if less) |
| Maternity allowance (MA) | for 39 weeks | £139.58 (or 90% of earnings if less) |

You can end your SMP, SAP or MA early and your partner can take parental leave instead of you and be paid SSPP. Or you can end your SMP, SAP or MA early and get SSPP yourself, as it gives you more flexibility in when you take your paid leave. See CPAG's *Welfare Benefits and Tax Credits Handbook* for more details.

# 4. **Claiming maternity, paternity and adoption benefits**

You claim statutory maternity, adoption, paternity and shared parental pay from your employer. You claim maternity allowance from your local Jobcentre Plus office.

# 5. **Challenging a decision**

If you think a decision about your maternity allowance is wrong, you can ask the DWP to look at it again. This process is known as a 'reconsideration' (the law refers to it as a 'revision'). Provided you ask within the time limit (usually one month), the DWP notifies you of the decision in a 'mandatory reconsideration notice'. If you are still not happy when you get this notice, you can appeal to the independent First-tier Tribunal. If it was not possible to ask the DWP to reconsider the decision within a month, you can ask for a late revision (within 13 months), explaining why it is late. You can also ask the DWP to look at a decision again at any time if certain grounds are met – eg, there has been an official error.

If you disagree with your employer's decision on your entitlement to statutory maternity, adoption, paternity or shared parental pay, or your employer fails to make a decision, you can ask HM Revenue and Customs to make a formal decision on your entitlement.

# 6. **Other benefits and tax credits**

There are a number of other benefits you may get when you have a baby, such as:
- child benefit when the baby is born;
- child tax credit (CTC) or an increase in your existing award. Tell HM Revenue and Customs within three months of the birth;
- if you are 19 or under and in full-time non-advanced education or approved training on which you were accepted, enrolled or started before you turned 19, income support (IS) as a parent;
- if you are a lone parent, IS whether or not you are a full-time student;
- universal credit (UC), if you come under the UC system (see p199);
- if there is no other child under 16 in the household, a Sure Start maternity grant within three months of the birth, provided you get a qualifying benefit (including IS, and CTC at a rate above the family element). If you are still waiting for a decision on your IS or tax credit, claim the grant anyway. If you are refused the grant, rather than your claim being held until your benefit or tax credit is awarded, make another claim within three months of being awarded the benefit or tax credit;
- Healthy Start vouchers.

Maternity allowance is taken into account when calculating whether the benefit cap applies (see p154 and p208). Statutory maternity, adoption, paternity and shared parental pay are not taken into account.

# Chapter 16

# Personal independence payment

**This chapter covers:**
1. What is personal independence payment (below)
2. Who is eligible (p192)
3. Amount of benefit (p193)
4. Claiming personal independence payment (p193)
5. Challenging a decision (p194)
6. Other benefits and tax credits (p194)

*Basic facts*
– Personal independence payment is for people who need help with daily living or who have mobility difficulties.
– Part-time and full-time students can claim.
– If you are a full-time student, getting personal independence payment allows you to claim income-related employment and support allowance and may also allow you to claim housing benefit. If you come under the universal credit system, getting personal independence payment allows you to claim universal credit, although you must meet a medical test.

---

## 1. **What is personal independence payment**

Personal independence payment (PIP) is a new benefit which replaces disability living allowance (DLA) for people of working age (aged 16 to 64).

In England and Wales, if you are already on DLA and are of working age, you are expected to be assessed for PIP by the end of 2017. If you were 65 or over on 8 April 2013, you remain on DLA. If you are getting DLA and are of working age, you must claim PIP instead if your DLA award is due for renewal, you have a change of circumstances or you are turning 16.

PIP is not means tested, so it is not reduced because of your student support or other income. It comprises two components: for daily living and mobility. Each component has two rates: a standard rate and an enhanced rate.

In Northern Ireland, the introduction of PIP is being debated but has not yet been confirmed. You should make a claim for DLA in the meantime (see Chapter 9).

## 2. Who is eligible

You qualify for personal independence payment (PIP) if you meet all the following conditions.

- You are aged 16 or over and under 65.
- You satisfy certain rules on residence and presence in the UK, and are not a 'person subject to immigration control'. See CPAG's *Welfare Benefits and Tax Credits Handbook* for details.
- You satisfy the disability conditions for the daily living component and/or the mobility component.
- You have satisfied the disability conditions for the last three months (unless you are terminally ill) and are likely to continue to do so for the next nine months.

Your ability to undertake various activities is assessed, usually at a medical examination. Depending on the type and level of help you need, you score points on different activities. If you score eight points, you get the standard rate of a component; if you score 12 points, you get the enhanced rate. For example, if you cannot dress or undress yourself, you score eight points.

See CPAG's *Welfare Benefits and Tax Credits Handbook* for more information about the activities and the points awarded.

### Daily living component

To get the standard rate of the daily living component, your ability to undertake certain specified day-to-day activities must be limited by your health or disability. If your ability to undertake the activities is severely limited, you get the enhanced rate.

You are assessed on your ability to carry out the following activities:

- preparing food;
- taking nutrition;
- managing your therapy or monitoring your health condition;
- washing and bathing;
- managing your toilet needs or incontinence;
- dressing and undressing;

- communicating verbally;
- reading and understanding signs, symbols and words;
- engaging face-to-face with other people;
- making budgeting decisions.

## Mobility component

You get the standard rate of the mobility component if your ability to undertake certain mobility activities is limited by your health or disability. If your ability to undertake the activities is severely limited, you get the enhanced rate.

You are assessed on your ability to plan and follow journeys, and to move around.

## Students

If you are a part-time or full-time student, you can get PIP if you meet the qualifying conditions. Starting studying should not affect your award, provided you still have daily living and/or mobility needs.

## 3. Amount of benefit

*Weekly rate from April 2015*
**Daily living component**

| | |
|---|---|
| Standard rate | £55.10 |
| Enhanced rate | £82.30 |

**Mobility component**

| | |
|---|---|
| Standard rate | £21.80 |
| Enhanced rate | £57.45 |

## 4. Claiming personal independence payment

Phone 0800 917 2222 (textphone 0800 917 7777) to make a claim for personal independence payment (PIP). If you cannot claim by phone, you can ask for a claim form to be sent to you. Claims cannot be backdated, so claim as soon as you think you qualify.

When you phone, some basic information is taken from you. You are then sent a form on which to give more information about your condition and how it affects you. You must normally return this form within one month. You must then usually attend a medical assessment.

Awards of PIP are usually made for a fixed period – eg, two years, or five years.

PIP is usually paid directly into your bank account, and is paid every four weeks in arrears.

## 5. Challenging a decision

If you think a decision about your personal independence payment is wrong, you can ask the DWP to look at it again. This process is known as a 'reconsideration' (the law refers to it as a 'revision'). Provided you ask within the time limit (usually one month), the DWP notifies you of the decision in a 'mandatory reconsideration notice'. If you are still not happy when you get this notice, you can appeal to the independent First-tier Tribunal. If it was not possible to ask the DWP to reconsider the decision within a month, you can ask for a late revision (within 13 months), explaining why it is late. You can also ask the DWP to look at a decision again at any time if certain grounds are met – eg, there has been an official error.

## 6. Other benefits and tax credits

If you are a full-time student and get personal independence payment (PIP), you are eligible for income-related employment and support allowance and, usually, housing benefit. If you get PIP, you come under the universal credit (UC) system and have limited capability for work, you are eligible for UC (see p199).

If you claim other benefits or tax credits, make sure the office dealing with your claim knows you get PIP, as it may qualify you for additional amounts in these.

If you, your partner or a young person you are responsible for get PIP, you are exempt from the benefit cap (see p154 and p208).

# Chapter 17

## The social fund

This chapter covers:
1. What is the social fund (below)
2. Sure Start maternity grants (p196)
3. Funeral payments (p196)
4. Budgeting loans (p197)
5. Local welfare assistance schemes (p197)
6. Challenging a decision (p198)

**Basic facts**

– To get help from the social fund, you must receive income support or another qualifying benefit.

– Most students do not qualify for help from the social fund because they do not get a qualifying benefit.

## 1. **What is the social fund**

The social fund consists of regulated payments and budgeting loans. Previous social fund payments (community care grants and crisis loans) were abolished in April 2013 and replaced by local welfare assistance schemes run by local authorities in England and the Discretionary Assistance Fund in Wales. The social fund is currently under review in Northern Ireland: for details of current support and potential changes see www.nidirect.gov.uk/help-from-the-social-fund.

Regulated social fund payments are:
- Sure Start maternity grants;
- funeral payments;
- cold weather payments;
- winter fuel payments.

You are entitled to regulated social fund payments if you satisfy the qualifying conditions. For more information on cold weather payments and winter fuel payments, see CPAG's *Welfare Benefits and Tax Credits Handbook*.

## 2. **Sure Start maternity grants**

A Sure Start maternity grant is a grant of £500 to help with the costs of a new baby. You are usually only eligible if there is no child under 16 in the household already. To qualify you must get:

- income support; *or*
- income-based jobseeker's allowance; *or*
- income-related employment and support allowance; *or*
- pension credit; *or*
- child tax credit at a rate above the family element (£545 a year); *or*
- working tax credit including a disability or severe disability element; *or*
- universal credit.

Claim at the local Jobcentre Plus office on Form SF100 up to 11 weeks before the birth or within three months of the birth. If you are waiting to hear about a claim for one of the qualifying benefits, make sure to claim the maternity grant within the deadline. Your entitlement is then protected and the grant can be awarded once the benefit decision is made, although you may need to fill in a second SF100.

## 3. **Funeral payments**

A funeral payment is made to help with burial or cremation costs. To qualify you must get:

- income support; *or*
- income-based jobseeker's allowance; *or*
- income-related employment and support allowance; *or*
- pension credit; *or*
- housing benefit; *or*
- child tax credit at a rate above the family element (£545 a year); *or*
- working tax credit including a disability or severe disability element; *or*
- universal credit.

Unless you are the partner of the deceased, you may not get a payment if there is a close relative who does not get one of these benefits.

Claim at the local Jobcentre Plus office on Form SF200 within three months of the funeral.

# 4. Budgeting loans

You can get a budgeting loan to help you pay for certain items – eg, furniture, clothes, removal expenses, rent in advance, home improvements, travelling expenses, maternity expenses, funeral expenses and jobseeking expenses. If you are claiming universal credit, you must apply for a budgeting advance instead of a budgeting loan.

The amount of budgeting loan you can get depends on the size of your family and how long you have been on benefit. To qualify, you must have been getting one of the following for at least 26 weeks before your claim is decided:

- income support;
- income-based jobseeker's allowance;
- income-related employment and support allowance; *or*
- pension credit.

See CPAG's *Welfare Benefits and Tax Credits Handbook* for details of who can get a loan and how to apply.

# 5. Local welfare assistance schemes

In England, Wales and Scotland, the discretionary elements of the social fund (community care grants and crisis loans) have been abolished. Their replacement varies depending on where you live. For Scotland, see CPAG's *Welfare Benefits and Tax Credits Handbook*.

## Local provision in England

Local authorities in England are now responsible for providing replacement schemes for community care grants and crisis loans. Schemes vary, so contact your local authority for details of its scheme. Although students are not excluded from applying, your local authority expects you to first claim assistance from your university's or college's hardship fund, if this is available. Funding is, in general, likely to be limited.

## Discretionary Assistance Fund in Wales

The Welsh government has set up a national scheme to replace social fund community care grants and crisis loans in Wales. The Discretionary Assistance Fund will exist until at least March 2016 and is administered through a partnership between Northgate Public Services, the Family Fund and Wrexham County Council.

The Fund consists of individual assistance payments to help people remain in or establish themselves in the community, and emergency assistance payments for people without money because of a disaster or emergency. To qualify, you must usually be getting a qualifying benefit (income support, income-based jobseeker's allowance or income-related employment and support allowance).

Students on a qualifying benefit are eligible for individual assistance payments if they meet the other criteria, but are excluded from emergency assistance payments. You are expected to apply to your college or university's discretionary fund instead.

More information on the Fund, and how to apply, is at www.moneymadeclearwales.org, under 'Other help'.

# 6. **Challenging a decision**

If you think a decision about your maternity grant or funeral payment is wrong, you can ask the DWP to look at it again. This process is known as a 'reconsideration' (the law refers to it as a 'revision'). Provided you ask within the time limit (usually one month), the DWP notifies you of the decision in a 'mandatory reconsideration notice'. If you are still not happy when you get this notice, you can appeal to the independent First-tier Tribunal. If it was not possible to ask the DWP to reconsider the decision within a month, you can ask for a late revision (within 13 months), explaining why it is late. You can also ask the DWP to look at a decision again at any time if certain grounds are met – eg, there has been an official error.

You can ask for a review of a budgeting loan decision within 28 days of the day the decision was issued to you (or sometimes later, if you have special reasons or if there is a mistake in the decision about the law or the facts of your case).

# Chapter 18

# Universal credit

**This chapter covers:**

*Basic facts*

– Universal credit is a new benefit, replacing tax credits and most means-tested benefits.
– It can include amounts for adults, children, illness, caring responsibilities, rent or mortgage interest, and childcare costs.
– You claim with your partner, and you are paid monthly in arrears in a single household payment.
– Universal credit is being introduced gradually in Great Britain, at first only if you meet certain 'gateway' conditions when you claim.
– If you are a full-time or part-time student, you do not meet the 'gateway' conditions, so you cannot claim universal credit.
– If you already get universal credit when you start studying, you can continue to do so in certain circumstances – for example, if you have a child.
– The amount you get is usually affected by any grant, loan or other income you have.

## 1. **What is universal credit**

Universal credit (UC) is a new means-tested benefit that has been introduced in some areas across Great Britain. It is expected that UC will be introduced in Northern Ireland at some point in the future, but at the time of writing the necessary legislation was still under discussion. The rules as currently proposed are very similar, but there are likely to be some differences.

UC replaces the following benefits and tax credits:

- income support;
- income-based jobseeker's allowance (JSA);
- income-related employment and support allowance (ESA);
- housing benefit (HB);
- child tax credit (CTC);
- working tax credit (WTC).

UC is being introduced gradually, so whether a new claim is for UC or an existing benefit depends on where you live and what your circumstances are. You may have to claim UC rather than make a new claim for JSA if, for example, you have recently lost your job. This may apply even if you already get HB or tax credits. If you get one of the other benefits above, you are likely to stay on this until the 'gateway' conditions change or you are transferred to UC.

If you have claimed UC and then start studying, you may be able to remain on UC if, broadly, you are a parent, disabled, a young student in non-advanced education who is without parental support, or if you have a partner who is not a student.

When you come under the UC system (ie, when you must claim UC), you claim UC instead of the existing working-age means-tested benefits. You also claim contributory ESA and contribution-based JSA under different rules to those that apply to existing claimants.

The amount you get is based on your circumstances (eg, whether you have a partner or child, or care for someone with a disability) and is usually affected by any grant, loan or other income you have.

## How students are affected by universal credit

- Students under 22 in non-advanced education do not get help with their housing costs in their UC, unless they are estranged from their parents or in some other circumstances (see p201). Currently, many young people in non-advanced education claim HB.
- Entitlement to UC for students with disabilities is more restricted than entitlement to current benefits. For UC, you must have 'limited capability for work' and also get disability living allowance (DLA) or personal independence payment (PIP) to qualify. Under the current system, a disabled student can get income-related ESA if s/he gets DLA or PIP, and HB if s/he is deaf and in receipt of a disabled students' allowance for deafness, or if s/he is certified as severely sight impaired or blind.
- There is no specific entitlement to UC for refugees who are learning English in their first year in the UK. In the current system, the rules allow access to certain benefits on this basis.

- There is no equivalent to WTC in UC, so students who are working but not in one of the groups who can claim UC get no extra help.
- Some full-time students who are eligible for UC and are not exempt from work-related requirements may be sanctioned. In this situation, amounts for children and housing costs are still paid, but a sanction on the UC 'standard allowance' could last up to three years – ie, beyond completing the course. Under the current system, such students can claim HB and CTC without any sanction being applied.
- Payment of UC is monthly in arrears. It is one payment, which includes help with rent. In the current system, help with rent through HB is usually paid directly to landlords, which is preferred by most claimants.
- Student loans and some other student funding reduce your UC pound for pound, beyond a monthly disregard. In the current system, student funding reduces HB at a rate of only 65p in the pound, and tax credits are generally not affected by student funding.

## 2. **Who is eligible**

### Students

To qualify for universal credit (UC), you must satisfy all the basic rules described on p204 and must be in one of the groups of students who can claim UC described below. At the time of writing, both full-time and part-time students are excluded from claiming UC under the 'gateway' conditions. However, once through the gateway (eg, you already get UC then start studying, or you are a student who starts living with a partner who gets UC), any change in your circumstances is taken into account under the normal UC rules. This means that you can stay on UC if you are in one of the groups of students who can claim UC and continue to satisfy the basic rules. If you are no longer eligible for UC because you start studying, and you no longer fit the gateway conditions (eg, because you are now studying), you may be able to claim housing benefit or another benefit that UC is replacing, provided you meet the rules for that benefit.

The basic rules specify that if you are a student (known as 'receiving education'), you cannot claim UC.

*Receiving education*
You are **'receiving education'** if you are:[1]
– a qualifying young person. This applies if you are in non-advanced education of at least 12 hours a week and have not yet reached 31 August after your 19th birthday;
– undertaking a full-time course of advanced education (see p160 – the rules are the same as for income support);[2]

– on another full-time course for which a loan, grant or bursary is provided for your maintenance;

– if none of the above apply, on a course that is not compatible with your 'work-related requirements' – ie, what you are expected to do in terms of looking for work.

## Who can claim universal credit

If you do not count as receiving education, you can claim UC in the same way as anyone else.

If you count as receiving education, you are only eligible for UC if you:[3]

- are responsible for a child or young person;
- are under 22 on a non-advanced course, you were under 21 when you started the course, and you are 'without parental support' (see below);
- have limited capability for work and also get disability living allowance or personal independence payment (PIP);
- are a single foster parent;
- are a member of a student couple and your partner is a foster parent;
- are over the qualifying age for pension credit and your partner has not yet reached that age;
- have a partner who is not a student;
- have taken time out because of illness or caring responsibilities, you have now recovered or your caring responsibilities have ended, and you are not eligible for a grant or loan.

If you are in one of the above groups and have a partner who is also a student, you can make a joint claim for UC with her/him, even if s/he is not in one of these groups.[4]

---

*Without parental support*

'**Without parental support**' means you:[5]

– are an orphan; *or*

– cannot live with your parents because you are estranged from them, or because there is a serious risk to your physical or mental health, or you would face significant harm if you lived with them; *or*

– are living away from your parents, and they cannot support you financially because they are ill or disabled, in prison or not allowed to enter Great Britain.

---

**Note:** if you are aged 16 or 17 and receiving education, you can only claim UC if you are in one of the first three bullet points above – ie, you have a child, are without parental support and in non-advanced education, or are ill/disabled. If you are a 16/17-year-old care leaver and are receiving education, you can only claim if you have a child or are ill/disabled, and you cannot get help with housing costs.[6]

*Examples*

Jodie is 18 and on UC. She starts a full-time course of non-advanced education. She is estranged from her parents. She is still eligible for UC.

Lewis is on UC. He moves in with his partner Liz, who is on a full-time advanced course and has a three-year-old child. They are eligible for UC.

Pauline is 23 and is on UC. She starts a full-time non-advanced course. She is single and not disabled. She is not eligible for UC while she is a student.

Karen is on UC. She moves in with her partner, Jake, who is unemployed. Karen starts a full-time advanced course. They are still eligible for UC.

## Work-related requirements

Even if you are a student who can claim UC, you may have 'work-related requirements' imposed as a condition of getting UC. It may not be possible to meet these while on your course and your UC may be reduced (sanctioned). See CPAG's *Welfare Benefits and Tax Credits Handbook* for more information about work-related requirements and sanctions.

There are no work-related requirements if you are receiving education and you are:[7]

- under 22 (and were under 21 when you started your course), in non-advanced education and have no parental support; *or*
- in receipt of student income which is taken into account for UC – ie, a student loan or a grant for maintenance. This only applies during the period of the year in which your student income is taken into account. Normally, this is over the academic year (see Chapter 22). Over the summer vacation you may be subject to work-related requirements.

If you are not exempt from work-related requirements under the rules above and not exempt for any other reason (eg, because you have a child under one or you are severely disabled), you must meet your work-related requirements, otherwise you can be sanctioned. This means that your UC is reduced by the level of your standard allowance (see p205). This reduction can last up to three years in some cases, even if you later meet your work-related requirements. You may be able to challenge a sanction. If you are sanctioned, you should seek advice as soon as possible.

*Examples*

Sukhi is a full-time postgraduate student studying for an MA. She is funding her course through savings. She has a 12-year-old daughter. She claims UC, but as she is not in receipt of a student loan or grant for her course, work-related requirements apply. If Sukhi cannot meet these requirements, her UC may be sanctioned.

Sean is a lone parent with one child aged eight, studying a full-time Higher National Diploma course. He claims UC and does not have any work-related requirements applied because he gets a student loan. His long vacation starts on 17 June 2016. For the assessment period covering 17 June and the next two assessment periods, which are wholly within his summer vacation, he is subject to work-related requirements. If Sean cannot meet these requirements, his UC may be sanctioned.

## 3. **Basic rules**

Universal credit (UC) is for people on a low income who are in or out of work. You can claim regardless of your circumstances, provided you meet basic rules about age, education, residence, income and capital. So, for example, lone parents, people with a disability, carers and unemployed people can all claim UC. However, UC is being introduced gradually, and you can only claim it if you meet certain 'gateway' conditions. Currently, it is mainly for single jobseekers. Once you are getting UC, you continue to do so if you start studying and are a student who can claim UC (see p201).

As well as being a student who is eligible to claim UC, you must satisfy all the following conditions.

- You are aged 18 or over. There are some exceptions for some 16/17-year-olds – eg, if you are estranged from your parents, are a parent yourself, are sick or disabled or if you are caring for someone with a disability.
- You are under the qualifying age for pension credit (PC).
- You are in Great Britain, satisfy the 'habitual residence' and the 'right to reside' tests, and are not a 'person subject to immigration control'. These terms are explained in CPAG's *Welfare Benefits and Tax Credits Handbook*.
- You have no more than £16,000 capital.
- Your income is less than your 'maximum amount' of UC (see p205).
- You have agreed a 'claimant commitment', setting out what you must do to receive your UC. If you have a partner, you must each agree a claimant commitment to get benefit.

# 4. **Amount of benefit**

Universal credit (UC) is payable after seven 'waiting days'. The amount of UC you get depends on your circumstances and, if you have a partner, her/his circumstances. The amount also depends on your and your partner's income and capital. Go through the following steps to work out the amount of UC to which you are entitled.

### Step one: capital

If your capital is over £16,000, you cannot get UC. Some kinds of capital are ignored. For details, see CPAG's *Welfare Benefits and Tax Credits Handbook*.

### Step two: work out your maximum amount

This is worked out by adding together the monthly amounts of the standard allowance and any other elements for which you are eligible.

### Step three: work out your monthly income

Chapter 22 explains how your loan, grant or other income is taken into account.

### Step four: deduct monthly income from maximum amount

If your income is *less* than your maximum amount, UC is the difference between the two. If your income is *the same as or more than* your maximum amount, you cannot get UC.

## Your maximum amount

Work out your maximum amount by adding together your standard allowance and any elements that apply. For the amounts, see xviii. Note that rates are monthly and are from April 2015. **Note:** the government plans to freeze most of the rates for the next four years.[8]

### Standard allowance

You get one standard allowance for yourself and any partner. There are different rates depending on whether you and your partner are under 25, or 25 or over.

### Child element

You get one child element for each dependent child who 'normally lives' with you.[9] The child must be under 16, or aged 16 to 19 and in full-time non-advanced education or approved training.[10] You can only claim for a child up to 31 August following her/his 19th birthday, and s/he must have been under 19 when s/he started her/his education or training. You cannot claim for a child who claims UC, employment and support allowance (ESA) or jobseeker's allowance in her/his own right.

You get an additional amount for a child/young person who gets disability living allowance or personal independence payment. If the child is severely disabled, you get a higher amount.

## Elements for illness

If you meet the medical test for 'limited capability for work' or 'limited capability for work-related activity', you get an extra amount of UC. This is the same as the test used for ESA to assess how much your health or disability limits your ability to work or undertake work-related activity.

## Carer element

You qualify for a carer element if you are entitled to carer's allowance (CA), or you would be entitled to CA except for the fact that your earnings are too high. You must be caring for someone for at least 35 hours a week who is in receipt of certain disability benefits. You cannot get an element for being a carer and for your own illness at the same time.

## Housing costs element

You get an amount for rent or mortgage interest, if you are liable for rent on your home or you own your own home and have a mortgage on it. The amounts are limited and may not pay all your rent or mortgage interest. The housing element of UC is paid directly to you, for you to then pay your landlord. See CPAG's *Welfare Benefits and Tax Credits Handbook* for more information.

## Childcare element

If you are working and have childcare costs, you can get help with up to 70 per cent of these costs (rising to 85 per cent from April 2016), up to a maximum monthly amount. You must be in paid work, but there is no minimum number of hours that you must work. If you have a partner, you must both be in paid work, unless your partner is ill or disabled, or a carer.

### Example

Colum is 23, a full-time, second-year undergraduate in Canterbury and a lone parent of Toni aged two. He lives with his parents and so has no housing costs. He gets a tuition fee loan of £9,000, a loan for living costs of £5,740, a special support grant of £3,387, a parents' learning allowance of £1,523 and a childcare grant of £3,900. He also receives £20.70 a week child benefit.

**During the academic year September 2015 to June 2016:**

| Step one | Colum has no savings or capital. | |
|---|---|---|
| Step two | His maximum amount of UC is: | £ |
| | Standard allowance for himself | 251.77 |
| | Child element | 277.08 |
| | **Total** | **528.85** |

**Step three**     His monthly income is:

Student loan                                                £607.50

The tuition fee loan, special support grant, parents' learning allowance and childcare grant are all disregarded, as is his child benefit. His loan is divided over eight months of the academic year, and £110 of the remaining amount is disregarded (see Chapter 22).

**Step four**     His income is above his maximum amount, so he cannot get UC.

**During the long vacation from June 2016 to September 2016:**

**Step two**     Colum's maximum amount of UC is still £528.85 (at 2015/16 rates).

**Step three**     His weekly income for UC purposes is nil. This is because his student income only counts during the academic year.

**Step four**     From June 2016 to September 2016, his monthly UC is £528.85, so Colum should reclaim over the summer. As Toni is under five years old, Colum may have to undertake certain work-related activity, such as an interview with a work coach, but is not subject to other work-related requirements during this period. If Toni were five or over, he may be subject to work-related requirements such as being available for work, and would face sanctions if he could not meet these requirements.

# 5. **Claiming universal credit**

You usually make a claim for universal credit (UC) online at www.gov.uk/ universal-credit. **Note:** currently, you can only claim if you meet the 'gateway' conditions. Help with online claims over the telephone, telephone claims and face-to-face claims should also be possible if required. If you have a partner, you claim jointly with her/him.

The DWP administers UC, and payments are made monthly in arrears. In exceptional circumstances, you can request alternative payment arrangements – eg, to get paid more regularly, to get the rent element paid directly to your landlord, or to get the payment split between you and your partner. This is a discretionary decision. See CPAG's *Welfare Benefits and Tax Credits Handbook* for more information.

If you are an employee, you do not usually need to report any changes in your earnings, as HM Revenue and Customs provides this information directly to the DWP.

If you do not have enough money to live on while you are waiting for your first payment of UC, you can ask for a short-term advance payment. Short-term advances can also be made when your needs have increased and you are waiting for an extra element of UC to be paid with your next monthly regular payment – eg, when you first have a new baby or become responsible for a child. Awards are at the DWP's discretion. You must repay an advance, usually from the next three months' UC payments. You can also ask for a loan, called a budgeting advance of UC, to meet certain needs once you have been getting UC for six months. Budgeting advances of UC normally must be repaid from your next 12 months' UC payments. See CPAG's *Welfare Benefits and Tax Credits Handbook* for more information.

# 6. Challenging a decision

If you think a decision about your universal credit is wrong, you can ask the DWP to look at it again. This process is known as a 'reconsideration' (the law refers to it as a 'revision'). Provided you ask within the time limit (usually one month), the DWP notifies you of the decision in a 'mandatory reconsideration notice'. If you are still not happy when you get this notice, you can appeal to the independent First-tier Tribunal. If it was not possible to ask the DWP to reconsider the decision within a month, you can ask for a late revision (within 13 months), explaining why it is late. You can also ask the DWP to look at a decision again at any time if certain grounds are met – eg, there has been an official error.

# 7. Other benefits and tax credits

If you come under the universal credit (UC) system, you cannot claim income support, income-based jobseeker's allowance (JSA), income-related employment and support allowance (ESA), housing benefit, child tax credit or working tax credit.

You can still get other benefits, such as carer's allowance, contributory ESA or contribution-based JSA, but they may count as income.

## The benefit cap

Your UC is reduced if your total income from benefits is over the maximum level that you or your partner can receive. The amount is £2,167 a month if you are a lone parent or member of a couple, and £1,517 if you are a single person. **Note:** the government plans to reduce the caps to £1,667 and £1,117 respectively.[11]

The benefits that count towards the cap include child benefit and carer's allowance. If you or your partner are working and earning at least £430 a month, or if you are disabled or a war widow/er, you are exempt from the cap. You are exempt from the cap because of disability if you or your partner get certain disability benefits, including disability living allowance (DLA), personal independence payment (PIP), ESA with a support component, or UC with a limited capability for work-related activity element. You are also exempt if a child or young person for whom you are responsible gets DLA or PIP.

There is protection for nine months before the cap applies if you are no longer working, or are earning less than £430 a month, but were working and earning at least £430 a month for each of the 12 months before this.

## Passported benefits

Provided you meet any other conditions, getting UC entitles you to:
- social fund funeral payments and Sure Start maternity grants;
- free health benefits – eg, dental treatment and prescriptions (see p131 for income thresholds introduced in England from 1 November 2015);
- Healthy Start vouchers and vitamins on a discretionary basis (see p134);
- free school lunches from your local authority.

Note: a requirement may be introduced to have income below a certain level for some or all of these passported benefits.

# Notes

**2. Who is eligible**
1   Reg 12 UC Regs
2   paras H6031 and H6047 ADM
3   Regs 3(2)(b), 13(4) and 14 UC Regs
4   Reg 3(2)(b) UC Regs
5   Reg 8(3) UC Regs
6   Reg 8 and Sch 4 para 4 UC Regs
7   Reg 89 UC Regs

**4. Amount of benefit**
8   clause 9 Welfare Reform and Work Bill 2015
9   Reg 4(2) UC Regs
10  Reg 5 UC Regs

**7. Other benefits and tax credits**
11  clause 7 Welfare Reform and Work Bill 2015

# Chapter 19

# Child tax credit

**This chapter covers:**
1. What is child tax credit (below)
2. Who is eligible (below)
3. Amount of child tax credit (p212)
4. Claiming child tax credit (p214)
5. Challenging a decision (p214)
6. Tax credits and benefits (p215)

### Basic facts
– Child tax credit is paid to families with children.
– Both part-time and full-time students with children can claim.
– The amount you get depends on your income, but most student support is ignored in the assessment.
– You claim from HM Revenue and Customs.

## 1. **What is child tax credit**

Child tax credit (CTC) is a payment made to people with children. It is administered by HM Revenue and Customs and paid whether you are working or not working. Full-time and part-time students with children are eligible to claim. You get a higher amount if you have a child with a disability. The amount of CTC depends on your income in the tax year.

## 2. **Who is eligible**

You qualify for child tax credit (CTC) if you meet all the following conditions.[1]
• You are aged 16 or over.
• You have a dependent child. You can get CTC for a child until 1 September after her/his 16th birthday. If s/he stays on at school, is in other full-time non-advanced education or is on approved training, you can get CTC for her/him

until her/his 19th, or sometimes 20th, birthday.[2] This includes during gaps between one course ending and another starting, provided the young person starts the next course. You can only continue to get CTC for a 19-year-old on a course or training which s/he was accepted on, enrolled on, or started before s/he reached 19 until s/he leaves the course or turns 20, whichever is earlier. You may be able to continue to get CTC for a young person under age 18 for 20 weeks after s/he leaves non-advanced education if s/he has registered for work or training with a qualifying body – eg, the place where your local authority provides careers advice for young people or the Ministry of Defence. If your child lives with someone else part of the time, you should decide between you who has main responsibility, otherwise HM Revenue and Customs decides who gets CTC.

- You are 'present and ordinarily resident' in Britain, are not a 'person subject to immigration control' and have a 'right to reside'. You must normally have been living in the UK for three months before you claim. These terms are explained in CPAG's *Welfare Benefits and Tax Credits Handbook*. Overseas students can get further advice from UKCISA (see Appendix 2).
- Your income is not too high (see Chapter 23).

There are no special rules for students. Both part-time and full-time students are eligible to claim.

## Your parent gets child tax credit for you

If you live with your parent(s), s/he cannot get CTC for you if you are in higher education. As explained above, s/he can continue to get CTC for you until your 19th, or sometimes 20th, birthday if you are in full-time non-advanced education. The course must be one recognised by the government and be more than 12 hours a week, on average, in term time. The course hours include tuition, supervised study, exams, practical work and any exercise or project in the curriculum. Do not count meal breaks or unsupervised study. You count as full time between courses if you are enrolled on another non-advanced course.

Your parent(s) cannot get CTC for you if you get income support, income-based jobseeker's allowance, CTC, working tax credit, employment and support allowance or universal credit in your own right.

If you live with a partner, or are married or in a civil partnership, your parent(s) can only claim CTC for you if your partner is also a young person in full-time non-advanced education or approved training.

In some circumstances, special rules apply – eg, if you are being looked after by a local authority or are in prison or a young offenders' institution.

# 3. **Amount of child tax credit**

The amount of child tax credit (CTC) you get if you are not working and eligible for working tax credit (WTC) depends on your maximum CTC and how much income you have. If you are eligible for WTC (see Chapter 20), you claim both tax credits together and the amount is worked out together. Tax credits are calculated according to a maximum annual amount that you could receive in line with the tax year (6 April – 5 April). However, often an annual award is worked out by adding together amounts calculated over separate periods within the year because, for example, you start a new claim or your circumstances change – eg, you have another child, you cease to be a member of a couple or you start work or increase your hours. What follows, therefore, is a simplification of what is often a very complicated calculation and assumes you are claiming CTC (but not WTC) for a full tax year and have no changes in your circumstances during that year. See CPAG's *Welfare Benefits and Tax Credits Handbook* for the detailed rules.

HM Revenue and Customs (HMRC) has a tax credits calculator at www.gov.uk/ tax-credits-calculator, where you can check how much CTC you are likely to get.

**Note:** the government plans to make various changes to the amount of tax credits you can get from April 2016. This includes freezing many of the amounts, increasing the taper from 41 per cent to 48 per cent and reducing the disregarded increase in income from £5,000 to £2,500.[3]

## Step one: work out your maximum child tax credit

The maximum CTC you can get is made up of:

- **child element** of £2,780 a year for each child; *plus*
- **family element** of £545 a year; *plus*
- **disability element** of £3,140 a year for each child who gets disability living allowance (DLA), personal independence payment (PIP) or is certified as severely sight-impaired or blind; *plus*
- **severe disability element** of £1,275 a year for each child who gets the highest rate care component of DLA or the enhanced rate daily living component of PIP.

These are the maximum amounts for the tax year April 2015 to April 2016. They usually increase each April. You get less than the maximum if your income is above a set threshold.

*Example*
Mairi has two children: Daisy, aged two, and Meena, aged four. Meena has asthma and gets the lowest rate care component of DLA. Mairi's maximum CTC for the tax year April 2015 to April 2016 is:

|                      | £     |
|----------------------|-------|
| Two child elements   | 2,780 |
|                      | 2,780 |
| Family element       | 545   |
| Disability element   | 3,140 |
| **Total maximum CTC**| **9,245** |

Whether she gets maximum CTC or a reduced amount depends on her income.

If your circumstances change so that you should gain or lose an element, tell HMRC so your award can be adjusted. If you should gain an element (eg, you have a new baby), you must tell HMRC within one month, otherwise you do not get the increase fully backdated. The exception to this is that the disability or severe disability elements can be fully backdated if you notify HMRC within one month of the DLA or PIP being awarded.

Other changes must be notified within one month – eg, if you stop being part of a couple. For details, see CPAG's *Welfare Benefits and Tax Credits Handbook*.

### Step two: getting a means-tested benefit

You automatically get maximum CTC if you are getting income support (IS), income-based jobseeker's allowance (JSA), income-related employment and support allowance (ESA) or pension credit (PC).

### Step three: not getting a means-tested benefit

If you do not get IS, income-based JSA, income-related ESA or PC, you must compare your income with a set threshold. The income threshold is £16,105, unless you are working and eligible for WTC. If your income is the same as or below this, you get maximum CTC. If your income is above this threshold, you get a reduced amount. If you or your partner are working and you are eligible for WTC, the income threshold is £6,420 instead of £16,105 (and Step one includes WTC elements).

### Step four: work out your income

How income is calculated for tax credits is covered in Chapter 23. A CTC award for a tax year is usually based on your income in the previous tax year. However, if you expect your income over the current tax year to be more than £2,500 lower than the previous year, or more than £5,000 higher than the previous year, tell HMRC and it reassesses your tax credit. Your award is then based on the current year's income plus £2,500 if it is more than £2,500 lower than in the previous year, or based on the current year's income minus £5,000 if it is more than £5,000 higher than the previous year's award.

### Step five: calculate your child tax credit

If your income is less than or the same as the threshold, you get maximum CTC. If your income is higher than the threshold, work out 41 per cent of the difference.

Your CTC is the amount worked out at Step one minus 41 per cent of the difference between your income and the threshold.

**Note:** this simplified calculation gives an approximate amount of CTC. Amounts are actually calculated using daily rates. See CPAG's *Welfare Benefits and Tax Credits Handbook* for more details.

# 4. Claiming child tax credit

Claim child tax credit (CTC) on Form TC600. You can get a form by phoning the Tax Credit Helpline (see p214) or from a Jobcentre Plus office.

When completing the form, remember to describe your circumstances, such as how many children you have or how many hours you work, as they stand at the time of your claim, but you must list your income as it was in the previous tax year. Bear in mind that HM Revenue and Customs (HMRC) requires your income for a tax year, April to April, even though your student award may run from September.

Your claim can be backdated for up to one month. Your award runs until the end of the tax year, at which point you are sent a renewal form. Your award can change or end during the year. Tell HMRC about changes in your circumstances. You should also tell HMRC if you expect your income that counts for tax credits to decrease by more than £2,500 in the current tax year, or if you expect it to increase by more than £5,000.

CTC and working tax credit are paid directly into a bank account.

## Contacting HM Revenue and Customs

You can report changes of circumstances or make enquiries to the Tax Credit Helpline on 0345 300 3900 (textphone 0345 300 3909) between 8am and 8pm, Monday to Friday, and 8am and 4pm on Saturdays. It is often very difficult to get through to the Helpline. If you cannot get through during the week, try on Saturdays when it is sometimes less busy.

# 5. Challenging a decision

If you think a decision about your child tax credit is wrong, you can ask HM Revenue and Customs (HMRC) to look at it again. This process is known as a 'reconsideration' (the law refers to it as a 'review'). Provided you ask within the time limit (usually 30 days), HMRC notifies you of the decision in a 'mandatory reconsideration notice'. If you are still not happy when you get this notice, you can appeal to the independent First-tier Tribunal. If it was not possible to ask HMRC to reconsider the decision within 30 days, you can ask for a late review (within 13 months), explaining why it is late. You can also ask HMRC to look at a decision again at any time if certain grounds are met – eg, there has been an official error.

If you want to complain about the way your claim has been dealt with, write to the Tax Credit Office, Preston PR1 4AT.

If you have been overpaid, the leaflet COP26, *What Happens if We've Paid You Too Much Tax Credit,* explains when the overpayment can be written off and what you need to do. HMRC sets out what you are expected to do to ensure your claim is correct and what you can expect of HMRC. If you have met all your responsibilities and HMRC has failed to meet one of its, the overpayment should not be recovered. This leaflet also explains when you can ask to repay an amount owed over a longer period. If an overpayment is challenged, it should not be recovered until the dispute is resolved. If you want to dispute recovery of an overpayment, HMRC expects you to do so within three months.

# 6. **Tax credits and benefits**

## **Means-tested benefits**

Child tax credit (CTC) is not taken into account as income for income support, income-based jobseeker's allowance or income-related employment and support allowance, although working tax credit (WTC) is.

Tax credits are taken into account as income for housing benefit. If a tax credit overpayment from a previous year is being deducted, the amount of the tax credit award less the deduction is taken into account. If you have been overpaid in the same year as the award and the tax credit award is consequently reduced, the lower amount of the award still to be paid to you is taken into account.

Arrears of tax credits are treated as capital for means-tested benefits and disregarded for 52 weeks.

CTC is taken into account when calculating whether the benefit cap applies (see p154). If you or your partner get WTC, the benefit cap does not apply.

## **Child benefit**

Child benefit is paid in addition to tax credits. It is ignored as income in the tax credit assessment.

## **Passported benefits**

Getting CTC or WTC may entitle you to other benefits. You may be able to get the following.
* Free school lunches from the local authority. Your income for tax credit purposes must be no more than £16,105 a year. You must get CTC but not be

eligible for WTC, unless your income for tax credit purposes is no more than £6,420, or you are getting the four-week run-on of WTC because you have reduced your hours or stopped work.[4]

- Health benefits, such as free prescriptions, dental treatment and vouchers for glasses. Your income for tax credit purposes must be no more than £15,276 and you must be getting CTC or WTC with a disability element. See Chapter 11 for other ways to qualify for health benefits.
- Sure Start maternity grant (if there is no child under 16 in the household already) or a funeral payment. Your CTC must be paid at the maximum rate or at a level above just the family element alone – eg, above £545. You also qualify if you get WTC with a disability or severe disability element.
- Healthy Start food vouchers. If you have a child under four, or you are pregnant, and get CTC but are not entitled to WTC (except during the four-week run-on period) and have an annual income for tax credit purposes of no more than £16,190, you may be eligible for Healthy Start food vouchers and free vitamins.[5]

# Notes

**2. Who is eligible**
1 Regs 3-5 CTC Regs
2 Reg 5 CTC Regs

**3. Amount of child tax credit**
3 Summer Budget 2015, paras 1.137,
  1.144 and 2.104

**6. Tax credits and benefits**
4 The Education (Free School Lunches)
  (Prescribed Tax Credits) (England)
  Order 2003, No. 383; The Education
  (Free School Lunches) (Prescribed Tax
  Credits) (Wales) Order 2003, No.879
5 HSS&WF(A) Regs

# Chapter 20

## Working tax credit

**This chapter covers:**
1. What is working tax credit (below)
2. Who is eligible (p218)
3. Amount of working tax credit (p219)
4. Claiming working tax credit (p221)
5. Challenging a decision (p222)
6. Tax credits and benefits (p222)

*Basic facts*

- Working tax credit is paid to top up low wages.
- Both part-time and full-time students are eligible to claim.
- You may be eligible if you are over 25 and working at least 30 hours a week.
- You may be eligible if you are working at least 16 or 24 hours a week and you have a child, a disability or are over 60.
- You can get help with childcare costs in your working tax credit.
- The amount you get depends on your income, but most student support is ignored in the assessment.
- You claim from HM Revenue and Customs.

## 1. **What is working tax credit**

Working tax credit (WTC) helps supplement low wages. It is administered by HM Revenue and Customs. It is paid to people who are working (employed or self-employed) for at least 16 hours a week or, in some cases, 24 or 30 hours a week. Full-time and part-time students are eligible to claim. You get a higher amount if you work 30 hours a week or have a disability. You can get childcare costs paid with WTC. The amount of WTC you get depends on your income in the tax year.

## 2. **Who is eligible**

You qualify for working tax credit (WTC) if you meet all of the following conditions.

- You are working sufficient hours and have a child or a disability, or you meet certain age conditions (see below).
- You are 'present and ordinarily resident' in the UK and not a 'person subject to immigration control'. These terms are explained in CPAG's *Welfare Benefits and Tax Credits Handbook*.
- Your income is not too high (see p221).

There are no special rules for students. Both part-time and full-time students are eligible to claim.

### Qualifying hours

To get WTC, you must work sufficient hours and meet other conditions. There are four ways to qualify.[1]

- **You have a child living with you.** You are eligible if:
  - you are aged 16 or over; *and*
  - you are working at least 16 hours a week and you are single or your partner is incapacitated, in hospital or prison, or gets carer's allowance, or you are a member of a couple and you are working at least 16 hours a week and between you and your partner you are working at least 24 hours a week; *and*
  - you have a dependent child. The rules are the same as for child tax credit (see p210).
- **You are a disabled worker.** You are eligible if:
  - you are aged 16 or over; *and*
  - you are working 16 hours or more a week; *and*
  - you have a disability that puts you at a disadvantage in getting a job and you pass a disability benefit test. This has a list of activities or functions concerned with mobility, manual dexterity, vision, hearing, speech, fits, mental disability, severe pain and rehabilitation. If you are unable to satisfy one of these, you pass the disadvantage test. HM Revenue and Customs (HMRC) may contact a doctor or medical professional to confirm this. You pass the disability benefit test if you get certain benefits such as disability living allowance or personal independence payment, or in the past six months you have been getting other benefits such as the higher rate of short-term or long-term incapacity benefit, employment and support allowance for at least 28 weeks, or a disability premium in a means-tested benefit. For more details, see CPAG's *Welfare Benefits and Tax Credits Handbook*. The test is also detailed in the notes for the claim form, TC600.

- **You are over 25.** You are eligible if:
  - you are aged 25 or over; *and*
  - you are working 30 hours or more a week.
- **You are over 60.** You are eligible if:
  - you are aged 60 or over; *and*
  - you are working 16 hours or more a week.

In each case, the work you do must be paid work. It must be expected to continue for at least four weeks from the time you claim WTC. This means you can claim WTC for work during long vacations but not during short vacations unless you will be working for at least four weeks. You can also claim during term time if you normally work sufficient hours to qualify. You must tell HMRC when you stop work, or if your hours reduce below the level required to qualify for WTC. In either case, your WTC award continues for another four weeks (called the 'four-week run-on').

## 3. **Amount of working tax credit**

The amount of working tax credit (WTC) you get depends on your maximum WTC and how much income you have. Tax credits are calculated according to a maximum annual amount that you could receive in line with the tax year (6 April – 5 April). However, often awards must be calculated on part years because of changes in your circumstances – eg, you have another child, you cease to be a member of a couple or you change your hours of work. What follows, therefore, is a simplification of what is often a very complicated calculation and assumes you are claiming for a full tax year and have no changes in your circumstances during that year. See CPAG's *Welfare Benefits and Tax Credits Handbook* for the detailed rules.

**Note:** the government plans to make various changes to the amount of tax credits you can get from April 2016. This includes freezing many of the amounts, reducing the income threshold from £6,420 to £3,850, increasing the taper from 41 per cent to 48 per cent and reducing the disregarded increase in income from £5,000 to £2,500.[2]

The government website has tax credit pages at www.gov.uk/topic/benefits-credits/tax-credits. You can use these to check whether you qualify and how much WTC you are likely to get.

The way in which WTC is calculated is the same as for child tax credit (CTC – see p212), except that the threshold with which your income is compared is always £6,420. First, work out your maximum WTC (and add the maximum CTC, if applicable). Then work out your income (see Chapter 23). Use your income for the previous tax year, unless the current year's income is more than £2,500 lower (in which case use the current year's income plus £2,500), or more than £5,000 higher than this (in which case use the current year's income minus £5,000). Finally, work out 41 per cent of the amount by which your income exceeds £6,420, and subtract this from your maximum WTC.

**Note:** this simplified calculation gives an approximate amount of WTC. Amounts are actually calculated using daily rates. See CPAG's *Welfare Benefits and Tax Credits Handbook* for more details.

The maximum WTC you can get is made up of a **basic element** of £1,960 a year plus whichever one or more of the following elements apply:

- **lone parent/couple element** of £2,010 a year;
- **30-hour element** of £810 a year if you work at least 30 hours a week (you can add your hours to your partner's if you have a child);
- **disability element** of £2,970 a year if you qualify for WTC as a disabled worker (see p218);
- **severe disability element** of £1,275 a year if you get the highest rate care component of disability living allowance (DLA) or the enhanced rate of the daily living component of personal independence payment;
- **childcare element.** You can get up to 70 per cent of your childcare costs up to a limit of £175 a week for one child or £300 for two or more children – ie, a maximum of £122.50 or £210. The childcare must be of a certain type, including a registered childminder, nursery or playscheme, an out-of-hours club or sitters service. You do not get help with childcare at home provided by a relative. To get the childcare element you must be a lone parent, or a couple and either both of you are working 16 hours or more a week, or one of you is incapacitated, in hospital or in prison.

These are the amounts for the tax year April 2015 to April 2016. The maximum amounts usually go up each April. You will get less than the maximum if your income is more than a set threshold.

*Examples*

Sian is 26. She does not work during the academic year, but in the summer vacation she gets a job for 30 hours a week and expects to work for nine weeks. Sian is eligible to claim WTC. Whether any WTC is payable depends on the level of her wages and other income.

Katherine and Spencer have a four-year-old child at nursery school. Katherine is a student and Spencer works 24 hours a week. Katherine works 16 hours a week during the summer only. They are eligible for WTC throughout the year. During the summer they can get a 30-hour element included in their WTC and they can also claim help with nursery charges.

Morag is a full-time student on a Higher National Certificate course. She has an eight-year-old daughter. She works 20 hours a week. Her income is a student loan, a parents' learning allowance, a childcare grant of £110 and earnings of £7,800 in the tax year, April 2015 to April 2016. In the previous tax year 2014/15, she worked full time and earned £15,000. Her maximum tax credits are:

|  | £ |
|---|---|
| CTC family element | 545 |
| CTC child element | 2,780 |
| WTC basic element | 1,960 |
| WTC lone parent element | 2,010 |
| **Total maximum tax credits** | **7,295** |

Her income this year is more than £2,500 lower than last year when she was working full time, so this year's income plus £2,500 is used.
Her income is £7,800 + £2,500 = £10,300
(her student income is ignored – see Chapter 23)
The threshold is £6,420.
Income minus threshold is £10,300 – £6,420 = £3,880
41% x £3,800 = £1,590.80
Maximum tax credits of £7,295 is reduced by £1,590.80.
Morag gets tax credits of £5,704.20, or about £110 a week.

The income threshold is £6,420. If your income is below this, you get maximum WTC. If your income is above this threshold, you get a reduced amount. See Chapter 23 for what income counts in the assessment.

If your circumstances change so that you could gain or lose an element, tell HM Revenue and Customs so your award can be adjusted. If you should gain an element (eg, because your hours of work increase or you incur eligible childcare costs), you must tell HMRC within one month, otherwise you do not get the increase fully backdated. The exception to this is that the disability or severe disability elements can be fully backdated if you notify HMRC within one month of DLA being awarded.

Some changes must be reported within one month – eg, if you stop working.

## 4. **Claiming working tax credit**

There is one claim form (Form TC600) for both child tax credit (CTC) and working tax credit (WTC). This is available by phoning the Tax Credit Helpline (0345 300 3900) or from a Jobcentre Plus office.

Your claim can be backdated for up to one month.

Any childcare element of WTC is paid to the main carer directly into a bank account. Otherwise WTC is paid into the bank account of the person in work.

When you claim, the form asks for your income in the previous tax year (see Chapter 23). Your income might be very different this year. When you get your initial award, tell HMRC straight away how much your income is expected to be in the current year if it will be more than £2,500 lower or more than £5,000 higher than the previous year.

## 5. Challenging a decision

If you think a decision about your working tax credit is wrong, you can ask HM Revenue and Customs (HMRC) to look at it again. This process is known as a 'reconsideration' (the law refers to it as a 'review'). Provided you ask within the time limit (usually 30 days), HMRC notifies you of the decision in a 'mandatory reconsideration notice'. If you are still not happy when you get this notice, you can appeal to the independent First-tier Tribunal. If it was not possible to ask HMRC to reconsider the decision within 30 days, you can ask for a late review (within 13 months), explaining why it is late. You can also ask HMRC to look at a decision again at any time if certain grounds are met – eg, there has been an official error.

If HMRC has overpaid you, see p215.

## 6. Tax credits and benefits

If you or your partner get working tax credit (WTC), the benefit cap does not apply.

See p215 for details of how WTC affects benefits.

## Notes

### 2. Who is eligible
1 Reg 4 The Working Tax Credit
(Entitlement and Maximum Rate)
Regulations 2002, No.2005

### 3. Amount of working tax credit
2 Summer Budget 2015, paras 1.137,
1.144 and 2.104

# Part 3

············································································

# Treatment of student income

# Chapter 21

# How income affects means-tested benefits

**This chapter covers:**

*Basic facts*
- Student loans for living costs are normally divided over 42 or 43 weeks from the beginning of September to the end of June and taken into account as income for means-tested benefits during that period. If your income is too high, you do not get income support, income-based jobseeker's allowance or income-related employment and support allowance during those weeks, and your housing benefit is reduced.
- Student loans for living costs are normally not taken into account as income for means-tested benefits from around the end of June until the beginning of September. You may be able to get income support or more housing benefit during these months, even if your income was too high during the academic year.
- Some student support does not affect the amount of means-tested benefits you can receive.

This chapter explains how your weekly income affects your entitlement to income support, income-based jobseeker's allowance, income-related employment and support allowance and housing benefit. For information on how income affects universal credit, see Chapter 22. See also Chapter 23 for how your income is assessed for tax credits and Chapter 24 for health benefits.

# 1. **Working out your income**

The way that student income is taken into account for income support (IS), income-based jobseeker's allowance (JSA), income-related employment and support allowance (ESA) and housing benefit (HB) is essentially the same. Chapters 10, 12 and 13 outline the ESA, IS and HB assessments step by step. This chapter explains how much weekly income counts in these assessments.

**Note:** if you or your partner have reached the qualifying age for pension credit (PC) and are not getting IS or income-based JSA, your student support is ignored as income for HB.

| | |
|---|---|
| Step one | **Add together the annual income from grants and loans.** Add together the annual amount of any student grants and/or loans for living costs, ignoring elements that are wholly disregarded. |
| Step two | **Apply annual disregards.** From the total annual grants and loans for living costs, deduct any disregarded amounts for books, equipment and travel. |
| Step three | **Divide income into a weekly amount.** Divide the annual amount of grants and loans for living costs by the number of benefit weeks in the period over which the grant and loan are counted as income for benefit purposes. |
| Step four | **Deduct any weekly disregard.** If you have a student loan for living costs, deduct £10 a week – this is the weekly disregard. |
| Step five | **Add other income to the weekly amount of grant and loan for living costs.** Add together any other weekly income – eg, from hardship funds (p238), professional and career development loans (p239), earnings (p240), tariff income from capital (p242), and benefits and tax credits (p241) – ignoring any amount that is disregarded. This total, added to the weekly grant and loan total in Step four, is the amount of income used in the benefit assessment. |

If you want to work out benefit entitlement during the long vacation, p234 explains when the long vacation starts and finishes for benefit purposes – ie, when your student loan or grant counts as nil income. You should then total on a weekly basis any other income you have over the vacation.

## 2. **Grants and loans**

### Grants

In general, grants intended for living costs are taken into account as income, and grants for other costs (such as books, travel, equipment, childcare or course-related support for disabilities) are disregarded. For the way that hardship funds are treated, see p238.

If you are a full-time undergraduate assessed for support in England, Wales or Northern Ireland and receive a special support grant, this is disregarded as it is paid for course-related costs.[1] If you receive a maintenance grant (eg, if you are the partner of a jobseeker's allowance (JSA) or income support (IS) claimant), this is taken into account in full as it is paid for living costs.

If you are *not* eligible for a student loan, deduct from your grant the following disregarded amounts:

- £390 for books and equipment;
- £303 for travel.

### Higher education grants

The following higher education grants are completely disregarded:

- grant for tuition fees;[2]
- grant for full-time 'old system' (see p25) undergraduate students in England and Wales;[3]
- special support grant for full-time undergraduate students in England, Wales and Northern Ireland;[4]
- childcare grant;
- disabled students' allowance;[5]
- Welsh government learning grant for 'old system' (see p48) students;
- parents' learning allowance;
- travel expenses;[6]
- course costs grant for part-time undergraduate students;[7]
- institutional bursaries paid for anything other than living costs.[8]

The following grants are taken into account:

- maintenance grant for full-time undergraduate students assessed in England and Northern Ireland;
- Welsh government learning grant for 'current system' (see p48) students in Wales;
- maintenance bursary for full-time 'old system' (see p61) undergraduate students assessed in Northern Ireland;
- adult dependants' grant;
- institutional bursaries paid for living costs.

## Healthcare student allowances
The following grants are taken into account:
- means-tested NHS bursary for degree-level healthcare courses in England and Wales;
- means-tested Department of Health, Social Services and Public Safety (DHSSPS) bursary for degree-level healthcare courses in Northern Ireland;
- non-means-tested NHS bursary for nursing, midwifery or operation department practitioner students in England and degree-level nursing courses in Wales;
- non-means-tested DHSSPS bursary for nursing and midwifery students in Northern Ireland;
- dependants' grants for healthcare students (for housing benefit (HB) and some existing IS, JSA and employment and support allowance (ESA) claimants with no child tax credit (CTC) award);[9]
- single parent addition.

The following grants are disregarded:
- childcare allowances;
- disabled students' allowance;[10]
- parents' learning allowance;
- travel expenses.[11]

## Other grants for vocational courses
The following are taken into account:
- NHS social work student bursary in England;[12]
- Care Council for Wales social work student bursary in Wales;
- DHSSPS social work incentive bursary in Northern Ireland;
- initial teacher training incentive bursaries.[13]

The following are disregarded:
- travel expenses.

## Postgraduate grants
Postgraduate maintenance grants and dependants' grants awarded by a research council, or for postgraduate social work students, are taken into account in the same way as for undergraduates (see p227). **You should ignore the following:**
- disabled students' allowance;
- grants for tuition fees;
- grants for residential study away from your normal home;
- grants intended to meet the costs of books and equipment.

## Further education grants
The following further education grants are disregarded:
- education maintenance allowance;[14]

- 16–19 bursary fund payments;[15]
- Care to Learn grants paid for childcare costs;
- childcare bursaries paid through the discretionary support funds;
- residential bursaries paid through the discretionary support funds (IS/JSA/ESA only);
- Welsh government learning grant for further education;
- the Northern Irish further education grant;
- additional grant allowances for disabled students.

The maintenance element of further education and advanced further education awards in Northern Ireland, subject to the standard disregard for travel, books and equipment, is **taken into account in full**.

## Student loans

### Student loan for fees
Loans for fees are disregarded.[16]

### Student loan for living costs
You should include in the student loan:
- the maximum loan for which you are eligible. This is taken into account as your income whether or not you apply for it.[17] This means that students cannot choose to apply for maximum IS rather than applying for a loan. You are simply treated as though you had taken out the full loan and your benefit is reduced accordingly;
- the assessed contribution from a parent or partner, whether or not you receive it. For IS, however, if you are a lone parent or a disabled student, only include contributions that are actually paid;[18]
- any payments for extra weeks of attendance.

Deduct from the annual student loan £390 for books and equipment and £303 for travel.[19] There is a further disregard of £10 a week that applies once the student loan has been divided into the relevant weekly amount (see p234).

**Note:** the government plans to abolish maintenance grants and special support grants for new students from September 2016 (see p30). Poorer students will be entitled to a higher student loan, to offset their loss. Part of this loan will be disregarded for students who previously would have received a special support grant. However, at the time of writing, regulations had not yet been laid.

### Professional and career development loan
How professional and career development loans are treated depends on what they are paid for. Disregard any amounts paid for:
- tuition fees;
- course costs.

Any amounts paid for living costs are treated as income. This amount should be divided over the period for which the loan is paid.[20]

## Professional studies loan

Loans paid to postgraduate students by banks for vocational study are treated in the same way as professional and career development loans (see p229). These have been discontinued in most cases, but may be relevant to older claim periods.

## Grants and loans checklist

| Student support | Treatment |
|---|---|
| **Further education income** | |
| 16–19 bursary fund | Disregarded |
| 24+ advanced learning loan | Disregarded |
| Care to Learn grant | Disregarded |
| Discretionary support funds/Financial Contingency Fund/hardship funds payment | Taken into account if paid for basic living costs regularly; disregarded if paid for other items |
| Education maintenance allowance | Disregarded |
| Northern Ireland bursary | Taken into account except:<br>– £390 a year for books and equipment;<br>– £303 a year for travel |
| Welsh government learning grant | Disregarded |
| **Undergraduate income** | |
| Adult dependant's grant | Taken into account in full |
| Care leavers' vacation grant (Northern Ireland) | Taken into account in full |
| Childcare grant | Disregarded |
| Course costs grant (part-time undergraduates) | Usually disregarded (as it is less than the general books/equipment and travel disregards) |
| Disabled students' allowance | Disregarded |
| Hardship funds | Taken into account if paid for basic living costs regularly (as capital if not regular payments); disregarded if paid for other items |
| Higher education grant ('old system' full-time undergraduates) | Disregarded |
| Higher education maintenance grant ('current system' full-time undergraduates) | Taken into account in full |

| | |
|---|---|
| Higher education special support grant ('current system' full-time undergraduates) | Disregarded |
| NHS bursary/nursing and midwifery bursary | Taken into account, except: <br>– £390 a year for books and equipment; <br>– £303 a year for travel |
| NHS dependants' grant | Taken into account |
| Parents' learning allowance | Disregarded |
| Social work bursary (England and Wales) | Any element for non-living costs, such as travel or tuition fee costs, disregarded; remainder taken into account in full |
| Social work bursary (Northern Ireland) | Taken into account in full except any element for travel costs |
| Student loan for fees | Disregarded |
| Student loan for living costs | Taken into account except: <br>– £390 a year for books and equipment; <br>– £303 a year for travel; <br>– £10 a week; <br>– amount of student's contribution to loan; <br>– partner's contribution |
| Travelling expenses | Disregarded |
| Welsh government learning grant ('old system' full-time undergraduates) | Disregarded |
| Welsh government learning grant ('current system' full-time undergraduates) | Taken into account in full |
| **Postgraduate income** | |
| Research council maintenance grant | Taken into account except: <br>– £390 a year for books and equipment; <br>– £303 a year for travel |
| Research council tuition fees | Disregarded |
| Research supplementary grants | As for undergraduate income |
| Social work bursary | Taken into account in full |
| Teaching training bursary/salary | Taken into account in full |
| **Other** | |
| Institutional bursary | Tuition and course cost payments disregarded; payments for living costs taken into account |

| Professional and career development loan | Tuition and course cost payments disregarded; payments for living costs taken into account |
| Professional study loan | Tuition and course cost payments disregarded; payments for living costs taken into account |

## 3. **Dividing student income throughout the year**

The annual amount of your loan and grant is divided over the number of weeks in, usually, a standard academic year to arrive at the weekly amount that is used to calculate your income support (IS), income-based jobseeker's allowance (JSA), income-related employment and support allowance (ESA) and housing benefit (HB). Rules specify the weeks over which the loan and grant are taken into account.

If your loan covers extra weeks of study beyond the usual academic year (a long course loan), the extra weeks' loan is added to the rest of the loan. However, it does not extend the number of weeks over which your loan is taken into account for benefit purposes.

### Grants

#### Higher education grant

The higher education maintenance grant for full-time 'current system' undergraduate students who do not have a benefits claim in their own right, and the adult dependants' grant paid by the Department for Business, Innovation and Skills, the Welsh government or the Department for Employment and Learning in Northern Ireland (DELNI), are taken into account over the duration of the course, whether it comprises 52 weeks or fewer. They are treated as income over the same period as the student loan, if you have one or are eligible for one.[21] This is the case even though government guidance says that such grants cover 52 weeks.

*Examples*

Dave receives a student loan of £8,009 and a maintenance grant of £3,387 to do his full-time undergraduate degree in London. This is his first year and his first term begins on Monday 5 October 2015. Dave lives with his partner, Kareen, and their two children. Kareen claims JSA and her benefit week starts on a Monday. Dave's student loan and maintenance grant are taken into account when working out Kareen's JSA. His student loan and maintenance grant are divided over the 42 weeks from Monday 7 September 2015 to Sunday 26 June 2016. However, as he is a first-year student, his loan and grant are not taken into account until he starts his course on Monday 5 October. So, from Monday 7 September until Sunday 4 October 2015, his student loan and grant income are not taken into account for Kareen's benefit purposes. From Monday 5 October 2015 to Sunday 26 June 2016, his student loan and grant income are included in the calculation to determine the amount of JSA Kareen receives. From Monday 27 June until Sunday 4 September 2016, his student loan and grant income is nil again for benefit purposes.

## Healthcare student bursaries

There are two types of bursary available to students on healthcare courses. A non-means-tested bursary is available in England for nursing, midwifery and operation department practitioner students studying a diploma course, and in Northern Ireland for nursing and midwifery students on both degree and diploma courses. If you are studying for a degree in England, Wales or Northern Ireland, a means-tested bursary and a non-means-tested grant are available. In addition, you can receive a non-means-tested reduced-rate loan.

Dependants' grants and other allowances may be means tested (see Chapter 2).

The income from both types of bursary, dependants' allowance and single parent addition are taken into account. As these are paid in monthly instalments, they are taken into account over 52 weeks. The reduced-rate loan should be treated over the same period as other student loans. The NHS childcare grant is disregarded in full.

## Social work bursaries

Social work bursaries in England and Wales should be taken into account for the period they are paid. In England, this is 52 weeks.

In England, the element paid for travelling expenses should be disregarded.[22] However, this is not usually specifically identified, so benefits offices may take the full bursary into account. Speak to an adviser for assistance.

Any amount paid for tuition fees (eg, to an 'old system' student) should also be disregarded.

In Northern Ireland, the social work incentive bursary is taken into account in full, but any element paid for travel costs should be disregarded.

## Postgraduate grants

A postgraduate award that is assessed for study throughout the calendar year is taken into account for the number of benefit weeks within the full calendar year.[23]

Students on a Postgraduate Certificate in Education (or Postgraduate Diploma in Education) course may get the same student loan and grants as undergraduates, and these are treated in the same way as undergraduate loans and grants. Teacher training bursaries/salaries are treated as grants.

### If you leave your course early

For IS, income-based JSA and income-related ESA, if you abandon your course or are dismissed from it, your grant continues to be taken into account until the end of the term or vacation in which you stop being a full-time student or, if earlier, until you repay the grant or the period for which the grant is payable ends.[24]

For HB, your grant is taken into account until the grant provider asks you to repay it.[25]

## Student loan for living costs

For autumn term starters, student loans are normally divided over 42 or 43 weeks from the beginning of September to the end of June. During this period, your student loan is taken into account as income in the assessment of IS, income-based JSA, income-related ESA and HB. If your income is too high, you are not eligible for these benefits. However, your student loan is not taken into account from around the end of June to the beginning of September. Because your income decreases in these months (unless you have other income – eg, earnings), you may be able to get benefit during the summer. It is important, therefore, to make a claim from the end of June, even if you were refused benefit at the start of the academic year. Make your claim in mid-June or earlier so that your benefit can start as soon as you are entitled.

### Courses starting in the autumn term lasting more than a year

The student loan is divided over the number of weeks starting from the first day of the first benefit week in September until the last day of the last benefit week in June.[26] In 2015/16 this is 42 weeks for benefit weeks that begin on a Monday or Saturday and 43 weeks for benefit weeks that begin on a Tuesday, Wednesday, Thursday or Friday. If your course starts in August, you count the weeks starting from the first day of the first benefit week on or after the start of your course, until the last day of the last benefit week in June.

This is the period over which your loan is taken into account as income in the benefit assessment, unless you do not count as a student at all. For example, at the start of your first year, you do not count as being a student until you actually start attending or undertaking the course. In other words, in the first year, the loan is still divided over 42/43 weeks, but the weekly amount arrived at is ignored as income until you start your course.

In the final year of study, the loan is divided over the number of benefit weeks starting from the first day of the first benefit week in September (or the start of the last day of the final term if it starts in August) until the end of the benefit week on or before the last day of the final academic term.[27]

For HB, the start of the benefit week is a Monday. For IS, JSA and ESA, it depends on your national insurance (NI) number.

*Example: first year, 'current system' higher education student in England*
Jean is in her first year at university. She has one child aged two and is claiming HB as a lone parent. She gets a loan of £9,000 for her fees, which is disregarded, and a student loan for living costs of £8,009 for studying in London, which is not. She also gets a special support grant of £3,387, a parents' learning allowance of £1,573 and a childcare grant of £100 a week, all of which are disregarded for IS and HB.
Her first term begins on Monday 5 October 2015. Her IS benefit week starts on a Monday. Her student loan is divided over the weeks from Monday 7 September 2015 until Sunday 26 June 2016 (42 weeks). However, as she is a first-year student, her loan is not taken into account until she starts her course on Monday 5 October. So, from Monday 7 September until Sunday 4 October 2015, her student loan income is not taken into account for benefit purposes. From Monday 5 October 2015 to Sunday 26 June 2016, her weekly student loan income is £164.19 for benefit purposes. From Monday 27 June until Sunday 4 September 2016, her student loan income is nil again for benefit purposes.

| | £ |
|---|---|
| The weekly loan income taken into account is: | |
| Loan | 8,009 |
| *Less* disregards for books and equipment (£390) and travel (£303) = | 7,316 |
| Divided by 42 weeks = | 174.19 |
| *Less* £10 weekly loan disregard = | 164.19 |

£164.19 is taken into account as weekly income from her loan between 5 October 2015 and 26 June 2016. She also receives £63.94 a week child tax credit which brings her weekly income for HB purposes to £228.13.

Her IS applicable amount is £73.10 and her HB applicable amount is £157.45 a week. From Monday 5 October 2015 to Sunday 26 June 2016, she is not entitled to IS because her income is higher than the IS applicable amount; her HB is reduced by £45.94 a week – 65 per cent of the excess (see p151). From Monday 27 June until Sunday 4 September 2016, her weekly income from her loan and grants is nil. Jean should claim IS again on 27 June 2016. **Note:** as UC is rolled out, a new claim may need to be for UC.

*Example: final year, 'current system' higher education student in Northern Ireland*
Graham is in his final year. He is claiming IS as a disabled student studying at Queens University, Belfast. He gets a student loan of £4,480. His parents are assessed to make a contribution of £890 towards his living costs, but this year they are refusing to pay. The parental contribution is not taken into account in the calculation because he is a disabled student.

His first term started on Tuesday 8 September 2015 and his final term ends on Friday 10 June 2016. His student loan is divided over the weeks from Monday 7 September 2015 until Sunday 5 June 2016 (39 weeks).

| The weekly loan income taken into account is: | £ |
|---|---|
| Loan | 4,480 |
| *Less* disregards for books and equipment (£390) and travel (£303) = | 3,787 |
| Divided by 39 weeks = | 97.10 |
| *Less* £10 weekly loan disregard = | 87.10 |

£87.10 is taken into account as weekly income from his loan between 7 September 2015 and 5 June 2016.

## Courses not starting in the autumn term

Your student loan is divided over the number of weeks starting from the first day of the first benefit week on or after the beginning of a standard academic year and ending on the last day of the last benefit week on or before the last day of the academic year, but excluding benefit weeks that fall entirely within the quarter that is taken by the DWP to be the longest vacation.[28]

### Academic years

'Academic years' are the 12 months beginning on 1 January, 1 April or 1 July for courses that begin in winter, spring or summer respectively.[29]

'Quarters' are 1 January to 31 March, 1 April to 30 June, 1 July to 31 August, 1 September to 31 December.[30]

### Example

Madeleine's course begins on Monday 4 January 2016. The main vacation is 3 June to 12 September 2016. She is claiming HB. Her loan is divided over the weeks from Monday 4 January 2016 to Sunday 26 June 2016 and from Monday 5 September 2016 until Sunday 25 December 2016. From 27 June 2016 to 4 September 2016, her student loan income is nil for benefit purposes.

## Courses lasting one year or less

Your loan is divided over the number of weeks from the first day of the first benefit week on or after the start of a standard academic year until the last day of the last benefit week on or before the last day of the final term. The academic year is taken to begin on 1 September, 1 January, 1 April or 1 July, depending on whether your course begins in the autumn, winter, spring or summer. The resulting weekly amount is then taken into account from the point you actually start attending or undertaking the course.

## If you leave your course early

If you abandon your course early or are dismissed from it before you have had the final instalment of your student loan in that academic year, the loan continues to be taken into account up until the end of the term in which you leave. The end of term is taken to be the end of December if you leave in the autumn term, the end of March if you leave in the winter term, the end of June if you leave in the spring term and the end of August if you leave in the summer.

The amount of loan taken into account is that which remains from the loan that was paid from the start of the standard academic year (eg, 1 September for students whose courses begin in the autumn – see p234) to the end of the term in which you left, having subtracted that part of the loan (including disregards for books, equipment and travel) that would have been treated as your weekly income in a normal benefits calculation up until the day you left.[31] The example below illustrates how this amount is calculated.[32]

*Example*

Nick studies in Birmingham. He abandons his course on 2 November 2015. He is in the second year of a three-year course and is claiming IS. His benefit week starts on a Monday.

**Work out weekly amount of annual loan**

|  | £ |
|---|---|
| Loan | 5,740 |
| *Less* disregards (£693) = | 5,047 |
| Divided by 42 weeks = | 120.17 |

**Work out amount of loan prior to leaving the course**
Multiply the weekly amount of annual loan by the number of benefit weeks from the week after the one that includes the start of the academic year until the end of the benefit week that includes the day Nick left the course.
Multiply weekly loan (£120.17) by nine weeks
(7 September to 8 November 2015) = 1,081.53

**Work out amount of loan since leaving the course**
To do this, add the loan instalments paid for the terms up to the one in which Nick left, deduct disregards and deduct the loan worked out for the period prior to leaving.

|  | £ |
|---|---|
| Loan up to end of term (33% x 5,740) = | 1,894.20 |
| *Less* disregards (£693) = | 1,201.20 |
| Deduct amount of loan prior to leaving (£1,081.53) = | 119.67 |

> **Work out weekly amount of loan from leaving course to end of term**
> Divide the total amount of loan for the period since leaving the course by the number of weeks left in the term. Count from the benefit week that includes the day Nick left the course until the benefit week that includes the end of term – ie, end of December, March, June or August.
> Divide £119.67 by seven weeks
> (9 November 2015 to 27 December 2015) =          £17.10
> £17.10 a week is taken into account from 9 November 2015 until 27 December 2015.

If you leave your course nearer to the end of term, this formula could result in there being no loan income taken into account for the remainder of the term. **Note:** if you repay the loan, it is nevertheless taken into account as income until the end of term.[33] So you could be refused benefit despite having no other money to live on. However, if your funder asks you to repay the loan rather than your repaying voluntarily, guidance tells DWP decision makers to disregard the loan as income from the date of the request.[34]

---

# 4. **Discretionary funds and other payments**

## Hardship funds

Discretionary funds paid by colleges and universities for course or living costs may be called hardship funds, the Access to Learning Fund (although this no longer exists, institutions may still refer to it), the Financial Contingency Fund or other discretionary support funds.[35] Hardship funds are treated differently from student grants and loans. In general, if these funds are paid for course costs, they should be disregarded. If they are paid for living costs, they should be treated as capital if paid in a lump sum,[36] or as income if paid regularly.[37] Your learning provider should be able to give you a letter for the relevant benefit office explaining the purpose of the payment.

Payments from the 16–19 bursary fund in England are exempt from income-related benefits calculations.[38] Learning providers have also been sent guidance that any payments made on a regular basis from the fund should be clearly marked as being for course costs. You should receive a letter from your provider stating what any payment is for to take to the benefits office.

Grants from further education funds specifically for childcare are disregarded altogether.[39]

## Lump-sum payments

Lump-sum payments are taken into account as capital if they are intended and used for food, ordinary clothing or footwear, household fuel, rent met by housing benefit (HB), housing costs met by income support (IS), council tax or water charges.[40] Although taken into account as capital, they only affect your benefit if they bring your capital above the £6,000 lower limit (see p241). Payments for school uniforms or sports clothes or sports shoes are ignored, as these do not count as 'ordinary clothing or footwear'.

### Regular payments

Regular payments are taken into account as income if they are intended and used for food, ordinary clothing or footwear, household fuel, rent met by HB, housing costs met by IS, council tax or water charges.[41] Up to £20 a week is disregarded. You cannot get the £20 disregard in full as well as the full disregards available on a student loan, widowed parent's allowance or war pensions (see p241). If you get one of these other payments in addition to a hardship payment, your maximum weekly disregard is £20. For example, if you have a student loan and receive a war pension, £10 a week is disregarded from each. If you also receive regular payments from a hardship fund, these would count in full as you have already used up your £20 disregard.

Regular payments intended and used for anything else, such as childcare expenses, are completely disregarded.

Regular payments from the 16–19 bursary fund should be disregarded regardless of their purpose, but colleges and other providers have also been given guidance to ensure that any regular payments from the fund are clearly identified as being for course costs, and so disregarded.

### Payments before a course starts or before a loan is paid

A payment from a hardship fund made before the course starts is always ignored as income, even if it is for living costs. A payment made before you get the first instalment of your student loan is ignored as income, provided it is intended to tide you over until your loan is paid.

## Institutional bursaries

Bursaries paid by institutions for living costs are treated as income over the period for which they are paid.

## Voluntary or charitable payments

Regular voluntary or charitable payments are ignored for IS, income-based jobseeker's allowance (JSA), income-related employment and support allowance (ESA) and HB. For IS and JSA, if paid as a lump sum, the payment is taken into account as capital whatever it is intended for.

## Professional and career development loans

Professional and career development loans are always treated as income rather than capital, no matter how they are paid.[42] The loan is taken into account if it is intended, and used, for food, ordinary clothing or footwear, household fuel, rent met by HB, housing costs met by IS, council tax or water charges. Once the period of education supported by the loan is completed, the loan is disregarded altogether, whatever it was originally intended for.

# 5. Earnings

Your earnings and the earnings of your partner are taken into account in the benefit assessment. It is your net weekly earnings that are taken into account – ie, after deducting:

- income tax;
- Class 1 national insurance contributions;
- half of any contribution you make towards a personal or occupational pension.

Some of your earnings are disregarded. The highest disregard that applies in your circumstances is deducted:

- £25 for lone parents claiming housing benefit (HB) who are not claiming income support (IS), income-based jobseeker's allowance (JSA) or income-related employment and support allowance (ESA);
- £20 for lone parents claiming IS, JSA or ESA;
- £20 for someone who gets a disability premium;
- £20 for someone who gets a carer premium;
- £20 for part-time firefighters and some other emergency auxiliaries;
- £10 for couples, whether one or both of you are working;
- £5 for single people.

For HB only, there is an additional disregard (£17.10) for some people working 16/30 hours a week.

For HB, childcare costs for registered childminders, nurseries and playschemes can be disregarded from earnings in some circumstances. Childcare costs of up to £175 a week for one child or £300 for two or more children are deducted from weekly earnings for:

- lone parents who are working;
- couples who are both working;
- couples, where one is working and one is incapacitated or in hospital or prison.

In each case, the work must be for 16 hours or more a week.

For full details of the way earnings are treated, see CPAG's *Welfare Benefits and Tax Credits Handbook*.

# 6. **Benefits and tax credits**

Some benefits are taken into account in the assessment of income support (IS), income-based jobseeker's allowance (JSA), income-related employment and support allowance (ESA) and housing benefit (HB), and others are ignored or partially ignored.

**Benefits and tax credits taken into account in full include:**
- child tax credit (CTC) for HB;
- carer's allowance;
- contributory ESA;
- contribution-based JSA;
- incapacity benefit;
- most industrial injuries benefits;
- retirement pension;
- working tax credit.

**Benefits and tax credits completely disregarded include:**
- attendance allowance;
- child benefit;
- CTC for IS, JSA and income-related ESA;
- disability living allowance;
- personal independence payment;
- social fund payments.

**Benefits and tax credits partly disregarded include:**
- widowed mother's allowance and widowed parent's allowance, which have £10 a week disregarded for IS, JSA and ESA, and £15 a week for HB (but you do not get this disregard if you already have £10 disregarded from a student loan or £20 disregarded from hardship fund payments).

# 7. **Maintenance**

For housing benefit, income support, jobseeker's allowance and income-related employment and support allowance, child maintenance paid to you by a former partner or your child's other parent is disregarded completely.

# 8. **Savings and capital**

There are limits on the amount of savings or capital you can have and still claim benefit. Some kinds of capital are not counted in the assessment. For details see CPAG's *Welfare Benefits and Tax Credits Handbook*.

- You cannot get income support, income-based jobseeker's allowance, income-related employment and support allowance or housing benefit (HB) if your savings or other capital are above £16,000.
- If your capital is £6,000 or less it does not affect your benefit at all.
- If your capital is between £6,000.01 and £16,000, you are treated as though you have income from this capital of £1 a week for every £250, or part of £250, between these limits. This is referred to as 'tariff income'. For example, if you have savings of £6,525, your tariff income is £3 a week.
- These limits are different if you or your partner have reached the qualifying age for pension credit (PC). All your capital is ignored if you or your partner get PC guarantee credit. Otherwise, tariff income of £1 for each £500 or part of £500 between £10,000.01 and £16,000 is taken into account in the assessment of HB.

# Notes

**2. Grants and loans**
1   **IS** Reg 62(2) IS Regs
    **JSA** Reg 131(2) JSA Regs
    **ESA** Reg 132(2) ESA Regs
    **HB** Reg 59(2) HB Regs
    See also para 30326 DMG
2   **IS** Reg 62(2)(a) IS Regs
    **JSA** Reg 131(2)(a) JSA Regs
    **ESA** Reg 132(2)(a) ESA Regs
    **HB** Reg 59(2)(a) HB Regs
3   **IS** Reg 62(2) IS Regs
    **JSA** Reg 131(2) JSA Regs
    **ESA** Reg 132(2) ESA Regs
    **HB** Reg 59(2) HB Regs
    See also para 30328 DMG
4   **IS** Reg 62(2) IS Regs
    **JSA** Reg 131(2) JSA Regs
    **ESA** Reg 132(2)(2) ESA Regs
    **HB** Reg 59(2) HB Regs
    See also para 30328 DMG
5   **IS** Reg 62(2)(c) IS Regs
    **JSA** Reg 131(2)(b) JSA Regs
    **ESA** Reg 132(2)(b) ESA Regs
    **HB** Reg 59(2)(b) HB Regs

6   **IS** Reg 62(2)(h) IS Regs
    **JSA** Reg 131(2)(g) JSA Regs
    **ESA** Reg 132(2)(g) ESA Regs
    **HB** Reg 59(2)(g) HB Regs
7   **IS** Reg 62(2)(g) and (h) IS Regs
    **JSA** Reg 131(2)(f) and (g) JSA Regs
    **ESA** Reg 132(2)(f) and (g) ESA Regs
    **HB** Reg 59(2)(f) and (g) HB Regs
8   **IS** Reg 62(2) IS Regs
    **JSA** Reg 131(2) JSA Regs
    **ESA** Reg 132(2)(b) ESA Regs
    **HB** Reg 59(2) HB Regs
    See also para 30330 DMG
9   Reg 59(6) HB Regs
10  **IS** Reg 62(2)(c) IS Regs
    **JSA** Reg 131(2)(b) JSA Regs
    **ESA** Reg 132(2)(b) ESA Regs
    **HB** Reg 59(2)(b) HB Regs
11  **IS** Reg 62(2)(h) IS Regs
    **JSA** Reg 131(2) JSA Regs
    **ESA** Reg 132(2) ESA Regs
    **HB** Reg 59(2)(g) HB Regs
12  paras 30121-25 DMG
13  para 30131 DMG

14 **IS** Sch 9 para 11(a) IS Regs
**JSA** Sch 7 para 12 JSA Regs
**ESA** Sch 8 para 13 ESA Regs
**HB** Sch 5 para 11 HB Regs
15 **IS** Schs 9 para 11 and 10 para 63 IS Regs
**JSA** Schs 7 para 12 and 8 para 52 JSA
Regs
**ESA** Schs 8 para 13 and 9 para 52 ESA
Regs
**HB** Sch 5 para 11 HB Regs
16 **IS** Reg 66C IS Regs
**JSA** Reg 136B JSA Regs
**ESA** Reg 139 ESA Regs
**HB** Reg 64A HB Regs
17 **IS** Reg 66A(3) and (4) IS Regs
**JSA** Reg 136(5) JSA Regs
**ESA** Reg 137(5) ESA Regs
**HB** Reg 64(3) and (4) HB Regs
18 **IS** Reg 67 IS Regs
**JSA** Reg 136(4) JSA Regs
**ESA** Reg 139(5) ESA Regs
**HB** Reg 64(4) HB Regs
19 **IS** Reg 64(5) IS Regs
**JSA** Reg 136(5) JSA Regs
**ESA** Reg 139(6) ESA Regs
**HB** Reg 64(5) HB Regs
20 **IS** Reg 41(6) IS Regs
**JSA** Reg 104(5) JSA Regs
**ESA** Reg 105(4) ESA Regs
**HB** Reg 41(4) HB Regs

**3. Dividing student income throughout
the year**
21 **IS** Reg 62(3B) IS Regs
**JSA** Reg 131(5A) JSA Regs
**ESA** Reg 132(6) ESA Regs
**HB** Reg 59(7) HB Regs
22 **IS** Reg 62(2)(h) IS Regs
**JSA** Reg 131(2)(g) JSA Regs
**ESA** Reg 132(3)(g) ESA Regs
**HB** Reg 59(2)(g) HB Regs
23 **IS** Regs 61 and 62(3)(a) IS Regs
**JSA** Regs 130 and 131(4)(a) JSA Regs
**ESA** Regs 131 and 132(4)(a) ESA Regs
**HB** Regs 53 and 59(5)(a) HB Regs
24 **IS** Reg 29(2B) IS Regs
**JSA** Reg 94(2B) JSA Regs
**ESA** Reg 91(4) ESA Regs
25 *Leeves v Chief Adjudication Officer,*
reported as R(IS) 5/99
26 **IS** Reg 66A(2)(c) IS Regs
**JSA** Reg 136(2)(c) JSA Regs
**ESA** Reg 137(3)(e) ESA Regs
**HB** Reg 64(2)(d) HB Regs
27 CIS/3734/2004

28 **IS** Reg 66A(2)(b) IS Regs
**JSA** Reg 136(2)(b) JSA Regs
**ESA** Reg 137(3)(d) ESA Regs
**HB** Reg 64(2)(d) HB Regs
29 **IS** Reg 66A(2)(aa) IS Regs
**JSA** Reg 136(2)(c) JSA Regs
**ESA** Reg 137(3)(e) ESA Regs
**HB** Reg 64(2)(b) HB Regs
30 **IS** Reg 61(1) IS Regs
**JSA** Reg 136(2)(aa) JSA Regs
**ESA** Reg 137(3)(b) ESA Regs
**HB** Reg 53(1) HB Regs
31 **IS** Reg 66A(2)(aa) IS Regs
**JSA** Reg 136(2)(c) JSA Regs
**ESA** Reg 137(3)(e) ESA Regs
**HB** Reg 64(2)(b) HB Regs
32 **IS** Reg 40(3A) IS Regs
**JSA** Reg 103(5) JSA Regs
**ESA** Reg 104(4) ESA Regs
**HB** Reg 40(7) HB Regs
33 See also HB/CTB Circular A31/2001 Part
6 and Annex D for guidance and a
sample calculation, together with HB/
CTB Circular A39/2001 para 19
34 CJSA/549/2003

**4. Discretionary funds and other
payments**
35 para 30305 DMG
36 **IS** Reg 61 IS Regs
**JSA** Reg 130 JSA Regs
**ESA** Reg 131 ESA Regs
**HB** Reg 53 HB Regs
37 **IS** Reg 61(1) IS Regs
**JSA** Reg 130(1) JSA Regs
**ESA** Reg 131(1) ESA Regs
**HB** Reg 53(1) HB Regs
38 **IS** Reg 68 IS Regs
**JSA** Reg 138 JSA Regs
**ESA** Reg 142 ESA Regs
**HB** Reg 68 HB Regs
39 **IS** Reg 66B IS Regs
**JSA** Reg 136A JSA Regs
**ESA** Reg 138 ESA Regs
**HB** Reg 65 HB Regs
40 **IS** Reg 41(6) IS Regs
**JSA** Reg 104(5) JSA Regs
**ESA** Reg 105(4) ESA Regs
**HB** Reg 41(4) HB Regs
41 **IS** Reg 66B IS Regs
**JSA** Reg 136A JSA Regs
**ESA** Regs 2(1) and 138 ESA Regs
**HB** Regs 2(1) and 68(3) and (4) HB Regs
42 **IS** Reg 41(6) IS Regs
**JSA** Reg 104(5) JSA Regs
**ESA** Reg 105(4) ESA Regs
**HB** Reg 41(4) HB Regs

# Chapter 22

## How income affects universal credit

**This chapter covers:**

This chapter explains how much weekly income is taken into account when working out your entitlement to universal credit (UC). If you do not yet come under the universal credit system and are claiming income support, income-based jobseeker's allowance, income-related employment and support allowance or housing benefit, see Chapter 21. If you are claiming child tax credit or working tax credit, see Chapter 23.

*Basic facts*

- Student loans and some grants count as income when working out how much universal credit you can get.
- Loans and grants are taken into account as income during the academic year, but ignored in the summer vacation.
- The maximum amount of student loan to which you are entitled is taken into account as income, whether or not you apply for it.

# 1. **Working out your income**

If you have student income (student loans and grants paid to you for your course), it usually counts as income for universal credit (UC).[1] This chapter explains how much monthly income counts in the assessment.

| | |
|---|---|
| Step one | **Add together the annual income from your student loan and grants.** Add the annual amount of any grants, ignoring those that are disregarded, to the annual amount of any loan (see below). |
| Step two | **Work out the period over which your student income counts.** Calculate this from the month in which you start your course until the month before the summer vacation, or end of your course, as applicable (see p248). |
| Step three | **Divide income throughout the year.** Divide the amount in Step one by the number of months over which your student income counts for that year (see p248). |
| Step four | **Deduct disregard.** Deduct a set amount of £110 from the monthly amount of income from grants and loan. |
| Step five | **Add other income.** Add any other income taken into account (eg, earnings) to the monthly amount of your grant and loan (see p249). This, added to the total at Step four, is the amount of income used in the UC assessment. |

# 2. **Grants and loans**

## If you get a student loan for living costs

If you are eligible for a loan for maintenance, it counts as income when working out universal credit (UC). The maximum loan you could be entitled to is taken into account, as though there were no reduction for household income or another grant.[2] **Note:** professional and career development loans do not count as student loans for this purpose. See p249 for more information on how they are treated.

Any other grants you receive are disregarded, except for any amount for the maintenance of your partner and/or child(ren), and any specific amount for rent if your UC includes an amount for rent.[3] A discretionary payment from an institutional hardship fund is ignored, provided it is not for the maintenance of your partner or child(ren) and not a specified amount for rent that is met by UC.

**Note:** the government plans to abolish maintenance grants and special support grants for new students from September 2016 (see p30). Poorer students will be entitled to a higher student loan, to offset their loss. Part of this loan will be disregarded for students who previously would have received a special support grant. However, at the time of writing, regulations had not yet been laid.

| Taken into account | Ignored |
|---|---|
| **England** | **England** |
| Maintenance loan | Tuition fee loan |
| Adult dependants' grant | Maintenance grant |
| NHS bursary dependants' grant | Special support grant |
| Some hardship fund payments (see p245) | Parents' learning allowance |
| **Wales** | Childcare grant |
| Maintenance loan | Disabled students' allowance |
| Adult dependants' grant | Travel/placement grant |
| NHS bursary dependants' grant | NHS bursary (means-tested and non-means-tested) |
| Some hardship fund payments (see p245) | means-tested) |
| | Teacher training bursary |
| | Social work bursary |
| | Most hardship fund payments (see p245) |
| | **Wales** |
| | Tuition fee loan |
| | Tuition fee grant |
| | Welsh government learning grant |
| | Special support grant |
| | Parents' learning allowance |
| | Childcare grant |
| | Disabled students' allowance |
| | Travel/placement grant |
| | NHS bursary |
| | Teacher training grant |
| | Social work bursary |
| | Most hardship fund payments (see p245) |

## If you do not get a student loan for living costs

If you do not get a loan, but you receive a grant, the grant income is taken into account for UC (subject to the disregards below).[4] A grant is an educational grant or award, and does not include 16–19 bursary payments, education maintenance allowance payments or other payments for people under 21 to enable them to complete a course of non-advanced education.[5]

Grant income is completely disregarded if you do not get a loan and the grant is paid for:[6]

- tuition fees or exams;
- your disability;
- extra costs of residential study away from your usual place of study during term time;

- the costs of your normal home (if you live elsewhere during your course), unless these are included in your UC;
- the maintenance of someone not included in your UC claim;
- books, equipment, course travel costs or childcare costs.

If you get a grant but no loan, and receive a discretionary payment in either further or higher education, this is disregarded if it is paid for any of the above and otherwise counts as income.

You should ensure your funder, university, college or learning provider gives you clear information on what any payment is for, especially if a grant is paid for course costs, as this may not be obvious from its title.

| Taken into account | Ignored |
|---|---|
| **England** | **England** |
| Some learner support fund payments (see above) | 24+ advanced learning loan |
| | Tuition fee grant |
| Some bursary loan fund payments (see above) | 16–19 bursary fund payment |
| | Some learner support fund payments (see above) |
| NHS bursary | |
| NHS bursary dependants' grant | Some bursary loan fund payments (see above) |
| Social work bursary | |
| Postgraduate stipend/studentship | Parents' learning allowance |
| Some hardship fund payments (see above) | Childcare grant |
| | Disabled students' allowance |
| **Wales** | Travel grant |
| NHS bursary | **Wales** |
| NHS bursary dependants' grant | Tuition fee grant |
| Social work bursary | Education maintenance allowance |
| Postgraduate stipend/studentship | Welsh government learning grant |
| Some hardship fund payments (see above) | for further education |
| | Parents' learning allowance |
| | Childcare grant |
| | Disabled students' allowance |
| | Travel grant |

# 3. **Dividing student income throughout the year**

Universal credit (UC) is paid monthly, for an 'assessment period'. Each assessment period runs from the day of the month you claimed UC, for one month – eg, if you claim on the second of the month, each assessment period runs from the second of the month to the first of the following month. The annual amount of your student income needs to be divided over the number of assessment periods in the course year, to arrive at the monthly amount that is used to work out UC.

Student income counts for each assessment period during your course, excluding the one at the end of each academic year and those in the long vacation.[7]

Student income counts as income:
• from the start of the assessment period in which the course/course year begins; *and*
• for every subsequent assessment period during the course/course year.

Student income is ignored:[8]
• in the assessment period in which the last week of the course or the start of the long vacation falls;
• in any assessment periods that fall completely within the long vacation; *and*
• if you abandon or leave your course completely, in the assessment period in which you leave.

**Long vacation**
The '**long vacation**' is the longest holiday in a course which lasts at least two years, and must last for at least one month.[9]

Once you have calculated the number of assessment periods in the course year, divide the total annual amount of loans and/or grants by this number, and apply the monthly disregard. In each assessment period, £110 of student income is disregarded.[10]

**Example**
Laura has a five-year-old daughter and is single. She starts a full-time degree course at her local university in Liverpool. Year one of her course runs from 5 October 2014 to 20 May 2016. Her assessment periods run from the third of the month to the second of the following month. Laura gets a tuition fee loan of £9,000, a maintenance loan of £5,740, a special support grant of £3,387, a parents' learning allowance of £1,573 and a childcare grant of £3,900. She also receives child benefit of £20.70 a week.

| Step one | Laura ignores the tuition fee loan, special support grant, parents' learning allowance and childcare grants, as well as her child benefit. |
| Step two | Her maintenance loan counts as income over seven assessment periods in the first year of her course (from 2 October 2014 to 1 May 2015). |
| Step three | £5,740 ÷ 7 = £820 |
| Step four | She disregards £110 per assessment period. £820 − £110 = £710 |
| Step five | She has no other income. Laura's UC is calculated on student income of £710 a month from 3 October 2015 to 2 May 2016. From 3 May 2016, the weekly income from her student funding is nil. Laura's next UC payment in June will be based on £0 student funding. Paula is 27, has a three-year-old son and is single. She is undertaking a full-time access to higher education course in Plymouth. Her course runs from 7 September 2015 to 27 May 2016. Her assessment periods run from the 14th of the month to the 13th of the following month. She has taken out a 24+ advanced learning loan of £1,700 to pay for her course. She also receives £700 over the year from the loan bursary fund for childcare. Both her loan and her bursary payment are disregarded, although she must provide evidence that the bursary payment has been made for childcare, not general costs. Her student income over the year is £0. |

## 4. **Other payments**

### Professional and career development loans

These educational loans count as capital if paid as a lump sum. If paid in instalments, they normally also count as capital.[11]

## 5. **Earnings**

Your earnings and your partner's earnings are taken into account in the universal credit assessment. Your net monthly earnings are taken into account – ie, after deducting:

- income tax;
- Class 1 national insurance contributions; *and*
- any contribution you make towards a personal or occupational pension.

Some of your earnings are disregarded. This is known as a 'work allowance'. The standard work allowance is £111 a month. You get a higher work allowance if you have children or if you are ill or disabled. Earnings above your work allowance are deducted at 65 pence for every pound above the allowance.

For full details of the way earnings are treated, see CPAG's *Welfare Benefits and Tax Credits Handbook*.

# 6. Benefits

Some benefits are taken into account in the assessment of your universal credit, and others are ignored. **Benefits taken into account include:**

- carer's allowance;
- contribution-based jobseeker's allowance;
- contributory employment and support allowance;
- most industrial injuries benefits;
- maternity allowance;
- retirement pension.

**Benefits that are ignored include:**

- child benefit;
- disability living allowance;
- personal independence payment;
- attendance allowance.

# 7. Savings and capital

There are limits on the amount of savings or capital you can have and still claim universal credit (UC). Some kinds of capital are not counted in the assessment. For details, see CPAG's *Welfare Benefits and Tax Credits Handbook*.

You cannot get UC if your savings or other capital are above £16,000.

If your capital is £6,000 or less, it does not affect your UC at all.

If your capital is between £6,000.01 and £16,000, you are treated as though you have income from this capital of £4.35 a month for every £250 or part of £250 between these limits. For example, if you have savings of £6,525, your assumed income is £13.05 a month.

# Notes

### 1. Working out your income
1  Reg 66(1)(e) UC Regs

### 2. Grants and loans
2  Regs 68 and 69 UC Regs
3  Reg 68(3) UC Regs
4  Reg 68(2) and (4) UC Regs
5  Reg 68(7) UC Regs
6  Reg 70 UC Regs

### 3. Dividing student income throughout the year
7  Reg 68 UC Regs
8  Reg 13 UC Regs
9  Reg 68(7) UC Regs
10  Reg 71 UC Regs

### 4. Other payments
11  Reg 46(4) UC Regs

# Chapter 23

. . . . . . . . . . . . . . . . . . . . . . . . . . . . . . . . . . . . . . . . . . . . . .

# How income affects tax credits

**This chapter covers:**
1. Income and tax credits (below)
2. Grants and loans (p253)
3. Earnings (p255)
4. Benefits (p255)
5. Other income (p256)

. . . . . . . . . . . . . . . . . . . . . . . . . . . . . . . . . . . . . . . . . . . . . .

*Basic facts*

– Most student income is ignored when working out your entitlement to tax credits.
– The higher education adult dependants' grant and some elements of professional and
   career development loans are taken into account.
– Earnings, some benefits and certain other income are also taken into account.

. . . . . . . . . . . . . . . . . . . . . . . . . . . . . . . . . . . . . . . . . . . . . .

## 1. Income and tax credits

If you are getting income support (IS), income-based jobseeker's allowance,
income-related employment and support allowance or pension credit, you are
entitled to maximum tax credits without any income test. If you are not on one
of these benefits, the tax credit assessment is based on your income over a full tax
year (6 April to 5 April). When you claim, HM Revenue and Customs (HMRC) uses
your income from the previous complete tax year. For example, if you claim tax
credits between 6 April 2015 and 5 April 2016, it uses your income from 6 April
2014 to 5 April 2015 to work out your entitlement. **Note:** although your income
from the previous year is used in the initial tax credit assessment, all other
relevant circumstances, such as the age of your child, are taken from the current
year of the tax credit award.

Your tax credits are first assessed using the previous year's income, even if
HMRC knows at the outset that your circumstances have changed. If you expect
your income over the current tax year to be more than £2,500 lower or more than
£5,000 higher, tell HMRC and it reassesses your tax credit entitlement. If you do

not tell HMRC, you will have an overpayment to repay at the end of the tax year, or an underpayment that you will get back as a lump sum.

At the end of the tax year, HMRC sends you an annual review form to check whether your income and circumstances have stayed the same over the year. It reassesses your award for the previous year based on the current year's income plus £2,500 if it is more than £2,500 lower than in the previous year, or based on the current year's income less a disregard of £5,000 if it is more than £5,000 higher.

If your income increases by £5,000 or less since the previous tax year used to assess your claim, you do not need to tell HMRC as this does not affect the amount to which you are entitled (but you should let it know if the change means you are now eligible for working tax credit (WTC) or more WTC). However, any increase will be taken into account from the following April (April 2016 for an increase in the 2015/16 tax year), so it is important to tell HMRC of any increase by this date, otherwise you are likely to incur an overpayment.

If you have a partner, your tax credits claim is made jointly and her/his income counts as well as yours.

Unless you or your partner are working and eligible for WTC, your maximum child tax credit is reduced if your income is above the threshold of £16,105 a year. If you are eligible for WTC, this threshold is £6,420.

When working out your income for tax credit purposes, some income is disregarded.

## 2. **Grants and loans**

Most grants and loans are disregarded when calculating a student's income for tax credit purposes (see below).[1] The following are the exceptions.

- **Adult dependants' grant**. Any grant received for an adult dependant is included in the calculation.
- **Professional and career development loan**. Any part of this paid for living costs for the period supported by the loan is taken into account in full.[2]

### Grants and loans checklist

| Student support | Treatment |
|---|---|
| **Further education income** | |
| 16–19 bursary fund | Disregarded |
| 24+ advanced learning loan | Disregarded |
| Adult learning grant | Disregarded |
| Care to Learn grant | Disregarded |

| | |
|---|---|
| Childcare fund | Disregarded |
| Education maintenance allowance | Disregarded |
| Further education award (Northern Ireland) | Disregarded |
| Discretionary support funds grant | Disregarded |
| Special educational needs allowance | Disregarded |
| Travel grant or expenses | Disregarded |
| Welsh government learning grant | Disregarded |

**Undergraduate income**

| | |
|---|---|
| Access to Learning Fund grant | Disregarded |
| Adult dependants' grant | Taken into account in full |
| Childcare grant | Disregarded |
| Disabled students' allowance | Disregarded |
| Hardship funds | Disregarded |
| Higher education grant | Disregarded |
| Institutional bursaries or scholarships | Disregarded |
| Maintenance grant | Disregarded |
| NHS dependants' grant for children | Disregarded |
| NHS healthcare bursary | Disregarded |
| Northern Ireland higher education bursary | Disregarded |
| Nursing and midwifery bursary | Disregarded |
| Parents' learning allowance | Disregarded |
| Part-time students' grant for course costs | Disregarded |
| Part-time students' grant for fees | Disregarded |
| Social work bursary | Disregarded |
| Special support grant | Disregarded |
| Student loan for living costs (including any means-tested element where appropriate) | Disregarded |
| Travelling expenses | Disregarded |
| Tuition fee grant | Disregarded |
| Tuition fee loan | Disregarded |
| Welsh government learning grant | Disregarded |

**Postgraduate income**

| | |
|---|---|
| Books and equipment expenses | Disregarded |
| British Academy grant | Disregarded |
| Research Council studentship or scholarship | Disregarded |
| Residential study | Disregarded |
| Social work bursary | Disregarded |
| Supplementary grants | As for undergraduate income |
| Teacher training grant | Disregarded |
| Tuition fees grant or loan | Disregarded |

**Other income**

| | |
|---|---|
| Professional and career development loan | Disregarded, except for any amount applied or paid for living expenses during the period supported by the loan, which is taken into account in full |

## 3. Earnings

Your gross earnings from the last full tax year, plus those of your partner, are taken into account in the tax credit assessment. 'Gross earnings' means all income before any income tax or national insurance contributions are deducted. It also includes tips, overtime pay, taxable expenses and, ignoring the first £30,000, taxable payments related to the termination of employment such as redundancy pay and strike pay.[3] If you make any contributions to a personal or occupational pension approved by HM Revenue and Customs, these contributions should be disregarded.[4] The first £100 a week of statutory maternity, paternity, shared parental and adoption pay is disregarded, but payments above this are included.[5] Statutory sick pay is included in full.[6] Any payments that are exempt from income tax should be ignored for the purposes of tax credits.

For full details of the way earnings are treated, see CPAG's *Welfare Benefits and Tax Credits Handbook*.

## 4. Benefits

In general, benefits that are not taxable are disregarded when calculating tax credits, and benefits that are taxable are included. For full details of the way social security benefits are treated, see CPAG's *Welfare Benefits and Tax Credits Handbook*.

**Benefits disregarded include:**[7]

- child benefit;
- disability living allowance;
- personal independence payment;
- income-related employment and support allowance (ESA);
- guardian's allowance;
- housing benefit;
- lower rate of short-term incapacity benefit (IB);
- income support (except to strikers);
- income-based jobseeker's allowance (JSA);
- industrial injuries benefit;

- maternity allowance;
- social fund payments;
- most war pensions;[8]
- increases for a child or adult dependant paid with any of the above benefits.

**Benefits taken into account in full include:**
- bereavement allowance;
- carer's allowance;
- contributory ESA;
- long-term IB;
- higher rate of short-term IB;
- contribution-based JSA. **Note:** amounts above the 'taxable maximum' are ignored. In practice, people are not paid above this amount, so in the majority of cases all contribution-based JSA is included;
- increases for a child or adult dependant paid with any of the above benefits.

**Benefits partly taken into account include:**
- state retirement pension (and private and occupational pensions);
- widows' pensions.

These are included in the tax credit calculation, except for the first £300 of the total income from pensions, and income from capital and foreign income, which is disregarded.

## 5. **Other income**

This is a brief outline of how other income is treated. For further details, see CPAG's *Welfare Benefits and Tax Credits Handbook*.

### Income from self-employment

Your taxable profits are taken into account, less any personal pension contributions.

### Savings and investments

There is no capital limit for tax credits. You are eligible whatever amount of savings you have and whatever the value of other capital. However, income generated from your savings or other capital is taken into account. For example, interest from bank accounts is taken into account, unless it is in a tax-free savings account. However, if you have no income from property or pensions, or foreign income, interest on savings or other capital is only taken into account if it is over £300 a year.

## Property

The capital value of any property is ignored. Any taxable rental income is included, except for the first £300 of the total income from pensions, income from capital, and foreign income, which is disregarded.[9]

Note: you can rent a room in your own home without paying tax on the rental income, provided this does not exceed £4,250 a year. This income is not taken into account when working out your entitlement to tax credits.

## Maintenance

Regular maintenance from an ex-partner is ignored, regardless of how the arrangement was made. Similarly, any support received from an ex-partner for your child(ren) is also ignored.[10]

# Notes

**2. Grants and loans**
1 Reg 8 TC(DCI) Regs
2 Reg 19(c) Table 8 para 2 TC(DCI) Regs

**3. Earnings**
3 Reg 4 TC(DCI) Regs
4 Reg 3(7)(c) TC(DCI) Regs
5 Reg 4(1)(h) TC(DCI) Regs
6 Reg 4(1)(g) TC(DCI) Regs

**4. Benefits**
7 Reg 7(3) TC(DCI) Regs
8 Reg 5 TC(DCI) Regs

**5. Other income**
9 Reg 11 TC(DCI) Regs
10 Reg 19 Table 6 para 10 TC(DCI) Regs

# Chapter 24

# How income affects health benefits

**This chapter covers:**

*Basic facts*

- The NHS low income scheme helps with health costs if your income is low enough.
- Student loans and most grants count as income.
- The exact amount of help you receive depends on the amount of excess weekly income (if any) you are assessed as having, once it is offset against a personal allowance and your housing costs.

## 1. Working out your income

The way that student income is taken into account for health benefits is broadly the same as for means-tested benefits (see Chapter 21).

| | |
|---|---|
| Step one | **Apply annual disregard.**<br>From the student maintenance loan, deduct the disregarded amount of £693 for books, equipment and travel. |
| Step two | **Divide income throughout the year.**<br>Divide the annual amount of loan by 52 weeks, unless you are in the final or only year of your course, in which case you should divide by the number of weeks between the start and finish of your course. |

Step three     **Weekly disregard.**

Unlike the means-tested benefits assessment, there is no weekly disregard of £10 on the student loan, unless you receive a premium in your applicable amount, an allowance because of deafness (separate to any disabled students' allowance), or you are not a student but your partner is. If you come into any of these categories, disregard £10.

Step four     **Add other income to weekly loan amount.**

Add together any other weekly income (except for 'mandatory' awards such as research council awards or non-means-tested NHS bursaries) – eg, from hardship funds (see p263) or a professional and career development loan (see p264), earnings (see p264), tariff income from capital (see p265), and benefits and tax credits (see p264) – ignoring any amount that is disregarded.

Step five     **Divide mandatory grant income over 52 weeks.**

Divide any mandatory grant or bursary over 52 weeks and add this to the weekly loan amount where appropriate. Amounts in excess of a maintenance grant are disregarded. This total, added to the weekly loan total calculated at Step four, is the amount of income used in the health benefits assessment.

## 2. **Grants and loans**

### Grants

In general, grants intended for living costs (such as the old maintenance grant, the NHS bursary and the social work bursary) are taken into account, and grants for other costs are disregarded. For how hardship funds and grants are treated, see p263.

A maximum amount of any maintenance grant or Welsh government learning grant paid to 'current system' students subject to variable or flexible tuition fees is taken into account, but amounts above this are ignored.[1] The maximum amounts taken into account are as follows:

| Student cohort | Amount taken into account |
| --- | --- |
| | £ |
| **England** | |
| 2012 cohort | 1,693.50 |
| 2009 cohort | 1,555 |
| All other 'current system' students | 1,400 |
| **Wales** | |
| 2010, 2011 or 2012 cohort | 2,580 |

| All other 'current system' students | 1,329 |
|---|---|
| **Northern Ireland** | 1,318 |

Institutional bursaries and scholarships are taken into account if they are paid for living costs.

If you are *not* eligible for a student loan for living costs, £693 for books, travel and equipment is deducted from your grant.

Social work bursaries are usually divided over the number of weeks of study, except if your classroom weeks exceed 45, in which case they are divided by 52.

Teacher training bursaries are divided over the number of days they are paid, then multiplied by seven to give a weekly amount. The £693 disregard is not applied.

## Further education grants

The following further education grants are disregarded:
- 16–19 bursary fund;
- 24+ advanced learning loan;
- education maintenance allowance;
- adult learning grant;
- Care to Learn grant;
- travel expenses allowance.

## Higher education grants

The following higher education grants are completely disregarded:
- grant for 'old system' students;
- Welsh government learning grant for 'old system' students;
- part-time course costs grant;
- childcare grant;
- parents' learning allowance;
- disabled students' allowance;
- travel expenses;
- tuition fees grants and loans.

The following grants are taken into account:
- adult dependants' grant;
- teacher training bursary;
- nursing and midwifery bursary;
- social work bursary.

## Postgraduate grants

Any research council or other maintenance grant and dependants' allowances are taken into account. Supplementary grants are treated in the same way as those for undergraduates (see p259). Ignore:

- grants for tuition fees;
- grants for residential study away from your normal home;
- grants intended to meet the costs of books and equipment.

## Student loan

A student loan includes:
- the maximum loan for living costs for which you are eligible, including any means-tested element (where applicable). This is taken into account as your income whether or not you apply for it. The government believes that it is the primary source of public support to students and, therefore, should be fully exhausted before further support is given;
- any payments for extra weeks' attendance.

The NHS Business Services Authority disregards £693 for books, travel and equipment from the annual student loan.

## Grants and loans checklist

| Student support | Treatment |
|---|---|
| **Further education income** | |
| 16–19 bursary fund | Disregarded |
| 24+ advanced learning loan | Disregarded |
| Adult learning grant | Disregarded |
| Care to Learn grant | Disregarded |
| Discretionary support funds/Financial Contingency Fund grant | Taken into account if paid for basic living costs, disregarded if paid for other items such as childcare |
| Education maintenance allowance | Disregarded |
| Travel expenses allowance | Disregarded |
| Welsh government learning grant | Disregarded |
| **Undergraduate income** | |
| Adult dependants' grant | Taken into account in full |
| Childcare grant | Disregarded |
| Disabled students' allowance | Disregarded |
| Hardship funds | Taken into account if paid for basic living costs (as capital if not regular payments), disregarded if paid for other items |
| Higher education grant | Disregarded |
| Institutional bursaries or scholarships | Taken into account if paid for living costs |

24

| | |
|---|---|
| Loan (including any means-tested element where appropriate) | Taken into account<br>Disregarded:<br>– £693 a year for books, travel and equipment; *and*<br>– £10 a week in certain circumstances (see p264) |
| Maintenance grants | Any sum in excess of a certain amount taken into account (see p259) |
| NHS healthcare bursary; nursing and midwifery bursary | Means tested: taken into account in full<br>Non-means tested: taken into account, except for £693 a year disregard for books, travel and equipment |
| Part-time grant for course costs | Disregarded |
| Part-time grant for tuition fees | Disregarded |
| Parents' learning allowance | Disregarded |
| Social work bursary | Taken into account, with £693 a year disregard if you are not entitled to a student loan |
| Special support grant | Disregarded |
| Teacher training bursary | Taken into account |
| Travelling expenses | Disregarded |
| Tuition fee grant | Disregarded |
| Tuition fee loan | Disregarded |
| Welsh government learning grant for 'old system' students | Disregarded |
| Welsh government learning grant for 'new system' students | Any sum in excess of a certain amount taken into account (see p259) |
| **Postgraduate income** | |
| Books and equipment | Disregarded |
| Research council studentship or scholarship | Taken into account, except for an annual £693 books, travel and equipment disregard |
| Residential study | Disregarded |
| Social work bursary | Taken into account |
| Supplementary grants | As for undergraduate income |
| Teacher training salary | Taken into account |
| Tuition fees grant or loan | Disregarded |

*Example*
Oliver is a first-year full-time undergraduate in Wales. He receives the maximum away-from-home student loan (£2,796), the maximum Welsh government learning grant for 'new system' students (£5,161) and £20 a week from his parents for food and bills.

When calculating his income for health benefits purposes, subtract £693 from his student loan, to give £2,103 and include the first £2,580 of his Welsh government learning grant. This gives £4,683. Divide this by 52 weeks (to give £90.06). The £20 a week he gets from his parents is added to this figure and his income is, therefore, assessed to be £110.06 a week.

This income is then set against the appropriate income support personal allowances, housing and other costs to determine whether or not it exceeds or falls short of Oliver's requirements. If it falls short, he receives full support. If his income exceeds this amount, he may receive partial support, depending on the level of excess.

# 3. **Discretionary funds and other payments**

## Hardship funds

Discretionary support provided by your university or college when you are in financial difficulty is treated differently from other student grants and loans. This support can include:

- higher education hardship funds, including what was previously the Access to Learning Fund in England and the Financial Contingency Fund in Wales (individual institutions may still refer to them by these names);
- further education discretionary support funds or support from the Financial Contingency Fund in Wales.

In general, if the payment is for living costs, it is taken into account in full if it counts as capital, or with up to a £20 a week disregarded if it counts as income. If the payment is for other costs, it is disregarded. For example, a further education discretionary support funds grant solely for childcare costs is disregarded. Ask your provider for a letter saying what the payment is for and how it is paid.

Lump-sum payments count as capital. Regular payments count as income.

## Lump-sum payments

Lump-sum payments are taken into account as capital if they are intended and used for living costs such as food, ordinary clothing or footwear, household fuel, rent, council tax or water charges. Payments for anything else are disregarded. Although taken into account as capital, this only affects your entitlement if it brings your capital above the £16,000 higher limit. See p265 for details.

## Regular payments

Regular payments are taken into account as income if they are intended and used for food, ordinary clothing or footwear, household fuel, rent, council tax or water charges. Up to £20 a week is disregarded. You cannot get the £20 disregard in full as well as the full disregards available on a student loan or voluntary and charitable payments (or on widowed parent's allowance or war pensions). If you get one of these other payments as well as a discretionary hardship payment, your maximum weekly disregard is £20.

For example, if you have a student loan for living costs and regular payments from the university's hardship fund, £10 a week is disregarded from each. If you also receive regular payments from a charity, these count in full as you have already used up your £20 disregard on the loan and the hardship fund payment.

Regular payments intended and used for anything else, such as childcare expenses, are completely disregarded.

### Voluntary or charitable payments

These are treated in the same way as hardship fund payments.

### Professional and career development loans

Professional and career development loans are always treated as income, not capital, no matter how they are paid. The loan is taken into account if it is intended and used for living costs – eg, food, ordinary clothing or footwear, household fuel, rent, council tax or water charges. Once the period of education supported by the loan is completed, the loan is disregarded altogether, whatever it was originally intended for.

## 4. Earnings

Your earnings and the earnings of your partner are taken into account in the health benefits assessment. Your net weekly earnings are taken into account – ie, deducting:

- income tax;
- Class 1 national insurance contributions;
- half of any contribution you make towards a personal or occupational pension.

## 5. Benefits and tax credits

If you receive income support (IS), income-based jobseeker's allowance (JSA), income-related employment and support allowance (ESA) or child tax credit, you automatically get free health benefits (see Chapter 11). You may also qualify if you get universal credit (see p131).

Housing benefit is effectively disregarded, as the NHS Business Services Authority only takes into account the rent paid directly by you when determining need.

Benefits and tax credits taken into account in full include:
- carer's allowance;
- contribution-based JSA;
- contributory ESA;
- incapacity benefit;
- most industrial injuries benefits;
- retirement pension;
- working tax credit.

Benefits and tax credits completely disregarded include:
- attendance allowance;
- child benefit;
- disability living allowance;
- personal independence payment;
- social fund payments.

Benefits and tax credits partly disregarded include:
- widowed mother's allowance and widowed parent's allowance, which have £10 a week disregarded. **Note:** you do not receive this disregard if you already have £10 disregarded from a student loan or £20 disregarded from hardship fund payments.

# 6. **Maintenance**

Regular maintenance payments (eg, child support and parental or spousal contributions towards maintenance) count as income. As a general rule, income is usually taken into account in the week in which it is paid, subject to a weekly disregard of £5, £10 or £20 depending on the circumstances. Irregular payments are averaged over the 13 weeks before your claim, and lump sums are treated as capital.

# 7. **Savings and capital**

There are limits on the amount of savings or capital you can have and still claim health benefits.

You cannot get health benefits if your savings or other capital is above £16,000.

If your capital is £6,000 or less, it does not affect your entitlement to health benefits at all. If your capital is between £6,000.01 and £16,000 (a higher limit of £23,250 if you are in a care home in England, or £24,000 in Wales), you are treated as though you have an income from this capital of £1 a week for every £250 (or part of £250) between these amounts. This is referred to as 'tariff income'. For example, if you have savings of £6,525, your tariff income is £3 a week.

# Notes

## 2. **Grants and loans**

1   The National Health Service (Travel
    Expenses and Remission of Charges)
    Amendment (No.2) Regulations 2006,
    No.2171, as amended

# Part 4

## Other issues

# Chapter 25

# Council tax

**This chapter covers:**
1. What is council tax (below)
2. Who pays council tax (p270)
3. Council tax reduction (p276)
4. Second adult rebate (p276)

*Basic facts*

– Council tax is a local tax on residential dwellings. It does not apply in Northern Ireland.
– You do not pay council tax if you are under 18.
– Full-time students sharing accommodation solely with other full-time students do not pay council tax.
– Full-time students sharing accommodation with non-students do not pay council tax.
– Full-time students who own the home in which they live, and who live with non-students may be liable, but may be exempt or get a discount or second adult rebate.
– Full-time and part-time students liable to pay council tax may be able to get help in the form of a council tax reduction.

## 1. **What is council tax**

Council tax is a tax on residential dwellings and is paid to the local authority. There is one amount to pay and one bill for each dwelling, unless it is exempt from council tax. A 'dwelling' includes a self-contained flat.

Each dwelling is allocated a valuation band from A to H, based on property values in 1991 (2005 in Wales). The amount of council tax is lowest for those in Band A.

Some dwellings are exempt from council tax. If a property is exempt, there is no council tax to pay for anyone who lives there or for a non-resident owner. There are also exemptions specifically for students (see p273).

Properties occupied solely by students are usually exempt, with the local authority receiving additional funds from central government instead of the council tax that would have been paid. Students who share with non-students are also exempt from paying council tax, although the property itself is not exempt.

If you are a student and you are liable, the amount you must pay may be reduced if you are eligible for council tax reduction (see p276) or a second adult rebate (see p276).

## 2. **Who pays council tax**

As a student, you may be exempt from paying council tax if:
- the accommodation in which you live is exempt (see p273); *or*
- you are not liable to pay (see p273).

If neither of these applies, it may be possible to reduce the council tax bill if:
- the liable person can get a discount (see p275); *or*
- the liable person can get council tax reduction (see p276) or a second adult rebate (see p276).

### Who counts as a student

If you are aged under 20, whether you count as a student for council tax purposes depends on whether you are on an advanced or non-advanced course. For older students, one rule applies whatever the level of your course.

### Under 20 in non-advanced education

You are regarded as a 'student' for council tax purposes if you are aged 19 or under and on a non-advanced course of more than 12 hours a week.[1]

*Non-advanced course*

A 'non-advanced course' is one below the level of a foundation degree, honours degree, Higher National Certificate, Higher National Diploma or National Vocational Qualification (NVQ) level four. It includes A levels, national diplomas and national certificates. The course must last more than three months.[2] It does not include: evening classes;[3] correspondence courses;[4] or courses taken as a result of your office or occupation.[5]

The hours that count are those required by the course rather than those you actually do, if they are different. To work out your hours, average out over term times the hours required under the course for tuition, supervised study, exams, and supervised exercises, experiments, projects and practical work.[6]

You are treated as a student on each day from the day you start the course until the day you complete it, abandon it or are dismissed from it.[7] So, you count as a student during term times, during short vacations at Christmas and Easter, and during the summer if your course continues after the summer. If your course ends in the summer and you begin a different one in the autumn, you do not count as a student in the summer between courses.[8] However, you might be able to get a discount (see p275).

*Example*

Drew is 18 and taking three A levels at college. Including his classes, exams and supervised study, his course hours are 18 a week. He is a student for council tax purposes.

## Under 20 in higher education

The rules are the same as for those aged 20 or over (see below).

## 20 or over in non-advanced or higher education

You are regarded as a 'student' for council tax purposes if the course requires you to undertake periods of study, tuition or work experience for at least 21 hours a week in at least 24 weeks each academic year.[9]

If you are on a sandwich course, required periods of work experience are included.

To count as a student, you must be enrolled on a course with an educational institution. You are a student from the day you begin the course until the day you complete it, abandon it or are no longer permitted by the educational institution to undertake it.[10] So if you take time out and are not enrolled on the course during that period, you do not count as a student for council tax purposes and you may become liable for council tax. If this is the case, check whether you are eligible for council tax reduction (see p276).

If you take time out but are still enrolled on the course, you continue to count as a student, provided you have not abandoned it completely and the institution has not said you can no longer undertake the course. Because the law says you are not a student if you are 'no longer permitted by the institution to undertake [the course]', it suggests that your dismissal from the course must be final. So you could argue that if you are temporarily suspended from the course but still registered, you still count as a student. In an informal letter, written in 1996, the former Department of the Environment (then responsible for council tax) stated:[11]

In our view a period of intercalation will remain within the period of a course... and therefore, provided that the person remains enrolled at the education establishment, they will continue to fall within the definition of a full-time student.

**Note:** a recent valuation tribunal decision indicates that students who are repeating a full-time course on a part-time basis may not be regarded as meeting the definition of 'full-time student', even if their normal attendance is on a full-time basis.[12] It is therefore important to ensure that your institution is clear about the normal expectations of your course in any documentation it provides.

Your college or university determines the number of hours of your course. You may need evidence from it to prove to the local authority that you count as a student. Colleges and universities are required to provide you with a certificate, if you ask for one while you are a student or for up to a year after you leave the course.[13] After that, they may still give you a certificate, but are not legally required to do so. The certificate must contain:[14]

- the name and address of the institution;
- your full name;
- your term-time address and home address (if known by the institution);
- a statement that you are (or were) a student – ie, that you are enrolled on a course requiring you to undertake periods of study, tuition or work experience of at least 21 hours a week over at least 24 weeks a year; *and*
- the date you became a student and the date your course ends.

## Postgraduate students

Full-time postgraduate students are regarded as 'students' for council tax purposes in the same way as other full-time higher education students.

In the past, some postgraduate research students have had difficulty in securing council tax exemption because local authorities have considered that their periods of 'study, tuition or work experience' do not meet the requirements of the regulations, and that, in particular, research does not count as 'study'. This has been successfully challenged in an appeal in Kent and, although it does not set a legal precedent, local authorities are obliged to take such decisions into account when making their own decisions.[15]

To further clarify the law in this area, the Department for Communities and Local Government and the Welsh government amended the regulations so that the requirement is to 'undertake' the course for the prescribed periods as opposed to 'attend' it, as was previously required. This should make it easier for postgraduate students who meet the requirements to argue they qualify.

Other postgraduate students have had difficulty in securing exemption during the thesis 'writing-up' period after the formal end of the course. While some local authorities are sympathetic and extend student status after the end of the course, others have regarded such students as liable as they are no longer 'within the period of their course'. A High Court ruling in 2008 in the case of *Fayad v Lewisham* has served to harden some local authorities' views (although in that case, the student was trying to claim exemption for a writing-up period lasting more than two years).[16] The case has been used by some local authorities to suggest that PhD students are ineligible for exemption even during the formal period of the course, but this should be challenged as the ruling related only to a writing-up period.

If this affects you, seek advice from your students' union or institution's advice centre.

**Note:** if you have completed an undergraduate course and intend to start a postgraduate course in the following academic year, you are not exempt as you are not within the period of either course. Depending on your circumstances, however, you may be able to claim council tax reduction (see p276) or a discount on the bill (see p275).

## Exempt dwellings

A dwelling is exempt from council tax if everyone who occupies it is:[17]
- a student; *or*
- a student's partner from abroad who entered the UK on a visa that prohibits her/him from working or claiming benefits. If the partner has the right to work but not to claim benefits, s/he should be covered by this exemption; *or*
- under age 18; *or*
- under age 20 and left non-advanced education at school or college after 30 April – this only applies between 1 May and 31 October of the year they left school or college; *or*
- 'severely mentally impaired'.

An unoccupied dwelling is exempt for up to four months if it is the main residence of a student (and not of anyone else who is not a student) and it was last occupied by one or more students. This allows an exemption to continue, for example, on the student's term-time accommodation through the summer vacation. Dwellings left unoccupied by a student owner are exempt indefinitely, provided the owner has been a student since s/he last occupied the dwelling or within six weeks of leaving it. Unoccupied dwellings that are substantially unfurnished are exempt for up to six months. If you are liable for council tax and anyone who is jointly liable with you is also a student, and the dwelling is no one's main residence, the dwelling is exempt indefinitely.

If the dwelling is exempt, there is no council tax to pay.

There are a number of other exemptions that are not specifically aimed at students. For details, see CPAG's *Council Tax Handbook*.

## Who is liable for council tax

Most full-time students are not liable to pay council tax. This is because either the dwelling is exempt because everyone who lives in it is a full-time student or, if a student lives with non-students, s/he is usually deemed exempt from liability for the council tax due on the property.

If the dwelling is not exempt from council tax, at least one person is liable for the bill. This depends on her/his position in a liability hierarchy. The person who comes the highest in the hierarchy is the one who is liable to pay. If there are two or more people at the same level in the hierarchy, they are usually jointly liable (see p274).

### Council tax liability hierarchy
Resident with a freehold interest in the property
Resident with a leasehold on the property, or the superior leaseholder if there is more than one
Resident tenant
Resident statutory or secure tenant
Resident who is a licensee
Other resident, including a squatter

If students share accommodation with non-students who are at the same level in the hierarchy, the non-students are liable, but the students are not.[18]

There is one situation in which a student may be liable for council tax. If a non-student adult lives in a property, it is not exempt from council tax. If you are a full-time student living with non-students, but you are higher on the hierarchy of liability than the non-students (eg, you are the owner of the property or the only person named on the tenancy agreement), the property is not exempt from council tax. However, because you are higher on the hierarchy of liability, you, not the non-students, are liable for the council tax. In this case, you may be entitled to a discount on the bill or to council tax reduction, depending on your circumstances.

### Example: joint tenants
Three students, Pooja, Joey and Zarah, share a flat as joint tenants. While they are all students the flat is exempt and there is no council tax to pay. Joey drops out of his course. The flat is no longer exempt and Joey is solely liable for the whole council tax bill (although there is a discount). Pooja and Zarah are not liable for any council tax. Joey should apply for a council tax reduction if his income is low.

### Examples: students who are liable
Antonia is studying full time and owns the flat in which she lives. She rents a room to a friend, Bill, who is not a student. Antonia is liable for the council tax. As there is only one non-student at the property, there is a 25 per cent discount on the bill. Bill is not liable for any council tax.

Raj is studying full time and rents the flat in which he lives. He sublets a room to a friend who is also a student. Raj is higher on the hierarchy of liability, but, as both of them are students, the flat is exempt from council tax and the bill is nil.

## Joint liability
'Joint and several liability' means that, in legal terms, you can be held liable for all of a bill on which you are named, or a share of it, even though there are other

named individuals. It gives the local authority the right to pursue as many, or as few, of the people named on the council tax bill for payment as it wants, regardless of how many liable residents there are, or were, in the property.[19]

In practice, local authorities try to bill as many liable people as possible. However, if a local authority cannot contact all the liable people (eg, because someone has moved out of the property and left no contact details), those who it can contact can be required to pay the total amount between them. If a local authority can only contact one individual, it can require that person to pay the whole bill.

Usually, couples (of the same or opposite sex, and whether married, in a civil partnership or cohabiting) who live together are jointly liable for the council tax. Students, however, are exempt from this rule. If you have a non-student partner who is liable for council tax, you are not jointly liable while you are a student.[20]

## Discounts

The full council tax bill assumes that there are two adults living in the property. If there is only one person living in the property, you get a discount of 25 per cent. If there is no one living in the property, you get a discount of 50 per cent.

Some people are disregarded when counting how many people live in the property. They are sometimes described as 'invisible' or having a 'status discount'.

The following people are disregarded in this way:
- anyone under 18 years old;
- anyone aged 18 or over for whom child benefit is payable;
- full-time students;
- partners of students who are not British citizens and whose immigration status prevents them from taking up paid employment or accessing social security benefits (though not necessarily both);
- someone under age 20 who was on a non-advanced course of education and who left school or college after 1 May. The discount applies from 1 May until 31 October;
- student nurses – ie, those studying for registration;
- apprentices training for an NVQ and on low pay;
- others – eg, carers, hospital patients and trainees. See CPAG's *Council Tax Handbook* for details.

## Disability reduction

The council tax bill is reduced to the valuation band below your own band if you or anyone else (adult or child) who is resident in the property is substantially and permanently disabled and uses a wheelchair indoors or needs an extra room.

# 3. **Council tax reduction**

Council tax reduction is administered by local authorities and helps you pay your council tax. It replaced council tax benefit (CTB) in April 2013, and may be referred to by your local authority as 'council tax support', or similar. Since April 2013, local authorities have had the discretion on how to run their own schemes. However, there is a 'default scheme', which is similar to CTB and which has been adopted by a large number of local authorities.[21] If you live in Wales, there is a national scheme and local authorities are funded by the Welsh government, so most people will have seen no change in their council tax support from the previous CTB.[22]

If you have reached pension age, your local authority should provide support that mirrors that previously available under the CTB scheme.[23]

Most full-time students do not need to claim help as they are not liable for council tax. If you are liable, you might be able to get council tax reduction, depending on your local scheme.

In general if your local authority has adopted the default scheme and you are a full-time student, you are not eligible for help unless you get certain other benefits, you are a lone parent or one of a student couple with children, or you are disabled.

If you are a part-time student, you may get help, depending on your circumstances and the details of your local scheme. The fact that you are a part-time student, in itself, is unlikely to affect your eligibility for a reduction.

However, schemes may have individual differences, so ask your local authority for details of its scheme. **Note:** scheme rules may change from year to year.

# 4. **Second adult rebate**

Students in England who are liable for council tax may be able to claim second adult rebate. The law refers to this rebate as 'alternative maximum council tax reduction'. It is intended for people whose bill is higher because they live with someone who cannot get a status discount (see p275), but who cannot make a full contribution towards the bill. You can only get a second adult rebate if you live with others who are not full-time students. **Note:** second adult rebate is not available in Wales.

Since April 2013, local authorities have been able to choose whether to offer second adult rebates. If so, your entitlement depends on the income of the person who shares with you. Your own income or capital is ignored.

You may be able to get a second adult rebate if:
- you are liable for council tax or you are jointly liable and all of those jointly liable are (or all but one are) students or have a status discount for some other reason (see p275); *and*

- you have a 'second adult' (see below) living with you; *and*
- the second adult is on income support (IS), income-based jobseeker's allowance (JSA), income-related employment and support allowance (ESA), pension credit (PC) or universal credit (UC), or has a low income.

### Second adult

A **'second adult'** is someone aged 18 or over who is a non-dependant – ie, someone who lives with you on a non-commercial basis, is not a student and does not have a status discount for any other reason.

If you are eligible for second adult rebate and for council tax reduction, the local authority decides which is worth the most to you. You cannot get both at the same time. If you get a second adult rebate, your council tax is reduced by 25 per cent, 15 per cent or 7.5 per cent depending on the income of the second adult. You may be able to get a reduction of 100 per cent if the second adult gets IS, income-based JSA, income-related ESA, PC or UC.

As the rules on second adult rebate are complex, get advice from your students' union, institution or local Citizens Advice Bureau.

# Notes

2. **Who pays council tax**
1 Sch 1 para 5(1) CT(DD)O
2 Sch 1 para 6(1)(a) CT(DD)O
3 Sch 1 para 6(1)(e) CT(DD)O
4 Sch 1 para 6(1)(c) CT(DD)O
5 Sch 1 para 6(1)(d) CT(DD)O
6 Sch 1 paras 5(3) and 6(2) CT(DD)O
7 Sch 1 para 3 CT(DD)O
8 Sch 1 para 5(2) CT(DD)O
9 Sch 1 para 4(1) CT(DD)O
10 Sch 1 para 3 CT(DD)O
11 Council tax information letter 5, 29 April 1996
12 Valuation Tribunal for England appeals 1765M88934/176C and 1765M88933/176C
13 Sch 1 para 5 LGFA 1992
14 Art 5 CT(DD)O
15 Kent Valuation Tribunal appeal 2220M23702/148C/1

16 *Fayad v Lewisham* [2008] EWHC 2531 (Admin)
17 Reg 3 CT(ED)O
18 s74 LGA 2003
19 s6 LGFA 1992
20 ss9 and 77 LGFA 1992

3. **Council tax reduction**
21 CTRS(DS)(E) Regs
22 CTRS(PR)(W) Regs
23 Reg 11 CTRS(PR)(E) Regs

# Chapter 26

## Tax and national insurance

**This chapter covers:**
1. Income tax (below)
2. National insurance contributions (p283)

*Basic facts*
- In general, students pay income tax and national insurance like everyone else.
- Most educational grants and scholarships, most research awards, and student loans and grants from discretionary funds do not normally count as taxable income, so most full-time students do not pay income tax or national insurance contributions on their student support.
- For all tax purposes, it is important to keep the relevant paperwork – eg, wage slips and tax forms from your employer, bank and building society statements and interest details, and invoices and receipts if you are self-employed.

## 1. Income tax

### Rates and allowances

Income tax is charged on 'taxable income' arising during a tax year (6 April to the following 5 April).[1] 'Taxable income' is your income from all sources, after deducting your personal allowance and any other allowable deductions, such as the blind person's allowance.

*Income tax rates 2015/16*
Percentage taxable income

| | |
|---|---|
| 20% basic rate | up to £31,785 |
| 40% higher rate | £31,786–£150,000 |
| 45% additional rate | £150,001 and above |

Every person resident in the UK has a personal allowance. This is an amount of annual income on which you do not have to pay tax. The allowance is deducted from your total taxable income before the relevant tax rate is applied. You may also be able to claim other tax allowances, such as the married couple's allowance, depending on your personal circumstances.

*Income tax personal allowances 2015/16*

| | |
|---|---|
| Personal allowance[2] | £10,600 |
| Blind person's allowance (additional)[3] | £2,290 |

**Note**: if your annual income is more than £100,000, your personal allowance is reduced by £1 for every £2 of additional income. If your income is high enough, your allowance can be reduced to nil.

**Note also:** if you take on a second part-time job while you are studying and you do not earn enough to pay tax in the first one, you can ask HM Revenue and Customs (HMRC) to split your tax allowance between your two jobs, so that your second job is not taxed at the higher (or basic) rate.

Up-to-date allowances and tax rates can be found at www.gov.uk/income-tax-rates.

The blind person's allowance can be claimed if you have a severe sight impairment. You do not have to be entirely without sight to be entitled. Claim the allowance by calling HMRC on 0300 200 3301 if either:

- you are registered blind with a local authority in England and Wales; *or*
- you live in Northern Ireland and your vision is so poor that it prevents you from doing any work for which eyesight is essential.

If you are married or in a civil partnership, the blind person's allowance can be transferred to your spouse or civil partner if you do not have enough taxable income to use any or all of it yourself.

*Example: working out the tax due*

Alice earns £18,000 in her placement year from September 2014 to August 2015, so £10,500 is earned in the seven months to 5 April 2015 (the 2014/15 tax year) and £7,500 from 6 April 2015 (the 2015/16 tax year). In each tax year, she has a personal allowance. In 2014/15, she pays no tax on the first £10,000 and 20 per cent on the remaining £500 – ie, £100. She should pay no tax in 2015/16, assuming she does not work after August 2015 for the rest of the tax year. Note, however, that she will have tax deducted from her pay in 2015/16, but will be able to claim it back after she stops work or at the end of the tax year.

## Students who are not domiciled in the UK

Most students from overseas are regarded as 'non-domiciled'. This means that different tax rules may apply, depending on your circumstances. More information is available in the HMRC guide *Coming to the UK to Study?*, available from www.hmrc.gov.uk/cnr/guide-int-students.pdf, and the Low Incomes Tax Reform Group website at www.litrg.org.uk/tax-guides/migrants/coming-to-the-uk-to-study.

## Spouses and civil partners

Spouses and civil partners are taxed separately; each is responsible for her/his own tax affairs. However, if one partner is claiming child benefit and one earns above £50,000, your individual tax affairs are affected. See www.gov.uk/child-benefit-tax-charge for more information.

## Sponsorships and scholarships

Sponsorships and scholarships are not usually taxable, provided they do 'no more than support a student during a period of study'.[4]

If you are receiving a scholarship, it is advisable to obtain written confirmation from the body making the award that it is, in fact, tax free.

If you are required to work in a company or organisation and its sponsorship is part payment for this, see p282.

## Benefits

Some benefits are taxable and others are not. A comprehensive guide is at www.litrg.org.uk or see CPAG's *Welfare Benefits and Tax Credits Handbook*. For example, income support is not normally taxable and housing benefit is not taxable, but jobseeker's allowance (both contribution-based and income-based) is taxable.

The tax due is not deducted when the benefit is paid, but reduces the refund you might otherwise receive through the Pay As You Earn (PAYE) system when you either return to work or reach the end of the tax year, whichever is sooner.[5]

## Bank and building society interest

Banks and building societies must deduct income tax at 20 per cent from interest payments before they are credited to your savings account. However, from April 2015, no tax is paid on interest if your total income (ie, your taxable income from all sources before any tax is deducted) is below £15,500. If you believe you qualify, you should complete Form R85 and give it to your bank or building society. If tax is deducted from your interest and you are not due to pay any tax, or if the amount deducted is more than you are due to pay, you can claim some or all of the tax back by completing Form R40.

Forms R40 and R85 can be found at www.gov.uk/government/collections/income-tax-forms.

*Tax rates for savings income 2015/16*
*Percentage savings income*

| | |
|---|---|
| 0% starting rate | £0 – £5,000 |
| 20% basic rate | £0 – £31,785 |
| 40% higher rate | £31,786 – £150,000 |
| 45% additional rate | above £150,000 |

The new 0 per cent rate only applies if your total income (from wages, benefits and savings) is less than your personal allowance plus £5,000. This means that in 2015/16 your savings are tax free if your total income plus savings is £15,600 or less.

If you have other taxable income (eg, from earnings), your savings may be taxed at a higher rate.

## Dividends on shares

Dividends are paid by companies on their shares and are a way of passing the profits to their shareholders. The dividend paid to shareholders is the net amount after a 10 per cent 'tax credit' has been attributed to it. So, a 'net dividend' is the amount of dividend you actually receive as a cheque or paid directly into your bank account. For example, if you are paid £900 as a net dividend, this is worth £1,000 before the tax credit is paid.

In 2015/16, tax is charged on dividends at:
- 10 per cent on dividends up to £31,785. As the 10 per cent has already been deducted, you do not need to pay any further tax on your dividends;
- 32.5 per cent (in practice, you pay tax at 22.5 per cent as you have already had 10 per cent deducted) up to £150,000;
- 37.5 per cent (in practice, you pay 27.5 per cent as you have already had 10 per cent deducted) on any amount above £150,000.

Unlike tax deducted from bank and building society interest, the dividend 'tax credit' is not refundable if you have paid too much tax in any tax year. However, it counts towards the amount of tax paid when calculating your overall tax position.

## Paying income tax

### Employed earners

Under the PAYE system, tax is deducted by your employer from each wage or salary payment, using a code number. Your code takes into account your tax allowances and any allowable deductions or restrictions. When you start a new job, your employer should ask you for 'new starter information' (previously, Form P46) to ensure that you pay the correct amount of tax. However, because of the way in which PAYE works, it is not uncommon for students to pay too much tax and then have to contact HMRC for a refund.

Check the tax code used against your income and be proactive in contacting HMRC if you think it is wrong or you do not understand it.

## Earnings during vacations

Students employed during vacations should expect to have tax deducted by their employer under the PAYE system. If at the end of the tax year you have overpaid tax, you can reclaim this from HMRC.

Before April 2013, employers could use a voluntary scheme, known as Form P38(S), which allowed them to pay students without deducting any tax, provided the student worked only in the vacations (and not at all during term time) and her/his overall income did not exceed her/his personal allowance over the whole tax year. However, from April 2013 and the introduction of 'real time' PAYE, the majority of employers can no longer do this. This means that, even if you are not going to earn over the annual tax threshold, you may pay tax on your vacation earnings. If you have paid too much tax in that tax year, you should contact HMRC for a refund.

## Placement students

Wages or salaries paid to placement students during periods of practical work experience (including sandwich courses) are taxable as earned income under PAYE, subject to the usual tax-free personal allowances and allowable employment expenses. However, if an employer sponsors your study, any wages/salary paid for periods spent at college can be paid tax free if:

- you are studying full time at a university, technical college or similar educational facility which is generally open to the public and offers more than one course – ie, employer 'in-house' training does not qualify;
- you are enrolled for at least one academic year (1 September to 31 August);
- you attend the course for at least 20 weeks in that academic year or, if the course is longer, for at least an average of 20 weeks in an academic year;
- your earnings, including lodging or subsistence allowances, are not more than £15,480 (excluding any fees paid by the employer).

These rules also apply if you are being released by your employer to study a course, but continue to be paid as a full-time employee. For further guidance, see www.gov.uk/student-jobs-paying-tax.

## Self-employed earners

If you are self-employed, you must usually complete a self-assessment return and pay income tax directly to HMRC. You must also let HMRC know when you first become self-employed. Call 0300 200 3504 or register your new business online at www.gov.uk/working-for-yourself.

There are strict rules on completing self-assessment tax returns – make sure you are aware of the deadlines and requirements so that you avoid penalties. Guidance is available from www.gov.uk/self-assessment-tax-returns.

If you need help with your return, call HMRC's self-assessment helpline on 0300 200 3310 or textphone 0300 200 3319.

# 2. National insurance contributions

National insurance (NI) contributions are paid by those who earn above a certain amount as a way of contributing to the social security system. Paying contributions during your working life can entitle you to a range of benefits, including retirement pension. HM Revenue and Customs (HMRC) keeps a record of everyone's contributions.

There are different types of contributions (called 'classes').

## Contributions and benefit entitlement

NI contributions can count towards your future entitlement to social security benefits.

- **Class 1 contributions** may later entitle you to contributory employment and support allowance (ESA), contribution-based jobseeker's allowance (JSA), retirement pension, maternity allowance, bereavement allowance and widowed parent's allowance. If you are a low earner, you can build up an entitlement to contributory benefits if you are earning between the 'lower earnings limit' (£112 a week in 2015/16) and the earnings threshold of £155 a week, even though you are not actually paying NI contributions.
- **Class 2 contributions** may later entitle you to contributory ESA, retirement pension, bereavement allowance and maternity allowance.
- **Class 3 contributions** are voluntary and allow you to top up your contribution record to qualify for a higher retirement pension, and for widows' and bereavement benefits.
- **Class 4 contributions** do not give entitlement to any social security benefits.

The exact amount of contributions required depends on the benefit concerned.

**Note:** paying NI contributions does not entitle you to benefits you would not otherwise be able to claim as a student.

## National insurance numbers

HMRC should issue you with an NI number shortly before your 16th birthday.

Employers must have an NI number for each employee. If you have been allocated a number but cannot find it, you should ring the NI numbers helpline on 0300 200 3502. If you have not been allocated a number (eg, if you are an international student who is permitted to work in the UK), contact Jobcentre Plus on 0345 600 0643. Who you need to contact in Northern Ireland varies depending on what you need the NI number for. See www.nidirect.gov.uk or contact your nearest NI number processing centre (Belfast area: 028 9013 8286, Southern area: 028 3877 3046 or Northern area: 028 7185 5406).

If a new number must be issued, the process can take several weeks to be completed. However, if you have lost your number, your employer can send the appropriate tax forms to HMRC without one, and attempts are automatically made to trace your number and inform your employer when it is found.

## Contribution rates

### National insurance contribution rates 6 April 2015 to 5 April 2016

| Contribution type | Weekly earnings | Employee's contribution |
|---|---|---|
| Class 1 (employed) | Below £155 | Nil |
| | £155.01 – £815 | 12% (if in additional state pension) |
| | | 10.6% (if contracted out of additional state pension) |
| | £815.01 and over | 2% |
| Class 2 (self-employed) | | £2.80 per week of self-employment |
| Class 3 (voluntary) | | £14.10 a week |
| Class 4 (self-employed) | Profits between £8,060 and £42,385 | 9% |
| | Profits above £42,385 | 2% |

## Who must pay national insurance contributions

### Age limits

No NI contributions are payable if you are under 16 or over state pension age, although you may have to apply for an exemption if your earnings would otherwise attract NI.

### Vacation or part-time work

Students do not pay NI contributions on any form of student support. However, if you work and earn more than the 'earnings threshold' of £155 a week, you must pay Class 1 (earnings-related) contributions. Your employer deducts these from your wages before you are paid. See p284 for the rates.

*Example*

Bob earns £900 a week. He pays no NI contributions on the first £155. He pays 12 per cent on the next £660 (£79.20) and 2 per cent on the remaining £95 (£1.90). His weekly NI contributions are, therefore, £81.10.

## Self-employed students

If you are self-employed, you must pay a flat-rate Class 2 NI contribution of £2.80 for each week of self-employment if your income is more than £5,965 in the 2015/16 tax year. If your profits are below £5,965, you can apply for an exemption on the basis of low income. However, you may decide to continue to pay your NI contributions as, if you stop, your future entitlement to certain social security benefits may be affected.[6]

You must pay Class 4 NI contributions of 9 per cent on your taxable business profits between £8,060 and £42,385 and 2 per cent on any amount above this.[7]

## Postgraduate students

If you are a research student, check whether you are liable for Class 1 or Class 2 and Class 4 contributions if you are paid for teaching or other similar work.

## Placement students

Placement students are liable to pay Class 1 NI contributions while receiving a salary for periods of work experience, although this income can be classed as 'exempt scholarship income' for periods spent attending college (see p280).

If you have been released from work to take a course but continue to be paid by your employer, some of this income can qualify as scholarship income and is exempt from contributions.

## Voluntary contributions

Your entitlement to state retirement pension depends on your having paid NI contributions at a certain level for a certain number of years during your working life. The exact number of years depends on when you reach state retirement age.

However, if your payment record is incomplete, you can pay voluntary contributions to make up the 'missing' years. These Class 3 NI contributions are paid at a flat rate – £14.10 a week in 2015/16.[8]

You can preserve your entitlement to retirement pension and also to widows' and bereavement benefits in this way. Voluntary contributions do not count towards short-term benefits, such as contribution-based JSA, contributory ESA and maternity allowance.

## Deciding whether to pay voluntary contributions

Before committing yourself to paying voluntary Class 3 NI contributions, contact the Future Pension Centre (tel: 0345 300 0168; textphone: 0345 300 0169) or see www.gov.uk/plan-retirement-income/pensions-from-the-government to establish your likely pension at retirement age and, therefore, whether it is necessary to make voluntary contributions. This is especially relevant if you are a mature or postgraduate student, have taken time out of work to care for children or adults (in which case, you might be 'credited' with NI contributions), or if you have lived abroad for long periods of time during your working life. Under the current rules, most younger students will not reduce their pension entitlement by not paying NI contributions during their studies, as they will have sufficient time after completing full-time education in which to do so.

Voluntary contributions can generally only be paid up to the end of the sixth tax year after they were 'due'.

# Notes

1. **Income tax**
   1  s1 FA 2013
   2  s2 FA 2013
   3  ss38-41 ITA 2007
   4  s776 IT(TOI)A 2005; HMRC,
      *Employment Income Manual,* para 06220
   5  ss671-75 IT(EP)A 2003 and part 8
      IT(PAYE) Regs

2. **National insurance contributions**
   6  s11 SSCBA 1992
   7  s15 SSCBA 1992
   8  s13 SSCBA 1992

# Chapter 27

# Time out from studies

**This chapter covers:**
1. Time out because of ill health (below)
2. Time out because of pregnancy and children (p289)
3. Time out to be a carer (p291)
4. Re-sits (p292)

*Basic facts*

– Students may be able to receive student support or get social security benefits during periods of absence from their course.
– Support is usually only available if you have taken time out because you are ill or pregnant, or because you have to care for someone.
– Support may also be available once you have recovered from your illness or your caring responsibilities have ceased and you are waiting to return to your course.

## 1. Time out because of ill health

### Full-time students

Which benefits you are eligible for depends on how long you have been ill, your age, whether you have paid any national insurance (NI) contributions, and whether you need personal care or have mobility difficulties. Once you have recovered, you may be able to 'sign on' for jobseeker's allowance (JSA) until you can return to your course.

This chapter provides a checklist of benefits for which you might be eligible if you meet the other conditions for that benefit. For more details about a benefit and how to claim it, see the relevant chapter.

You still count as a full-time student when taking time out of your course, unless you have completely abandoned or been dismissed from it.[1]

#### From the start of your ill health

If you have paid sufficient NI contributions in recent years, you are eligible for contributory employment and support allowance (ESA) after seven 'waiting days' (see Chapter 10).

## From three months

You can claim personal independence payment (PIP) if you need help getting around or with daily living activities because of a disability. You are eligible for this after three months if your disability is likely to last at least another nine months.

If you get PIP or disability living allowance (DLA), you can also claim income-related ESA. You are usually also eligible for housing benefit (HB) to help with your rent.

If you come under the universal credit (UC) system (see p199), you can claim UC if you get PIP or DLA and you have 'limited capability for work'.

## From 28 weeks

Once you have had 'limited capability for work' for 28 weeks, you can claim HB to help with your rent.

The 28-week period runs from the day your limited capability for work begins, not from the day you leave your course. See p122 for how limited capability for work is assessed. You do not need to have been working to count as having limited capability for work. **Note:** you can have limited capability for work but still be able to study, so HB can continue when you return to college or university.

### Example

Sean is ill and takes time out of his course. He is not eligible for PIP, and has not worked enough to qualify for contributory ESA. He gets no benefits until he has been ill for 28 weeks, when he can claim HB. He makes a claim for ESA, supported by a backdated medical certificate, in order to establish his limited capability for work, and also fills in a claim form for HB.

## Once you have recovered

Once you have recovered, you may need to wait some time to be readmitted to your course. During this time, you can claim JSA (you must 'sign on' at the Jobcentre Plus office) and HB.[2]

You can claim for up to one year from the day you recover until the day the college or university agrees you can return to your course. You are not eligible if you get a grant or loan during this time. Once the student support stops, you can claim benefit.

## Student support

Although regulations allow payment of student loans to be suspended after 60 days' absence because of ill health, Student Finance England, Student Finance Wales and Student Finance NI have the discretion to continue to pay you until the end of the academic year.

Your college or university should tell Student Finance England/Student Finance Wales/Student Finance NI the reason you have suspended your studies.

Your college or university should write to Student Finance England/Student Finance Wales/Student Finance NI explaining why it has suspended you from your course. You should also contact Student Finance England/Student Finance Wales/Student Finance NI in writing and request that it continues to pay you while you are ill. You are normally asked to provide medical evidence.

Any student who is personally eligible can also apply to the college or university for discretionary help from its hardship funds.

If you receive a bursary and want to take time out from your studies, check with the institution to see whether it continues to be paid during your time out and what happens when you return to your studies.

If you take time out from your course because of ill health and are not paid a student loan during this time, the unpaid student loan does not count as 'notional' income when calculating your ESA.[3] For HB, the unpaid loan is arguably not counted as 'notional' income because payment of it is discretionary.

## Part-time students

If you are a part-time student, you can claim income-related ESA as soon as you are ill or disabled (or UC, if you come under the UC system – see p199), whether or not you get DLA or PIP.

### From the start of your ill health

If you are already getting JSA, you can continue to do so for up to 13 weeks. After that, you must claim ESA instead.

You can claim ESA if your income is low or you have paid sufficient NI contributions, and HB.

### From three months

You can claim PIP if you need help getting around or with daily living activities because of a disability. You are eligible for this after three months if your disability is likely to last at least another nine months.

### Once you have recovered

You can claim JSA if you are available for work.

---

# 2. Time out because of pregnancy and children

## Student support

If you are a full-time undergraduate student receiving a student loan paid for living costs, Student Finance England, Student Finance Wales or Student Finance

NI normally stops your student support once you suspend your studies. However, they all have the discretion to continue making loan payments for the rest of that academic year.[4]

Your college or university should write to Student Finance England/Student Finance Wales/Student Finance NI explaining why it has suspended you from your course. You should also contact Student Finance England/Student Finance Wales/Student Finance NI in writing to request that it continues to pay you while you are taking time out. You are usually asked to provide medical evidence as well as evidence of potential hardship if applicable.

If you are an NHS-funded healthcare student in England or Wales, you can receive an NHS maternity bursary for up to 45 weeks while on maternity leave. Contact NHS Student Bursaries in England or the NHS Student Awards Unit in Wales for details.

You could also apply to your college or university for support from its hardship funds.

If you receive a bursary from your college or university and want to take time out from your studies, check with the institution to see whether this continues to be paid during your time out and what happens when you return to your studies.

## Benefits

There is no provision for pregnant full-time students to claim income support (IS), housing benefit (HB) or universal credit (UC).

As a part-time student, you can claim IS once you reach the 11th week before your expected week of childbirth, or earlier if your pregnancy has made you ill and incapable of work.

If you have an employer, you may be able to get statutory maternity pay. If you are not working now but have worked recently, you may be able to get maternity allowance.

Once the baby is born, there are various benefits you can claim.

Nursing and midwifery students can continue to receive their bursary for a period of up to 45 weeks' maternity leave.

## Lone parents

Once the baby is born, if you are a lone parent studying full time you can claim:
- child benefit;
- child tax credit (CTC);
- IS if your youngest child is under five or you are under 18;
- HB;
- if there is no child under 16 already in the household, a Sure Start maternity grant of £500. Claims must be made within three months of the birth or, in some cases, before the birth (see p196);
- Healthy Start food vouchers and vitamins (see p134).

If you are not eligible for IS as a lone parent because your child is over the age at which you count as a lone parent, you may be able to claim jobseeker's allowance (JSA) in the summer vacation only (see Chapter 14). You may also be able to claim IS over the summer instead, not because you are a lone parent (although you must have a dependent child) but, for example, because you are a carer or you are in the last few months of pregnancy. If you come under the UC system (see p199), you can claim UC instead of CTC, IS and HB.

## Fathers and partners

If your partner has had a baby and you have an employer, you may be able to claim statutory paternity pay. You can claim if you are the child's father or the mother's partner and you will be caring for the baby or the mother. You may also be able to claim statutory shared parental pay.

## Couples

A full-time student couple (ie, both are students) with a child can claim throughout the course:
- child benefit;
- CTC;
- HB;
- Healthy Start food vouchers and vitamins (see p134).

A full-time student couple with a child can claim in the summer vacation:
- IS (if eligible under the usual non-student rules);
- JSA.

Couples can also claim a Sure Start maternity grant if one partner gets a qualifying benefit and there is no child under 16 already in the household (see p196).

If you are a full-time student and a parent and you have a partner who is not a student, s/he can claim benefits for you under the usual benefit rules.

If you come under the UC system (see p199), you can claim UC instead of CTC, IS/JSA and HB.

# 3. **Time out to be a carer**

If you are a full-time student, you may have stopped attending your course in order to care for someone. If you suspend your studies, your funding is usually also suspended. However, Student Finance England, Student Finance Wales or Student Finance NI has the discretion to keep paying your student loan and grant for living costs, if you have been receiving one.[5]

You must write and request that it does this. In most cases, you must provide evidence of your circumstances, including evidence that you will be in hardship if you are not paid during this time. You could also apply to your college or university for support its hardship funds.

If, once your caring responsibilities have come to an end, you have to wait before you can return to the course, you can 'sign on' for jobseeker's allowance, and claim housing benefit (or universal credit if you come under the new system – see p199). You can claim for up to a year until the day from when the university or college agrees you can return to your course.[6] You are not eligible, however, if you get a grant or loan during this time.

If you receive a bursary from your college or university and want to take time out from your studies, you should check with the institution to see whether this continues to be paid while you take time out and what happens when you return to your studies.

Part-time students can claim income support (IS) and carer's allowance. If you come under the UC system (see p199), you can claim UC instead of IS.

See Chapter 7 for information on claiming carer's allowance.

## 4. Re-sits

If you are a full-time student taking time out to re-sit exams, you are still treated as a student during your absence from the course. You cannot claim income support (IS), jobseeker's allowance (JSA), income-related employment and support allowance (ESA), housing benefit or universal credit during this time, unless you would be eligible anyway as a student – eg, as a lone parent. However, if you are taking professional qualifications set by a professional institute or some other body unconnected to your own college or university, you may be able to claim IS, JSA or income-related ESA while taking time out for re-sits. You may need to appeal and argue that caselaw supports your getting benefit.[7]

**Note:** you also continue to count as a full-time student if you are doing re-sits after the official end date of your course.

# Notes

1. **Time out because of ill health**
   1 **ESA** Reg 2(1), definition of 'period of study', ESA Regs
     **HB** Reg 53(2)·HB Regs
     **UC** Reg 13(1)(a) UC Regs
   2 **JSA** Reg 1(3D) JSA Regs; para 30209 DMG
     **HB** Reg 56(6) HB Regs
     **UC** Reg 13(4) UC Regs
   3 Reg 137(4A) ESA Regs

2. **Time out because of pregnancy and children**
   4 Reg 112(12)-(13) E(SS) Regs

3. **Time out to be a carer**
   5 Reg 112(12)-(13) E(SS) Regs
   6 **JSA** Reg 1 JSA Regs
     **HB** Reg 56(6) HB Regs
     **UC** Reg 13 (4) UC Regs
     HB/CTB Circular A32/2000, para 6

4. **Re-sits**
   7 R(JSA) 2/02

# Appendices

# Appendix 1

## Information and advice

### Student support

#### Official guidance

The Department for Business, Innovation and Skills issues guidance on existing higher education student support legislation for England and forthcoming provisions. The guidance has no legal standing, but may be quoted in an appeal. It is available at www.practitioners.slc.co.uk and includes:

- notes for funding bodies on the student support regulations;
- *Student Support Information Notices;*
- notes announcing forthcoming student support provision.

The Department for Education and the Department for Business, Innovation and Skills also issue guidance to providers and partners on the learner support schemes in further education in England. These can be found at www.gov.uk/sfa and www.gov.uk/efa.

Information and guidance on funding in Wales is available at www.studentfinancewales.co.uk/practitioners.

Information and support fund guidance for higher education institutions in Northern Ireland is available on the Department for Employment and Learning website at www.delni.gov.uk/articles/higher-education-student-finance.

#### Advice

Contact student advisers within institutions and students' unions for advice on student support. A list of advisory services is available on the website of the National Association of Student Money Advisers at www.nasma.org.uk.

### Social security benefits and tax credits

#### Publications

The following are available from CPAG at 30 Micawber Street, London N1 7TB. You can order online at www.shop.cpag.org.uk, or telephone CPAG on 020 7837 7979.

- *Benefits for Students in Scotland Handbook* 2015/16, £20.
- *Welfare Benefits and Tax Credits Handbook* 2015/16, £59. The 2016/17 edition is due in April 2016 and is also available online. See www.shop.cpag.org.uk/publications for more information.
- *Council Tax Handbook*, 11th edition (autumn 2015), £22.
- *Universal Credit: what you need to know*, 3rd edition (autumn 2015), £15.
- *Disability Rights Handbook* 2015/16, £33.50.

## Official guidance

The following guidance, used by decision makers in the Department for Work and Pensions and local authorities, is available at www.gov.uk/dwp. It has no legal standing, but may be used in an appeal, revision or supersession.

- *Advice for Decision Making* (universal credit and personal independence payment).
- *Housing Benefit and Council Tax Benefit Guidance Manual.*
- *Decision Makers' Guide* (other benefits).

In Northern Ireland, guidance is provided by the Department for Social Development (DSD) and is available at www.dsdni.gov.uk.

## Legislation

- *The Law Relating to Social Security.* This is available at http://lawvolumes.dwp.gov.uk. These volumes are officially produced and contain updated Acts and regulations relating to social security.
- *Social Security Legislation*, Volumes 1 to 5. Published by Sweet and Maxwell, these volumes contain updated Acts and regulations covering social security and tax credits with explanatory commentary. Available from CPAG.
- CPAG's *Housing Benefit and Council Tax Reduction Legislation* contains updated Acts and regulations and a detailed commentary.
- Decisions of the Upper Tribunal are available from the HM Courts and Tribunals Service website at www.osscsc.gov.uk/decisions/decisions.htm.

## Advice

Contact your student services department or students' union for advice on studying and claiming benefits.

## Other financial help

### Publications

- *The Guide to Educational Grants* 2015/16 (published by Directory of Social Change).
- *The Guide to Grants for Individuals in Need* 2015/16 (published by Directory of Social Change).
- *The Directory of Grant Making Trusts* 2016/17 (published by Directory of Social Change).
- *Charities Digest* 2015 (published by Charity Choice).
- *The Grants Register* 2016 (published by Palgrave Macmillan), containing information on postgraduate student awards for both the UK and overseas.
- *British Music EducationYearbook* 2015/16 (published by Rhinegold Publishing).

Many of these publications can be found online, or in public libraries, university or college libraries. Advice centres may also carry some.

# Appendix 2
## Useful addresses

### General sources of information
#### National Union of Students UK

**England**
Macadam House
275 Gray's Inn Road
London WC1X 8QB
Tel: 0845 521 0262
nusuk@nus.org.uk
www.nus.org.uk

**Wales**
2nd Floor, Cambrian Buildings
Mount Stuart Square
Cardiff CF10 5FL
Tel: 02920 435 390
office@nus-wales.org.uk

**Northern Ireland**
NUS–Union of Students in Ireland
42 Dublin Road
Belfast BT2 7HN
Tel: 028 9024 4641
info@nistudents.org
www.nus-usi.org

NUS provides information on entitlement to student support, benefits and tax credits, along with other student welfare issues.

### Child Poverty Action Group
30 Micawber Street
London N1 7TB
Tel: 020 7837 7979
Advice line for advisers only:
020 7812 5231 (10am–12pm and 2–4pm Monday to Friday)
advice@cpag.org.uk
www.cpag.org.uk/advisers

CPAG provides advice, information and training to advisers.

## Low Incomes Tax Reform Group
1st Floor
Artillery House
11–19 Artillery Row
London SW1P 1RT
www.litrg.org.uk
www.taxguideforstudents.org.uk

The Low Incomes Tax Reform Group provides extensive information on students and the taxation system, including student loan repayment.

## The Money Charity
15 Prescott Place
London SW4 6BS
Tel: 020 7062 8933
hello@themoneycharity.org.uk
www.themoneycharity.org.uk

The Money Charity provides general advice on money management, including a free guide, *The Student Money Manual*.

## UKCISA (UK Council for International Student Affairs)
9–17 St Albans Place
London N1 0NX
Advice line: 020 7788 9214 (1–4pm, Monday to Friday)
www.ukcisa.org.uk

UKCISA provides advice and information for overseas students.

## Disability Rights UK
Ground Floor
CAN Mezzanine
49–51 East Road
London N1 6AH

Disabled students' helpline: 0800 328 5050 (11am–1pm Tuesdays and Thursdays)
Information service textphone: 18001 0800 328 5050
students@disabilityrightsuk.org
www.disabilityrightsuk.org

Disability Rights UK produces a number of booklets and information sheets.

## Support for learning
### Care Council for Wales
South Gate House
Wood Street
Cardiff CF10 1EW
Tel: 0300 303 3444
info@ccwales.org.uk
www.ccwales.org.uk

The Care Council for Wales provides bursary support to undergraduate social work students in Wales.

### Dance and drama awards
www.gov.uk/dance-drama-awards

### Department for Business, Innovation and Skills
1 Victoria Street
London SW1H 0ET
Tel: 020 7215 5000
enquiries@bis.gsi.gov.uk
www.gov.uk/bis

Responsible for student support for higher education in England and for adult learners in further education in England.

### Department for Education
Piccadilly Gate
Store Street
Manchester M1 2WD
Tel: 0370 000 2288
Textphone: 0370 000 2288
www.gov.uk/government/organisations/department-for-education

Responsible for learner support for 16–19-year-olds in England.

### Department for Employment and Learning
Student Finance Branch
Adelaide House
39–49 Adelaide Street
Belfast BT2 8FD
Tel: 028 9025 7777
info@delni.gov.uk
www.delni.gov.uk

Responsible for student financial support in Northern Ireland.

## Department of Health
Richmond House
79 Whitehall
London SW1A 2NS
Tel: 020 7210 4850
Textphone: 020 3741 8449
www.gov.uk/dh

Responsible for NHS-funded students in England.

## Department of Health, Social Services and Public Safety

### Nursing and midwifery bursaries
Bursary Administration Unit
Business Services Organisation
2 Franklin Street
Belfast BT2 8DQ
Tel: 028 9536 3817
studentnurse.bursaries@hscni.net
www.hscbusiness.hscni.net

### Social Work Student Incentive Scheme
Office of Social Services
Bursary Administration Section
Castle Buildings
Stormont
Belfast BT4 3SQ
Tel: 028 9536 3988
See also: www.nidirect.gov.uk/nhs-and-social-work-students

Provides bursaries for healthcare and social work students in Northern Ireland.

## Education Funding Agency
Student Bursary Support Team
Learner Support Provider Helpline: 0300 303 8610
Students/young parents: 0800 121 8989
1619bursary@studentbursarysupport.co.uk
C2L@studentbursarysupport.co.uk
www.gov.ac/efa
www.gov.uk/guidance/student-bursary-support-service

Funds further education for 16–19 year-olds in England.

## Get Into Teaching
https://getintoteaching.education.gov.uk
Tel: 0800 389 2500

Information on teacher training in England.

## NHS Business Services Authority

**NHS Student Bursaries**
  Ridgeway House
  Northgate Close
  Middlebrook
  Horwich
  Bolton BL6 6PQ
  Tel: 0300 330 1345
  nhsbsasbsms@nhs.net
  www.nhsbsa.nhs.uk/students

Provides information on funding and assessments for students undertaking allied
health professions courses in England.

**NHS Wales Student Awards Services**
  Floor 4
  Companies House
  Crown Way
  Cardiff CF14 3UB
  Tel: 02920 376 854
  www.nwsspstudentfinance.wales.nhs.uk

Provides information and assessments for students undertaking allied health
professions courses in Wales.

**Social work bursaries**
  PO Box 141
  Hesketh House
  200–220 Broadway
  Fleetwood FY7 9AS
  Tel: 0300 330 1342
  www.nhsbsa.nhs.uk/students

Administers social work bursaries for all social work students in England.

## Health Careers Helpline
  Tel: 0345 606 0655
  www.healthcareers.nhs.uk

Provides information on careers in the healthcare professions in the NHS in
England.

## Professional and career development loans
  Tel: 0800 100 900
  www.gov.uk/career-development-loans

## Research councils

### Arts and Humanities Research Council
Polaris House
North Star Avenue
Swindon SN2 1FL
Tel: 01793 416 000
enquiries@ahrc.ac.uk
www.ahrc.ac.uk

### Biotechnology and Biological Sciences Research Council
Polaris House
North Star Avenue
Swindon SN2 1UH
Tel: 01793 413 200
www.bbsrc.ac.uk

### Economic and Social Research Council
Polaris House
North Star Avenue
Swindon SN2 1UJ
Tel: 01793 413 000
www.esrc.ac.uk

### Engineering and Physical Sciences Research Council
Polaris House
North Star Avenue
Swindon SN2 1ET
Tel: 01793 444 000
epsrcstudentshipqueries@epsrc.ac.uk
www.epsrc.ac.uk

### Medical Research Council
Polaris House
North Star Avenue
Swindon SN2 1FL
Tel: 01793 416 200
rfpd@headoffice.mrc.ac.uk
www.mrc.ac.uk

### Natural Environment Research Council
Polaris House
North Star Avenue
Swindon SN2 1EU
Tel: 01793 411 500
stag@nerc.ac.uk
www.nerc.ac.uk

## Science and Technology Facilities Council
Polaris House
North Star Avenue
Swindon SN2 1SZ
Tel: 01793 413 195
studentships@stfc.ac.uk
www.stfc.ac.uk

## Skills Funding Agency
Cheylesmore House
Quinton Road
Coventry CV1 2WT
Tel: 0345 377 5000
info@sfa.bis.gov.uk
www.gov.uk/sfa

Allocates funding for adult further education and skills training in England.

## Student Loans Company
100 Bothwell Street
Glasgow G2 7JD
Tel: 0141 306 2000
www.slc.co.uk
**Student loan repayment**
Tel: 0300 100 0611
www.studentloanrepayment.co.uk

Responsible for administering the collection of student loans throughout the UK, in conjunction with HM Revenue and Customs.

## Student Finance England
PO Box 210
Darlington DL1 9HJ
Tel: 0300 100 0607

A part of the Student Loans Company, Student Finanace England is responsible for administering applications and payments of government-funded loans and grants in England.

Guides and information leaflets about financial support available for students are available from www.gov.uk/student-finance.

## Student Finance Wales
PO Box 211
Llandudno Junction LL30 9FU
Tel: 0300 200 4050
Minicom: 0300 100 1693
www.studentfinancewales.co.uk

Student Finance Wales is a Welsh government-led partnership, responsible for administering student financial support to students who normally live in Wales.

## Student Finance NI
County Hall
182 Galgorm Road
Ballymena
Co Antrim BT42 1HN
Tel: 0300 100 0077
Minicom: 0300 100 0625
www.studentfinanceni.co.uk
Further education awards: www.welbni.org/index.cfm/do/StudFin

Provides financial support to students who normally live in Northern Ireland, in partnership with the Department for Employment and Learning, the Student Loans Company and the five regional offices of the Education Authority in Northern Ireland.

## Student Finance Services Non-UK Team
Student Finance England
PO Box 89
Darlington DL1 9AZ
Tel: 0141 243 3570

Provides information about applications by European Union students for fee payment support in England, or migrant workers for fee and maintenance support.

## Teacher Training Cymru
www.teachertrainingcymru.org

Information on teacher training in Wales.

## Universities and Colleges Admissions Service
Rosehill
New Barn Lane
Cheltenham GL52 3LZ
Tel: 0371 468 0468 (undergraduates); 0371 468 0470 (performing arts);
0371 334 4447 (postgraduates); 0371 468 0469 (postgraduate teacher training)
Text relay service: 18001 plus relevant number
www.ucas.com

Contact UCAS for information on applying to higher education.

## Welsh government (education and skills)
Tel: 0300 060 3300
http://gov.wales/topics/educationandskills

Responsible for education funding in Wales.

## Benefits and tax credits
### Child tax credit and working tax credit helpline
Tel: 0345 300 3900
Textphone: 0345 300 3909
www.gov.uk/topic/benefits-credits/tax-credits

### Department for Work and Pensions
www.gov.uk/dwp
www.gov.uk/government/collections/dwp-detailed-benefit-guides
www. gov.uk/browse/benefits
www.gov.uk/government/publications

Responsible for social security in England, Wales and Scotland. The DWP website has information on general entitlement to benefits and contains the *Decision Makers' Guide* and *Advice for Decision Making* at www.gov.uk/government/publications.

### Department for Social Development
www.dsdni.gov.uk
www.nidirect.gov.uk/money-tax-and-benefits
Benefit Enquiry Line: 0800 220 674
Textphone: 028 9031 1092

Responsible for social security in Northern Ireland.

## Other issues
### Department of Health
Health and Social Care publications
PO Box 777
London SE1 6XH
Tel: 0300 123 1002
Minicom: 0300 123 1003
www.orderline.dh.gov.uk

For bulk orders of HC1 forms – eg, for students' union advice centres.

### NHS Business Services Authority Help with Health Costs
Bridge House
152 Pilgrim Street
Newcastle upon Tyne NE1 6SN
Tel: 0300 330 1343 or 0191 279 0565
www.nhsbsa.nhs.uk/helpwithhealthcosts.aspx

The NHS Business Services Authority Help with Health Costs advises students on getting help with their health costs on the grounds of low income.

## HM Revenue and Customs
For students: www.gov.uk/student-jobs-paying-tax
For the address of your nearest HMRC office and telephone numbers of helplines:
www.gov.uk/government/organisations/hm-revenue-customs/contact

## Local Government Ombudsman
PO Box 4771
Coventry CV4 0EH
Tel: 0300 061 0614
www.lgo.org.uk

The Local Government Ombudsman can investigate claims of maladministration by local authorities in England.

## Public Services Ombudsman for Wales
1 Ffordd yr Hen Gae
Pencoed CF35 5LJ
Tel: 0300 790 0203
www.ombudsman-wales.org.uk

The Public Services Ombudsman for Wales can investigate claims of maladministration by local authorities in Wales in respect of benefit claims or student support applications.

## Northern Ireland Ombudsman's Office
Freepost RTKS-BAJU-ALEZ
Belfast BT1 6BR
Tel: 0800 343 424/02890 233 821
Textphone: 02890 897 789
ombudsman@ni-ombudsman.org.uk
www.ni-ombudsman.org.uk

The Northern Ireland Ombudsman's Office can investigate claims of maladministration by local authorities in Northern Ireland in respect of benefit claims or student support applications.

# Appendix 3

## Abbreviations used in the notes

| | |
|---|---|
| AAC | Administrative Appeals Chamber |
| AACR | Administrative Appeals Chamber Reports |
| Art(s) | Article(s) |
| EWCA Civ | England and Wales Court of Appeal (Civil Division) |
| EWHC | England and Wales High Court |
| NICA | Northern Ireland Court of Appeal |
| para(s) | paragraph(s) |
| Reg(s) | regulation(s) |
| s(s) | section(s) |
| Sch(s) | Schedule(s) |
| UKUT | United Kingdom Upper Tribunal |
| vol | volume |

### Acts of Parliament

| | |
|---|---|
| CA 1989 | Children Act 1989 |
| EA 1996 | Education Act 1996 |
| ETA 1973 | Employment and Training Act 1973 |
| FA 2013 | Finance Act 2013 |
| HEA 2004 | Higher Education Act 2004 |
| ITA 2007 | Income Tax Act 2007 |
| IT(EP)A 2003 | Income Tax (Earnings and Pensions) Act 2003 |
| IT(TOI)A 2005 | Income Tax (Trading and Other Income) Act 2005 |
| JSA 1995 | Jobseekers Act 1995 |
| LGA 2003 | Local Government Act 2003 |
| LGFA 1992 | Local Government Finance Act 1992 |
| SSCBA 1992 | Social Security Contributions and Benefits Act 1992 |
| WRA 2007 | Welfare Reform Act 2007 |

## Regulations and other statutory instruments

| | |
|---|---|
| C(LC)SSB Regs | The Children (Leaving Care) Social Security Benefits Regulations 2001 No.3074 |
| CB Regs | The Child Benefit (General) Regulations 2006 No.223 |
| CBGA(A) Regs | The Child Benefit and Guardian's Allowance (Administration) Regulations 2003 No.492 |
| CT(DD)O | The Council Tax (Discount Disregards) Order 1992 No.548 |
| CT(ED)O | The Council Tax (Exempt Dwellings) Order 1992 No.558 |
| CTC Regs | The Child Tax Credit Regulations 2002 No.2007 |
| CTRS(DS)(E) Regs | The Council Tax Reduction Schemes (Default Scheme) (England) Regulations 2012 No.2886 |
| CTRS(PR)(E) Regs | The Council Tax Reduction Schemes (Prescribed Requirements) (England) Regulations 2012 No.2885 |
| CTRS(PR)(W) Regs | The Council Tax Reduction Schemes and Prescribed Requirements (Wales) Regulations 2012 No.3144 |
| E(ALGS)(W) Regs | The Education (Assembly Learning Grant Scheme) (Wales) Regulations 2002 No.1857 |
| E(SL) Regs | The Education (Student Loans) Regulations 1998 No.211 |
| E(SL)(R) Regs | The Education (Student Loans) (Repayment) Regulations 2009 No.470 |
| E(SS) Regs | The Education (Student Support) Regulations 2009 No.1555 |
| E(SS)(NI) Regs | The Education (Student Support) (No.2) Regulations (Northern Ireland) 2009 No.373 |
| E(SS)(W) Regs | The Education (Student Support) (Wales) Regulations 2015 No.54 |
| E(WMTTIS) Regs | The Education (Welsh Medium Teacher Training Incentive Supplement) Regulations 1990 No.1208 |
| ESA Regs | The Employment and Support Allowance Regulations 2008 No.794 |
| ESA(TP) Regs | The Employment and Support Allowance (Transitional Provisions) Regulations 2008 No.795 |
| HB Regs | The Housing Benefit Regulations 2006 No.213 |
| HSS&WF(A) Regs | The Healthy Start Scheme and Welfare Food (Amendment) Regulations 2005 No.3262 |
| IS Regs | The Income Support (General) Regulations 1987 No.1967 |
| IT(PAYE) Regs | The Income Tax (Pay As You Earn) Regulations 2003 No.2682 |
| JSA Regs | The Jobseeker's Allowance Regulations 1996 No.207 |
| JSA Regs 2013 | The Job Seeker's Allowance Regulations 2013 No.378 |
| NHS(CDA) Regs | The National Health Service (Charges for Drugs and Appliances) Regulations 2000 No.620 |

| | |
|---|---|
| NHS(DC) Regs | The National Health Service (Dental Charges) Regulations 2005 No.3477 |
| NHS(DC) (W) Regs | The National Health Service (Dental Charges) (Wales) Regulations 2006 No.491 |
| NHS(FP&CDA) (W) Regs | The National Health Service (Free Prescriptions and Charges for Drugs and Appliances) (Wales) Regulations 2007 No.121 |
| NHS(GOS) Regs | The National Health Service (General Ophthalmic Services) Regulations 1986 No.975 |
| NHS(OCP) Regs | The National Health Service (Optical Charges and Payments) Regulations 1997 No.818 |
| NHS(TERC) Regs | The National Health Service (Travel Expenses and Remission of Charges) Regulations 2003 No.2382 |
| NHS(TERC)(W) Regs | The National Health Service (Travelling Expenses and Remission of Charges) (Wales) Regulations 2007 No.1104 |
| SS(ICA) Regs | The Social Security (Invalid Care Allowance) Regulations 1976 No.409 |
| TC(DCI) Regs | The Tax Credits (Definition and Calculation of Income) Regulations 2002 No.2006 |
| UC Regs | The Universal Credit Regulations 2013 No.376 |
| WTC(EMR) Regs | The Working Tax Credit (Entitlement and Maximum Rate) Regulations 2002 No.2005 |

## Other abbreviations

| | |
|---|---|
| ADM | *Advice for Decision Making* |
| DMG | *Decision Makers' Guide* |
| GM | *The Housing Benefit and Council Tax Benefit Guidance Manual* |

References like CIS/142/1990 and R(SB) 3/89 are references to commissioners' decisions. References like *AD v SSWP* [2009] UKUT 46 (AAC) are references to decisions of the Upper Tribunal.

# Index

··············································

## How to use this Index

Entries against the bold headings direct you to the general information on the subject, or where the subject is covered most fully. Sub-entries are listed alphabetically and direct you to specific aspects of the subject.

| | | | |
|---|---|---|---|
| CA | Carer's allowance | I-ESA | Income-related employment and support allowance |
| C-ESA | Contributory employment and support allowance | I-JSA | Income-based jobseeker's allowance |
| C-JSA | Contribution-based jobseeker's allowance | JSA | Jobseeker's allowance |
| CTC | Child tax credit | NI | National insurance |
| DLA | Disability living allowance | PIP | Personal independence payment |
| ESA | Employment and support allowance | UC | Universal credit |
| HB | Housing benefit | WTC | Working tax credit |
| IS | Income support | | |